Elise C Otté

A simplified grammar of the Swedish language

Elise C Otté

A simplified grammar of the Swedish language

ISBN/EAN: 9783337724146

Printed in Europe, USA, Canada, Australia, Japan

Cover: Foto ©ninafisch / pixelio.de

More available books at **www.hansebooks.com**

TRÜBNER'S COLLECTION

OF

SIMPLIFIED GRAMMARS

OF THE PRINCIPAL

ASIATIC AND EUROPEAN LANGUAGES.

EDITED BY

REINHOLD ROST, LL.D., PH.D.

X.

SWEDISH.

BY E. C. OTTÉ.

TRÜBNER'S COLLECTION OF SIMPLIFIED GRAMMARS OF THE PRINCIPAL ASIATIC AND EUROPEAN LANGUAGES.

EDITED BY REINHOLD ROST, LL.D., Ph.D.

I.
HINDUSTANI, PERSIAN, AND ARABIC.
By the late E. H. Palmer, M.A.
Price 5s.

II.
HUNGARIAN.
By I. Singer.
Price 4s. 6d.

III.
BASQUE.
By W. Van Eys.
Price 3s. 6d.

IV.
MALAGASY.
By G. W. Parker.
Price 5s.

V.
MODERN GREEK.
By E. M. Geldart, M.A.
Price 2s. 6d.

VI.
ROUMANIAN.
By R. Torceanu.
Price 5s.

VII.
TIBETAN.
By H. A. Jaschke.
Price 5s.

VIII.
DANISH.
By E. C. Otté.
Price 2s. 6d.

IX.
OTTOMAN TURKISH.
By J. W. Redhouse.
Price 10s. 6d.

X.
SWEDISH.
By E. C. Otté.
Price 2s. 6d.

Grammars of the following are in preparation :—
Albanese, Anglo-Saxon, Assyrian, Bohemian, Bulgarian, Burmese, Chinese, Cymric and Gaelic, Dutch, Egyptian, Finnish, Hebrew, Kurdish, Malay, Pali, Polish, Russian, Sanskrit, Serbian, Siamese, Singhalese, &c., &c., &c.

LONDON: TRÜBNER & CO., LUDGATE HILL.

A

SIMPLIFIED GRAMMAR

OF THE

SWEDISH LANGUAGE.

BY

E. C. OTTÉ.

LONDON:
TRÜBNER & CO., LUDGATE HILL.

1884.

[*All rights reserved.*]

LONDON:
GILBERT AND RIVINGTON, LIMITED,
ST. JOHN'S SQUARE, CLERKENWELL ROAD.

INTRODUCTION.

The Swedish language belongs to a northern offshoot of the Old Germanic, which in course of time gave origin to two slightly differing forms of speech, known to Scandinavian grammarians as *Forn-Svenskan*, the Old Swedish, and *Forn-Norskan*, the Old Norse. The former of these was spoken by the Svear and Götar, or ancient Swedes and Goths; while the latter, as the name implies, was the language of the Norsemen, and probably identical with the *Norrœna*, or *Dönsk Tunga*, of the Northmen who first made themselves known to the nations of Christian Europe.

We have evidence that these two main branches of the Old Northern never deviated sufficiently from each other to interfere with their comprehension by all the Scandinavian peoples, although each possessed certain inherent and persistent characters peculiar to itself, of which traces may still be found in the modern forms of cultivated speech, which we distinguish as Swedish, and Dano-Norwegian. These distinctive survivals of the original twin forms of the

Old Northern have been best preserved in the provincial dialects of the northern kingdoms, and considerable light has been thrown on the history of the development of the Swedish language by a study of the various forms of the so-called "*bondespråk,*" or peasant-speech, which still maintain their ground in different parts of Sweden.

The *Forn-Svenskan,* or Old Swedish, can scarcely be said to have lost its status as the spoken tongue of the people till the beginning of the sixteenth century, when, with the emancipation of Sweden from the dominion of Denmark, and its political and social regeneration under Gustaf Vasa, a new era began in the language, as well as in the political and national life of the people. Gustaf, partly from policy perhaps as much as from conviction, early gave his support to the Reformers, whose zealous endeavours to provide the laity with trustworthy vernacular translations of the Scriptures he warmly seconded, encouraging the most learned of the Swedish adherents of the Lutheran doctrines to take part in this praiseworthy labour. Amongst these, the most eminent was Olaus Petri, who, although of peasant birth, was an elegant scholar, alike well versed in the literature of his native land, and in the learning of the schools, which he had acquired while studying at the German universities under the immediate direction of Luther. His translation of the New Testament, which appeared in 1536, and is the earliest Swedish version of the

Scriptures, may therefore be fairly accepted as a true representative of the highest literary standpoint of the language in the earlier half of the sixteenth century. Indeed it may be said that Olaus Petri's work marks the turning point between the older and more rugged form of the language, and that later development from which has resulted the spoken Swedish of our own times. The latter has naturally undergone various modifications, but it has retained far more of the characteristic vigour of the Old Northern than its sister-speech of Norway and Denmark, where even the best preserved provincial dialects betray the Germanizing influences to which both the spoken and the written language of the people have been subjected. From this vitiation of their northern mother-tongue the Swedes have been saved through their early severance from their political union with Denmark, and still more, perhaps, through their geographical position, which, while it has aided them in maintaining, almost unassailed, the independence which the first of the Vasas secured for them, has not been without powerful influence on the preservation of the genuine northern character of their language.

In modern Swedish, great dialectic differences of inflection and pronunciation are still to be met with even among the educated classes, although it cannot be denied that the present generation is showing a constantly increasing inclination to level provincialisms towards a more general standard, and thus to create a fixed form of cultivated spoken speech. The more circumscribed dialects are rapidly disappearing, and the most important Swedish linguistic differences may therefore now be comprehensively included under the two heads of *Upsvænsk*, and *Sydsvænsk*, "Upper or Northern Swedish," and "Southern Swedish." To the latter of these belongs the pronunciation of Södermanland, which is generally considered the best, and is that of an influential section of the cultivated classes of Stockholm, on which account it may be accepted by the student of Swedish as the best standard he can follow in his attempt to master the difficulties which appertain to the correct pronunciation of Swedish.

The Swedes rejected the use of the Gothic characters three hundred years ago, and since then they have employed the ordinary Latin letters, adding merely certain marks to indicate special vowel-sounds peculiar to the northern tongues. With the older alphabet, they did not, however, at once lay aside the cumbersome modes of spelling in use in the sixteenth and seventeenth centuries, and it is only within recent years that any systematic and rational reform has been introduced into the spelling of Swedish words. Since the meeting at Stockholm, in 1869, of the Scandinavian Linguistic Congress an important change has, however, been in progress, and although the end is not yet attained, much has already been done in Sweden to carry out the Resolutions of the Conference, whose leading aim was to purify the northern sister-tongues from foreign elements as far as existing conditions admitted of their elimination, and to revert as far as possible to the forms of the Old Northern, from which they have in common derived their descent.

In conformity with this principle, the spelling of modern Swedish is being greatly simplified. The double and mute letters of older times are being discarded, and while derivations and inflections are being made to agree orthographically with their roots and stems, the use of the vowels is being brought into closer harmony with the sounds of which these characters are the written representatives.

CONTENTS.

PART I.

	PAGE
The Alphabet (*Alfabetet*)	1
Articles (*Artikeln*)	8
Nouns (*Tingord*)	11
First Declension	11
Second and Third Declensions	12
Fourth and Fifth Declensions	13
Adjectives (*Egenskapsord*)	17
Adverbs (*Omständighetsord*)	20
Pronouns (*Ersättningsord*)	21
Personal Pronouns	21
Possessive Pronouns	22
Demonstrative Pronouns	22
Verbs (*Händelseord*)	24
Passive Verbs (*Passivum*)	30
Prepositions (*Förord*)	33
Conjunctions (*Bindeord*)	33
Interjections (*Utropsord*)	34

PART II.

ON THE USE AND CHARACTER OF THE DIFFERENT PARTS OF SPEECH.

	PAGE
The Indefinite Article .	35
The Definite Articles	36
The Noun .	39
Adjectives	44
The Numerals	46
Pronouns	48
Verbs .	52
Adverbs .	58
Prepositions	60
Conjunctions .	61
Modes of Inflection in Old Swedish	65

SWEDISH GRAMMAR.

PART I.

THE ALPHABET.

THE Swedish alphabet consists of the following twenty-eight letters (*Bokstäfver*) :—

A, called *ah*, pronounced like *a* in father.
B ,, *bey* ,, as in English.
C ,, *sey* ,, in genuine Swedish words like *k* before *a, o, u*; and like *s* in words of foreign origin and when it stands before *e, i, ä* and *y*.
D ,, *dey* ,, as in English.
E ,, *eh* ,, like *ai* in laid, and like *e* in felt.
F ,, *eff* ,, generally as in English, but like *v* at the end of words. It represents *ph* and φ.
G ,, *yay* ,, like hard English *g* before *l, r, t, a, o,* and *u*; like English *y* before *e, j, ä, ö, y*; before *n* it may take, with that letter, the sound of *en*, Fr.

H, called *haw*, aspirated except before *j* and *v*.

I　„　*ee*,　pronounced　like *ee* in tr*ee*, or like *i* in th*i*n

J　„　*yee*　„　like *y* in *y*ellow.

K　„　*kaw*　„　like English *k* before *l, r*, and *v*, and before the hard vowels *a, å, o, u*, as well as at the end of words. Before the soft vowels *ä, e, i, y*, and *ö*, it takes what the Swedes designate as the "*tje*" sound, which is nearly equivalent to the sound of English *ch*.

L　„　*ell*　„　generally as in English; but not heard before *j*, as *ljus* (pron. *juus*), 'light.'

M　„　*emm*　„　as in English.

N　„　*enn*　„　as in English; before *k, n* takes the sound of *ng*.

O　„　*oh*　„　when short like *o* in d*o*g, or like *o* in b*o*re, but also like *oo* in b*oo*n.

P　„　*pey*　„　as in English.

Q　„　*coo*.　This letter is followed in Swedish by *v*, instead of *u*, and is then pronounced like English *kv*.

R　„　*err*, pronounced like a strongly enunciated *r*, and always audible among the more cultivated classes.

S, called *ess*, pronounced like hard English *s* before *l*, and before *k* and *t*, where these letters are not followed by *j*, in which case *sk* and *st* acquire the sound of English *sh*. This sound is, moreover, heard at all times in *sj*; and in *sk*, where the latter is followed by the soft vowels *ä, e, i, ö, y*.

T   ,,   *tey*   ,,   as in English.

U   ,,   *oo*   ,,   like *oo* in sp*oo*n, or when short like *u* in f*u*ll. In addition to these, the Swedish *u* has, however, a sound not precisely analogous to any to be found in more southern European tongues, but which in many instances appears to have an intermediate sound between the English *u* in p*u*ll and the *u* in sh*u*tter.

V   ,,   *vey*   ,,   as in English.

X   ,,   *eks*   ,,   ,,   ,,

Y   ,,   *u*   ,,   like French *u* in p*u*re.

Z   ,,   *seyta*   ,,   as hard English *s*.

Å   ,,   *awe*   ,,   like *aw* in s*aw*.

Ä   ,,   *ey*   ,,   like *a* in s*a*le, and when short like *e* in wr*e*n.

Ö   ,,   *eu*   ,,   like *eu* in b*eu*rre (Fr.) and in p*eu* (Fr.).

The letter *c* is generally replaced by *k* where it has the hard sound of that letter, as *Karl* for 'Carl.' In foreign words which have been adopted with little or no modification, the *c* is often replaced by *s*, as *seder*, or *ceder*, 'cedar.'

The letter *d* is not sounded before *t*, as *godt* (*got*), 'good,' nor between *l* and *t*, as *mildt* (*millt*), 'mild.' It is dropped before *j* in certain words, as *djur* (*jur*), 'animal.'

The letter *f* is followed by *v*, and merged in that letter, when standing between two vowels, as *gifva* (*yeeva*), 'to give.'

The letter *g* has the sound of hard *g* or soft *k* at the end of words, as *skog*, m. (*skoägk*), 'wood;' but it takes the sound of Swedish *j* when preceded by *l* or *r*, as *talg* (*talj*), 'tallow;' *färg* (*färj*), 'colour.'

When *g* precedes a soft vowel at the beginning of a word, or of a syllable, it takes the sound of Swedish *j*, or English *y*; as, *gäst* (*yest*), 'stranger;' *begüra* (*beyera*), 'to require;' *gerna* or *gürna* (*yerna*), 'willingly.'

When *g* is followed by *n* in a root-word, it takes the so-called '*äng*' sound, as *regna* (*rengna*), 'to rain,' from *regn*, 'rain.'

The letter *h* is often dropped after *k*, or absorbed in that letter, as *bokhällare* (*bokkellare*), 'book-keeper.'

Although *k* has the sound of English *ch* before soft vowels in ordinary Swedish words, as *kyrka* (*chürka*), 'church,' it retains the hard sound in most foreign words, as *anarki* (*annarkee*), 'anarchy.' It is occasionally dropped before other consonants, as *spektakel* (*spetaakel*), 'theatre.'

L between two consonants is generally dropped, as *verld* (*verd*), 'world.' It is not heard before *j*, as *ljud* (*youd*), 'sound.'

Sj, which as already observed is equivalent to *sh*, as *sjuk* (*shuuk*), 'sick,' is occasionally used to express the sound of *si* in such foreign words as *asjette* (*assiette*, Fr.), 'plate;' *pasjon*, 'passion.'

Although as a rule *sk* takes the sound of *sh* before soft vowels, as *skepp* (*shepp*), 'ship,' while it retains its hard sound before the hard vowels, as *skall*, 'shall,' its use is, however, occasionally irregular under both conditions, as *handske* (*hanskē*), 'glove;' and *menniska* (*mennisha*), 'human being.'

T is often dropped before *s*, as *båtsman* (*bosman*), 'boatman;' *skjuts* (*shüss*), 'post-relay.' *Tj* has the sound of the Italian *c* before soft vowels, as *tjära* (*cera*, Ital.), 'tar.' *Ti* in foreign words has the sound of *tsh*, as *nation* (*naatshone*), 'nation.' The *th* of foreign words, pronounced like simple *t*, is rendered by that letter, although in the older forms of Swedish it constituted a distinct character of the alphabet.

Foreign words, although often rendered literally, as 'logis,' 'cake,' etc., are not unfrequently spelt phonetically, as *marki*, 'marquis,' *kuragè*, 'courage.'

A, *å*, *o*, *u* are reckoned as hard vowels, and *e*, *i*, *ä*, *ö*, *y* as soft vowels.

Final *e* is generally sounded, as in German.

In many words *e* has precisely the same sound as *ä*, which has been made to supersede it in the modern system of orthography wherever the root of the word pointed to an Old Northern derivation that warranted the adoption of this form of the vowel *a*. Thus while one writer gives *tjenare*, another will give *tjänare*, 'servant.' In older Swedish MSS. of the thirteenth and fourteenth centuries the *ä* (or *æ*) is found in all words in which the vowel has the sound of a long *e*, as *äftär*, 'after,' which is now written *efter*, and the object aimed at in this, as in other proposed changes of spelling, is to revert—as already observed—as far as circumstances admit, to the use of the letter which best represents the vowel-sound of the Old Northern. Similarly, it is proposed to exchange *o* for *å*, where the short sound of the latter has led to a deviation from the older Northern form, as in *boll* used for the more correct *båll*, 'ball.'

The vowel-sounds differ so widely with the varying degrees of stress or accentuation on the word, that a prolonged acquaintance with the spoken speech is absolutely necessary to enable a foreigner to know when the vowel should be long or short.

It must, moreover, be borne in mind that intonation, apart from the length or shortness of the vowel, constitutes an important element in the pronunciation of Swedish. According to Mr. Henry Sweet, who is one of the highest authorities on the sounds and intonation of spoken Swedish, there is in every word a simple and a compound tone. The simple tone he characterizes as "a rising modulation, as in asking a question in English," while in the compound tone he recognizes "a falling tone (as in answering a question) on the stress-syllable with an upward leap of the voice,

together with a slight secondary stress on a succeeding syllable. The latter occurs, therefore, only in polysyllables. The simple tone is the regular one in monosyllables." ....
In accordance further with the same competent authority.
.... "Foreign words and many names of places have the simple tone." .... while "The definite suffix (article) does not count as part of the word, so that *dăg*en, 'the day,' retains the simple tone of *dăg*, 'day.'"

In words ending in *eri*, as *bageri*, 'bakehouse,' and in various words of foreign origin and termination, as *nat*ur, 'nature;' *gener*al, 'general;' *juv*el, 'jewel,' the tone is on the last syllable.

In compounds the tone may be said to be grave on the first, and acute on the second syllable; as, *sōlskén*, 'sunshine;' *uppfóstra*, 'to bring up.'

Swedish, in conformity with its general affinity with the other northern representatives of the Old Gothic, adapts itself readily to the formation of compound words composed of various different parts of speech. In the modern system of spelling there is a tendency, however, to restrict this practice within more rational limits, more especially in regard to compound prepositions, adverbs and conjunctions, the component parts of which are now more and more frequently written separately; as, *till freds*, 'content;' *i hjäl*, 'dead;' instead of *tillfreds, ihjäl*.

THE ARTICLES. (*Artikeln.*)

Three genders are recognized in Swedish, viz. the masculine, feminine, and neuter.

The Articles agree in gender and number with the noun to which they refer.

There are three Articles: the "Indefinite" (*obestämd*), and two forms of the "Definite" (*bestämd*), (1) the Affixed or Terminal Article (*slutartikel*), and (2) the Independent (*fristående*) Article.

The *Indefinite Article*, which precedes the noun, or the adjective which qualifies the latter, is as follows:—

MASC. AND FEMIN. GENDERS.	NEUTER GENDER.
en, a, an.	*ett*, a, an.

Examples: *en gosse*, m., 'a boy,' *en flitig gosse*, 'a diligent boy;' *en flicka*, f., 'a girl,' *en vacker flicka*, 'a fine girl;' *ett barn*, n., 'a child,' *ett godt barn*, 'a good child.'

The *Affix* or *Terminal Definite Article* consists of the following particles, which are incorporated with the noun:—

Singular.

MASC. AND FEMIN. GENDER.	NEUTER GENDER.
en or *n*, the,	*et* or *t*, the.

Plural.

ne, na,	*en* or *a*, the.

Examples: *dag*, m., 'day,' *dag*en, 'the day;' *blomma*, f., 'flower,' *blomma*n, 'the flower;' *namn*, n., 'name,' *nam*net, 'the name;' *rike*, n., 'kingdom,' *rik*et, 'the kingdom;' *dalar*, m. pl., 'valleys,' *dalar*ne, 'the valleys;' *sagor*, f. pl., 'tales,' *sagor*na, 'the tales;' *namn*, n. pl., 'names,' *namn*en, 'the names;' *riken*, n. pl., 'kingdoms,' *riken*a, 'the kingdoms.'

The proper application of these affixes depends, (1) upon the form of declension to which the noun belongs; (2) on whether the word ends in a vowel or a consonant; and (3) on considerations of euphony.

This mode of incorporating the article with the noun is a special characteristic of the Scandinavian tongues which they derive from the Old Northern. It does not exist in Old Gothic, but it is met with under a modified form in Albanian, and in the kindred languages of Bulgaria, and Roumania.

In the Old Northern we may trace the origin of this method of noun-and-article agglutination to a grammatical construction which admitted of putting a demonstrative pronoun *after* the noun which it defined; as, *madr hinn*, m., 'man that;' *eik hin*, f., 'oak that;' *dyr hitt*, n., 'animal that;' *hestar hinir*, m. pl., 'horses those;' *tungur hinar*, f. pl., 'tongues those;' *börn hin*, n. pl., 'children those.'

In the course of time the noun and pronoun were connected in writing, as *madrhinn*; and finally, in following the current mode of pronunciation, the *h* was dropped, leaving only as suffixes *inn, in, itt*, pl., *ir, ar, in*. The Scandinavian twin branches of language, known as *Svenska*, Swedish, and *Dansk-Norsk*, Dano-Norwegian, which have been derived from the Old Northern as their common mother tongue, have followed a similar process. Thus for example, *dag hinn*, 'day that,' gradually assumed its present agglutinated form of *dagen*, 'the day.'

The demonstrative pronoun served in Old Northern to define the object, like a simple definite article, of which there is no other representative in the older Icelandic writings; nor is there any trace of a distinct indefinite article till a comparatively recent period, when its place was supplied by the numeral *einn*, mas., *ein*, fem., *eitt*, n., 'one.' From this has been derived the modern Swedish article *en*, *ett*, 'a,' 'an,' which is merely the unaccentuated form of the word which expresses the numeral 'one.'

The Swedish Independent Definite Article (*Fristående Artikel*), is:—

Singular.		Plural.
MASC. AND FEM.	NEUTER.	ALL GENDERS.
den, the	*det*, the	*de*, the.

This article is merely an unaccentuated form of the demonstrative pronouns, *dēn*, *dēt*, *dē*, derived from the Old Northern *hinn*, *hin*, *hitt*, *hinir*, *hinar*, *hin*. It directly precedes the noun which it defines, or the adjective which qualifies the latter; as, *den gosse*, 'the boy;' *den qvinna*, 'the woman;' *det barn*, 'the child;' *de dalar*, m., 'the valleys;' *de sagor*, f., 'the tales;' *de bälten*, n., 'the belts.' *Den flitige gossen*, 'the diligent boy;' *den ädla qvinnan*, f., 'the noble woman;' *det goda barnet*, 'the good child;' *de djupa dalarne*, m., 'the deep valleys;' *de gamla sagorna*, 'the ancient tales;' *de korta bältena*, 'the short belts.'

Here it will be observed that the noun, when preceded by an adjective, takes both the affixed article and the independent definite article. This pleonasm is peculiar to the Swedish branch of the Scandinavian languages, Dano-Norwegian dispensing with the terminal affix when the noun is preceded by an adjective with the requisite independent or adjective form of the definite article.

In many instances, however, and under certain conditions, the terminal article is dropped in Swedish when the noun is qualified by an adjective.

NOUNS. (*Tingord.*)

Swedish Nouns are of three genders, Masculine, Feminine and Neuter; as, *en fader*, m., 'a father;' *en moder*, f., 'a mother;' *ett barn*, n., 'a child.'

Nouns are grouped under *five* modes of declension (*böjningssätt*), viz.:—

The First Declension.

(Plural termination *or.*)

Without the terminal article.   *With the terminal article.*
Sing. Nom.   *blomma*, f. flower,   *blomma*n,   the flower.
... Gen.   *blomma*s,   ...   *blomma*ns, of ...
... Dat. Acc.   *blomma*,   ...   *blomma*n, ...
Pln. N. D. A.   *blommor*, flowers,   *blommor*na, the flowers.
... Gen.   *blommor*s,   ...   *blommor*nas, of ... ...

To this declension belong all feminine nouns ending in *a*.

The Second Declension.

(Plural termination *ar*.)

Without the terminal article.   *With the terminal article.*

Sing. Nom., etc., *dal,*   m.,   dale,   *dal*en,   the dale.
... Gen.,   *dal*s, ...   *dal*ens, of ... ...
Plu. Nom., etc., *dal*ar,   ...   dales,   *dal*arne (or *na*).
... Gen.,   *dal*ars, ...   *dal*arnes (or *nas*).
Sing. Nom., etc., *socken,*   f.,   parish,   *sockn*en, the parish.
... Gen.,   *sockens,*   ...   ...   *sockn*ens, of ... ...
Plu. Nom., etc., *sockn*ar,   ...   parishes, *sockn*arna, the parishes.
... Gen.,   *sockn*ars, f.,   ...   *sockn*arNAS, of the parishes.

To this declension belong both masculine and feminine nouns.

The Third Declension.

(Plural termination *er*.)

Without the terminal article.   *With the terminal article.*

Sing. Nom., etc.,   *vän,*   m. & f.,   friend,   *vänn*en,   the friend.
... Gen.,   *väns,*   ...   ...   *vänn*ens, of ... ...
Plu. Nom., etc., *vänn*er,   ...   friends, *vänn*erne (or *na*).
... Gen.,   *vänn*ers, ...   *vänn*ernes (or *nas*).
Sing. Nom., etc., *tryckeri,* n., printing office,   *tryckeri*et, the printing office.

NOUNS. 13

Sing. Gen., tryckeris, n., printing tryckeriets, of the
      office,   printing office.
Plu. Nom., etc., tryckerier, ... tryckerierna, the
      offices,   printing offices.
... Gen.,   tryckeriers, ... tryckeriernas, of ... ...

To this declension belong masculine, feminine, and neuter nouns.

The Fourth Declension.

(Plural termination *n.*)

Without the terminal article. *With the terminal article.*

Sing. Nom., etc., bälte, n., belt, bältet, the belt.
... Gen.,   bältes, ... bältets, of ... ...
Plu. Nom, etc., bälten, ... belts, bältena, the belts.
... Gen.,   bältens, ... bältenas, of ... ...

To this declension belong only neuter nouns ending in a vowel.

The Fifth Declension.

(The same termination in the plural as in the singular.)

Without the terminal article. *With the terminal article.*

Sing. Nom., etc., krigare, m., warrior, krigaren, the
             warrior.
... Gen.,   krigares, ... krigarens, of the
             warrior.
Plu. Nom., etc., krigare, ... warriors, krigarne, the
             warriors.

Plu. Gen.,   *krigares*, m., warriors, *krigarnes*, of the warriors.

Sing. Nom., etc., *namn*,   n., name,   *namn*et, the name.
... Gen.,   *namns*, ...   *namn*ets, of ... ...
Plu. Nom., etc., *namn*,   ... names,   *namn*en, the names.
... Gen.,   *namns*, ...   *namn*ens, of ... ...

To this declension belong masculine and neuter nouns.

In regard to differences of gender it may be observed that the following belong generally to the *masculine* :—

1. Nouns that indicate the male sex in persons or animals; as, *konung*, m., 'king;' *tupp*, m., 'cock.'

2. The names of seas, lakes, and woods, and the seasons, months, and days; as, *höst*, 'autumn;' *juli*, 'July;' *torsdag*, 'Thursday.'

3. Nouns generally that end in *ad, ande, are, dom, ing, ling, lek, när, skap*; as, *mån*ad, m., 'month;' *handl*ande, m., 'trader;' *tjen*are, m., 'man-servant;' *ung*dom, m., 'youth;' *men*ing, m., 'meaning;' *främl*ing, m., 'stranger;' *kärl*ek, m., 'love;' *konst*när, m., 'artist;' *veten*skap, m., 'science.'

To the feminine gender belong generally :—

1. Nouns that indicate the female sex in persons and animals; as, *drottning*, f. 'queen;' *höna*, 'hen.'

2. The names of small rivers and brooks, and of indigenous Swedish trees; as, *Dalelven; björk*, f., 'birch.'

3. Words ending in *a, an, and, ång, d, t, else,* and *i, ik, ion,* and *ur* in words of foreign origin; as, *kyrk*a, f.,

'church;' *verk*an, f., 'effect;' *r*and, f., 'edge;' *st*ång, f., 'pole;' *dyg*d, f., 'virtue;' *dräg*t, f., 'dress;' *föd*else, f., 'birth;' *geografi*, f., 'geography;' *fabr*ik, f., 'manufactory;' *relig*ion, f., 'religion;' *nat*ur, f., ' nature.'

To the neuter gender belong generally :—

1. The names of countries and places, letters of the alphabet, and words or sentences used as nouns; as, *Sverge*, n., 'Sweden;' *Stockholm*, n.; *ett a*, 'an a;' *ett Lef väl*, 'a farewell.'

2. Nouns ending in *a*, where they have the plural in *n*; as, *hjerta*, n., 'heart;' *öga*, n., 'eye' (pl., *ögon*); *öra*, n., 'ear' (pl., *öron*); in *e*, *el*, *er*, *on*, and in *um*, *eum*, and *ium* in words of foreign origin; as, *rik*e, n., 'kingdom;' *hag*el, n., 'hail;' *blomst*er, n., 'flower;' *ostr*on, n., 'oyster;' *fakt*um, n., 'fact;' *mus*eum, n., 'museum;' *kolleg*ium, n., 'college.'

Compound words, irrespective of their precise meaning, take the gender of the last member of the combined group; as, *qvin*folk, n., 'woman;' *stats*råd, n., 'councillor of state.'

The gender of many words varies in different parts of Sweden in accordance with local usage, depending among other conditions upon whether the district belongs to the ancient "*Svea*" or "*Göta*" dominions; thus i.a., *finger*, 'finger,' and *bolster*, 'bolster,' which are masculine in the former, are neuter in the latter territory.

Numerous words have different meanings in accordance with a difference in their gender; as, *pil*, m., 'an arrow,' *pil*, f., 'a willow;' *dam*, m., 'wear,' *dam*, f., 'lady,' *dam*, n., 'dust;' *gran*, f., 'pine-tree,' *gran*, n., 'grain.'

Many such words differ in the mode in which they form their plural; as, *kor*, m., 'a company of singers,' pl. *korer*; *kor*, n., 'church-quire,' pl. *kor*; *lår*, m., 'corn-bin,' pl. *lårar*; *lår*, n., 'thigh-bone,' pl. *lår*.

Some words may be used under two distinct modes of termination in the singular dependent upon uncertainty of declension; as, *almanacka* and *almanack*, pl., *almanackor*.

Others may differ both in the plural and singular; as, *Fur* or *fura*, f., 'fir-tree;' the former making *furer*, and the latter *furor*, in the plural.

Some nouns do not admit of being declined; as, (*i*) *går*, 'yesterday;' (*till*) *pass*, 'at the right time;' (*på*) *spe*, 'mockery.' Such words, however, as in the instances given, usually require to be used adverbially with a preposition.

Many words have different meanings in accordance with the declension to which they belong, and the consequent difference in their plural; as, *bok*, f., 'book,' pl. *böcker*; *bok*, f., 'beech,' pl. *bokar*.

Some nouns, as in English, can only be used in the singular; as, *bly*, n., 'lead;' *allmoge*, m., 'peasantry;' *stolthet*, f., 'pride,' and many other abstract nouns of a similar kind.

Some nouns can only be used in the plural; as, *bopålar*, m. pl., 'domicile;' *ränker*, m. pl., 'cabal.'

Many nouns form their plural by changing their radical vowel; as, *hand*, f., 'hand,' pl. *händer*; *son*, m., 'son,' pl. *söner*; *man*, m., 'man,' pl. *män* or *männer*; *gås*, f., 'goose,' pl. *gäss*; *mus*, f., 'mouse,' pl. *möss*. The two last take *en* as their plural terminal article.

ADJECTIVES. (*Egenskapsord.*)

Swedish adjectives agree in gender and number with the noun which they qualify; as, *en flitig man, och en flitig qvinna,* 'a diligent man and woman;' *ett flitigt barn,* 'a diligent child;' *gode (a) söner,* 'good sons;' *flitiga flickor,* 'diligent girls;' *ädla namn,* n., 'noble names.' Here it will be observed that in this indefinite so-called "weak" form of the adjective, which is also used as a predicate, the masculine and feminine in the singular are identical, while the neuter takes a *t*. The masculine plural in *e* is in accordance with the older forms of the language, but by modern and common usage an *a* is generally substituted for the *e*, and the plural of all genders is thus reduced to one mode of termination in the indefinite form of the adjective. Thus while the same form of the adjective is used for the masculine and feminine, or common gender in the singular, the neuter is marked by the addition of *t*, and the plural by *a*, as:

Singular.

COMMON GENDER.   NEUTER.
god, good.   *god*t, good.

Plural.

goda, good, for all genders,

excepting in some cases as above referred to, where the masculine takes final *e* instead of *a*.

This termination of *e* is also met with for all genders in

c

certain compound, and other, adjectives derived from a participle and ending in *ad*; as—

Sing., *godhjertad*, c. g., *godhjertadt*, n., good-hearted.
Plural for all genders, *godhjertade*, ,,

The "definite" or so-called "strong" form of the adjective is marked by the addition of *a* to the abstract form in the feminine and neuter singular and plural, while in regard to the masculine it must be borne in mind that the older specific termination *e*, which originally marked that gender, is still of frequent occurrence, as—

	MASCULINE.	FEMININE AND NEUTER.
Both Numbers	*goda*, or *gode*,	*goda*, good ;

as, den *gode* (or *goda*) *man*nen, the good man.
den *vackra blom*man, 'the lovely (the) flower.'
det *stora hus*et, 'the large (the) house.'
de *ædle kriga*rne, 'the noble (the) warriors.'
de *flitiga qvinnor*na, 'the diligent (the) women.'
de *ljusa bon*a, 'the light (the) dwellings.'

Here it will be observed that the noun has the terminal article, although the adjective qualifying it is preceded by the definite article *den*. The double use of the article is, as already noticed, not to be found in Dano-Norwegian, in which the terminal article is not applicable to words defined by the independent article *den, det, de*.

This form is also used when the noun is in the genitive, or is preceded by a pronoun; as, *konungens lyckliga regering*, 'the king's happy reign;' *min gamle vän*, 'my old friend.'

Adjectives ending in *t*, preceded by a consonant, do not take another *t* in the neuter, as *salt*, m. f., *salt*, n. 'salt.'

Adjectives ending in a vowel double the *t* in the neuter; as, *fri, fri*tt, n., 'free;' *ny, ny*tt, n., 'new.'

Adjectives ending in *al, el, en, er*, drop the *a* or *e* where this vowel occurs in the declension of the word, as in *gammal*, 'old,' which changes to *gam*le (a), while *trogen*, 'faithful,' *tapper*, 'brave,' etc., change to *trog*ne (a), *tap*pre (a), etc.

Some adjectives are indeclinable; as, *bra*, 'good;' *öde*, 'waste;' *gängse*, 'usual.'

Adjectives may be used in the sense of nouns; as, *den tappre*, 'the brave (man);' *den vackra*, 'the charming (woman);' *det ädla*, 'the noble (act, thing).'

The degrees of comparison are expressed by adding to the positive form *are* or *re*, and *ast* or *st*; as—

POSITIVE.	COMPARATIVE.	SUPERLATIVE.
stark, strong,	*starkare*, stronger,	*starkast*, strongest.
hög, high,	*högre*, higher,	*högst*, highest.

Mera or *mer*, 'more,' and *mest*, 'most,' may be used as in English to express comparison, and this more especially where the adjective has a participle form; as,—

POSITIVE.	COMPARATIVE.	SUPERLATIVE.
godhjertad, good-hearted,	*mera godhjertad*,	*mest godhjertad*

Many adjectives are wholly irregular; as—

POSITIVE.	COMPARATIVE.	SUPERLATIVE.
god, good,	*bättre*,	*bäst.*
liten, small,	*mindre*,	*minst.*
mycken, much,	*mera*,	*mest.*
elak or *ond*, bad,	*värre*,	*värst.*
gammal, old,	*äldre*,	*äldst.*

Some are defective, having either no positive, or neither positive nor comparative, especially where the word is derived from a preposition or adverb; as, *främre* (comp.), 'more forward,' *främst*, 'most forward' (*fram*, prep., 'forth, onward'); *yttre* (comp.), 'outer,' *ytterst* (super.), 'outermost' (*ut*, adv., 'out').

Some adjectives from their meaning do not admit of comparison; as, *död*, 'dead;' *stum*, 'mute.'

The adverb *desto*, 'the,' 'so much the,' is often used to give additional force to the comparative, as *desto bättre*, 'the better.' The particle-adjectives *aller, allra*, 'all,' give a similarly heightened form to the superlative, as *allerbäst, allrabäst*, 'the very best.'

ADVERBS. (*Omständighetsord.*)

Many Swedish adverbs are identical with the neuter of the corresponding adjective, as *tungt*, 'heavily,' from *tung*, m., f., *tungt*, n., 'heavy.' In such cases they follow the same rules of comparison as the corresponding adjective; as, *tyngre*, 'more heavily;' *tyngst*, 'most heavily.'

Many adverbs of irregular modes of comparison are similarly identical with the corresponding adjectives; as—

väl, well, comp. *bättre,* better, superl. *bäst,* best.
illa, badly, „ *värre,* worse, „ *värst,* worst.

The following are some of the more generally used adverbs of time, place, manner, mode, affirmation, negation, etc.—

nu, now.	*här,* here.	*gerna,* willingly.
då, then.	*dit,* thither.	*visst,* certainly.
snart, soon.	*hit,* hither.	*ja, jo,* yes.
strax, immediately.	*in, inne,* in.	*nej, ej,* no, not.
redan, already.	*ut, ute,* out.	*icke,* no, not.
länge, long.	*framdeles,* in future.	*ingalunda,* by no means.
ofta, often.		
huru, how.	*hvarför,* why.	*månne,* may be, perchance.
der, there.	*så,* so.	

PRONOUNS. (*Ersättningsord.*)

The *Personal Pronouns* in Swedish are:—

Singular.

Nom., *jag,* I; *du,* thou; *han,* he; *hon,* she; *det,* it.
Gen.,   —   —   *hans*;   *hennes*;   *dess.*
D., Acc., *mig*; *dig*;   *honom*;   *henne*;   *det*; *sig,* self (reflect).

Plural.

Nom., *vi,* we; *i, ni,* you; *de,* they.
Gen.,   —   —   *deras.*
D., Acc., *oss*; *eder (er)*; *dem.*

The reflective pronoun *sig* is used in all genders for the third person, both singular and plural. For the special use of the personal pronouns, see Part II.

The *Possessive Pronouns* are:—

Singular.		Plural.	
MASC. AND FEM.	NEUTER.	ALL GENDERS.	
min,	mitt, my.	mina,	my.
din,	ditt, thy.	dina,	thy.
sin,	sitt, his, her.	sina,	their.
vår,	vårt, our.	våra,	our.
eder, er,	edert (ert), your.	edra,	your.

Sin, sitt, sina are used (as in Danish) in a subjective reflective sense, whilst *hans, hennes, dess* are only used objectively; as, *Fadern älskar sitt barn, och söker befrämja dess väl,* 'a father loves his (own) child, and strives to promote his (the child's) welfare.

The *Demonstrative Pronouns* are:—

Singular.		Plural.	
MASC. AND FEM.	NEUTER.	ALL GENDERS.	
Nom.,etc., den,	det, the, this, that.	N., de,	the, these.
G., dess (dens),	dess, ,,	G., deras,	,, ,,
		D., Acc., dem,	,, ,,

Singular.

MASC.	FEM.	NEUTER.
Nom., *denne* (a),	*denna,*	*detta,* this.
Gen., *dennes* (as),	*dennas,*	*dettas,* ,,

Plural.

MASC.	FEM.	NEUTER.
Nom., *desse* (a),	*dessa,*	*dessa.*
Gen., *desses* (as),	*dessas,*	*dessas.*

Sing., *den samme* (a), m., *den samma*, f., *det samma*, the same.
Plur., *de samme* (a), ,, *de samma,* ,, *de samma,* ,, ,,

The *Reciprocal Pronouns hvarandra, hvarannan,* 'one another,' 'each other,' take *s* in the genitive.

The *Interrogative* and *Relative Pronouns* are:—

Nom.,	*ho, hvem,*	who;	*hvad,* what.
Gen.,	*hvars* (*hvems*),	,,	*hvars,* ,,
D., Acc.,	*hvem,*	,,	*hvad,* ,,

Hvad för en, m., f., *hvad för ett*, n., *hvad för*, pl., are occasionally used instead of the relative *hvilken*, m., f., *hvilket*, n., Gen. *hvilkens, hvilkets*, N. A. D. pl. *hvilka*, for all genders, Gen. *hvilkas*, 'which.'

Som, 'whom,' 'which,' 'that,' is not declinable.

The principal *Indefinite Pronouns* are:—

En, Gen. *ens,* pl. *ena,* 'one,' 'some one,' generally used only in the objective case.

Man, 'one,' 'they,' used only in the nominative singular.

Någon, m., f., *något*, n., pl. *några*, 'some one,' 'any one;' *ingen*, m. f., *intet*, n., pl. *inga*, 'no one,' 'none;' *bägge, båda,* 'both;' *mången*, m., f., *månget*, n., pl. *många*, 'many,' 'many a one;' *annan*, m., f., *annat*, n., pl. *andra*, 'other;' *ömse*, 'both,' 'each;' *sjelf*, m., f., *sjelft*, n., pl. *sjelfva*, 'other;' *dylik*, 'such;' *egen*, m., f., *eget*, n., pl. *egna*, 'own.'

VERBS. (*Händelseord.*)

In Swedish there are three forms of verbs—the active, passive, and deponent.

The auxiliary verbs are divided by Swedish grammarians into three classes: (1) *temporala*, or those which help to form compound tenses; as, *hafva*, 'to have,' and *skola*, 'shall' or 'will;' (2) *modala*, or those which serve to express different moods; as, *må*, *måste* (defect.), 'may,' 'must;' *kunna*, 'can;' *låta*, 'let;' *vilja*, 'will;' *böra*, 'ought;' (3) *passiva*, or those which serve to conjugate the passive; as, *vara*, 'be;' *varda, blifva*, 'become.'

Infinitive.

att hafva, to have.   *att vara*, to be.
Partic. Present, *hafvande*, having.   *varande*, being.
Partic. Past,   *haft*, had.   *varit*, been.

Indicative.

PRESENT TENSE.

Singular.

Jag, du, han, hon, den, det,   Jag, du, han, hon, den, det
har (*hafver*), I have, etc.   *är*, I am, etc.

VERBS.

Plural.

Vi hafva (ha), we have. *Vi äro,* we are.
I hafven (han), ye „ *I ären,* ye „
De hafva (ha), they „ *De äro,* they „

IMPERFECT TENSE.

Singular.

All 3 persons, *hade,* I had, etc.   *var,* I was, etc.

Plural.

Vi hade, we had. *Vi voro,* we were.
I haden, ye „ *I voren,* ye „
De hade, they „ *De voro,* they „

Subjunctive or Optative.

Present.

Singular.

All 3 persons, *hafve* or *må hafva,* have, or may have.
„   „   *vare,* I may be, etc.

Plural.

Vi hafve or *må hafva,* we have, or may have, etc.
I hafven „ *mån* „ ye „ „ „
De hafve „ *må* „ they „ „ „
Vi vare, we may be.
I varen, ye „ „
De vare, they „ „

Imperative.

2nd person sing., *haf; var;* have, be thou.
1st ,, plur., *hafvom; varom;* let us have, be.
2nd ,, ,, *hafven; varen;* have, be ye.

The other auxiliaries, which may also in certain cases be used independently, are conjugated as follows:—

Infinitive.	Pres. Indic.		Imperfect.		P. Part.
	Sing.	Plur.	Sing.	Plur.	
skola, shall.	*skall,*	*skola.*	*skulle,*	*skulle.*	*skolat.*
vilja, will.	*vill,*	*vilja.*	*ville,*	*ville.*	*velat.*
må, may.	*må, må*	*(måga).*	*måtte,*	*måtte.*	*måst.*
måste, may.	*måste,*	*måste.*			*måst.*
tör, töra, dare.	*tör,*	*töra.*	*torde,*	*torde.*	
kunna, can.	*kan,*	*kunna.*	*kunde,*	*kunde.*	*kunnat.*
böra, ought.	*bör,*	*böra.*	*borde,*	*borde.*	*bort.*
varda, become.	*varder,*	*varda.*	*vardt,*	*vordo.*	*vorden.*
blifva, be, remain.	*blifver,*	*blifva.*	*blef,*	*blefvo.*	*blifvit.*

Here, as in all other verbs, the second person plural ends in *en*; as, *I skolen; I bören;* etc.

There are *four modes of conjugation* in Swedish, the three first of which include so-called *weak* verbs, while the fourth comprises all so-called *strong* verbs.

First Conjugation (Active).

The *Imperf. Indic.* ends in *ade, Past Part.* in *ad, Supine* in *at.*
Example:—*Infinitive Pres.,* (att) *kalla,* 'to call;' *Perfect,*

VERBS.

hafva kallat, 'to have called;' *Pres. Part.*, *kallande*, 'calling;' *Sup.*, *kallat*, 'called.'

Indicative.

Present.	Imperfect.	Past Tenses.

Sing., all persons: *kallar*, *kallade*, *har*, or *hade kallat*,
                                            have, or had called.
Plur., 1st and 3rd persons: *kalla*.

FUTURE TENSES.

Simple Future and Conditional.   *Compound Future.*

skall, or *skulle kalla*,   *skall*, or *skulle hafva kallat*,
shall, or should call.   shall, or should have called.

Subjunctive or Optative.

Present.	Imperfect.	Perfect.
kalle.	The same as Imperf. Indicative.	*må hafva*, or *hade kallat*, may have, or had called.

Imperative.

Sing. 2 pers. *kalla* (*du*).
Plur. 1 „ *kallom* (*vi*).
    2 „ *kallen* (*I*).

It must be observed here, that in accordance with what has already been stated, the *second person plural* in this, as in the other conjugations, differs from the other persons by ending in *en* or *n*, according to the termination of the tense or mood; as, *I kallen*, 'ye call' (pres. indic.); *I kalladen*, 'ye were calling' (imperf. indic.). The first person plural of the imperative has also a special termination, viz. *om*, as *kallom*, 'let us call;' but beyond these differences, which, moreover, refer to the written language only, there is no exception to the rule that the first person of either number indicates the termination of the other persons of the tense or mood, and on this account we shall only give the first persons in the following conjugations.

The *Second Conjugation* takes *de* or *te* in the imperf. indic., *d* or *t* in the perfect past participle, and *t* in the supine.

Examples of these two classes:—

Infinitive.

(*att*) *böja*, to bend, Part. Pres. *böjande*, Past Part. *böjd*.
„ *köpa*, to buy, „ *köpande*, „ *köpt*.

Indicative.

Present.	Imperfect.
Sing. *böjer, köper*.	Sing. and Plur. } *böjde, köpte*.
Plur. *böja, köpa*.	

Optative.

Present.	Imperfect.	Imperative.
Sing. and Plur. } *böje, köpe*.	The same as Imperf. Indic.	Sing. 2 pers. *böj, köp*.
		Plur. 1 „ *böjom, köpom*.
		„ 2 „ *böjen, köpen*.

The *Third Conjugation* takes *dde* in the imperfect indicative, *dd* in the past participle, and *tt* in the supine. The infinitive does not take the terminal *a*, and the present participle takes *ende*.

VERBS.

Infinitive.

Example: (*att*) *tro*, 'to believe;' Part. Pres. *tro*ende;
Past Part. *tro*dd; Sup. *tro*tt.

Indicative.

Present.	Imperfect.	Imperative.
Sing. *tror*.	Sing. *tro*dde.	Sing. 2 pers. *tro*.
Plur. *tro*.	Plur. *tro*dde.	Plur. 2 ,, *tro*n.

Optative.

Present.
Sing. and Plur. } *må tro*.

Imperfect.
The same as Imperf. Indic.

The Fourth Conjugation.

This conjugation includes all the so-called *strong* verbs, i. e. verbs whose imperfect indicative tense is formed through some internal change of the radical vowel.

This conjugation is divided into two classes, viz.:

1. Verbs which undergo only *one* change of vowel, affecting the imperfect indicative; as, *gripa*, imperfect *grep*, past part. *gripen*, supine *gripit*, 'to grasp.'

2. Verbs which undergo a change of vowel, both in the imperfect indicative and in the perfect participle and supine; as, *binda*, imperfect *band*, part. past *bunden*, supine *bundit*.

Examples :—

Infinitive.

(*att*) *gripa* to grasp, Part. Pres. *gripande*, Part. Past, *gripen*,
                Sup. *gripit*.
,, *binda*, to bind, ,, *bindande*, Part. Past, *bunden*,
                Sup. *bundit*.

Indicative.

Present.	Imperfect.
Sing. *grip*er, *bind*er.	Sing. *grep*, *band*.
Plur. *grip*a, *bind*a.	Plur. *grep*o, *bund*o.

Optative.

Present.	Imperfect.
Sing. and Plur. } *grip*e, *bind*e.	Sing. and Plur. } *grep*e, *bund*e.

Imperative.

Sing. 2 pers. *grip*, *bind*.
Plur. 1 ,, *grip*om, *bind*om.
,, 2 ,, *grip*en, *bind*en.

PASSIVE VERBS. (*Passivum.*)

The modern Swedish form of the passive has originated from the Old Northern, in which it was a mere adaptation of the reflective pronoun *sik, sig,* and was conjugated with the help of the auxiliaries *vera, verda* (*varða*), 'to be,' and the past participle of the active form of the verb.

In modern Swedish the passive is formed by adding *s* (for *sig*) to the transitive active form of the verb; as—

Infinitive.
Present.

(*att*) *kall*as, to be called.
,, *böj*as, ,, bent.
,, *tros*, ,, trusted.
,, *bind*as, ,, bound.

VERBS. 31

Past.

att hafva kallats, to have been called.
,, ,, böjts, ,, ,, ,, bent.
,, ,, trotts, ,, ,, ,, trusted.
,, ,, bundits, ,, ,, ,, bound.

Supine.   Past Participle.
kallats.   kallad.
böjts.   böjd.
trotts.   trodd.
bundits.   bunden.

Indicative.
Present.

   kallas. (All persons but 2 plur.)
2 pers. plur. (kallens).
   böjes. ,, ,, ,, ,,
,, ,, (böjens).
   tros. ,, ,, ,, ,,
,, ,, (trons).
   bindes. ,, ,, ,, ,,
,, ,, (bindens).

Imperfect.

   kallades.
2 pers. plur. (kalladens).
   böjdes.
,, ,, (böjdens).
   troddes.
,, ,, (troddens).
   bands.
1 and 3 pers. plur. bundos.
2 ,, ,, bundens

Compound Tenses.

Sing. *har, hade kallats,* or *blifvit kallad.*
Plur. *hafva, hade* ,,   ,,   ,,   ,,
Sing. *har, hade böjts*   ,,   ,,   *böjd.*
Plur. *hafva, hade* ,,   ,,   ,,   ,,
Sing. *har, hade tr*otts   ,,   ,,   *tr*odd.
Plur. *hafva, hade* ,,   ,,   ,,   ,,
Sing. *har, hade bu*ndit   ,,   ,,   *bu*nden.
Plur. *hafva, hade* ,,   ,,   ,,   ,,

Deponents are conjugated after the passive form, while they have an active significance; as, *minnas*, 'to remember,' *jag minnas*, 'I remember.'

Some deponents are merely the passive of some other reflective active verb; as, *förifras*, 'to be in a passion,' from *förifra sig*, 'to put oneself in a passion.' Others have no relation to any corresponding active verb; as, *hoppas*, 'to hope.'

Most intransitive verbs are without the passive; as, *falla*, 'to fall,' *hända*, 'to happen,' etc., and such verbs may generally be used as impersonals; as, *det faller sig svårt*, 'it is difficult;' *det hände mig*, 'it happened to me.'

Intransitives may be used in some cases in the passive when they have an impersonal sense; as, *det dansas här i huset*, 'there is dancing going on in the house.'

For an explanation of the principal forms of deviations from the normal modes of conjugation, see Part II.

PREPOSITIONS. (*Förord.*)

The chief prepositions are:—

af, of, by.
efter, after.
bland, among.
från, from.
för, for, before.
utför, down.
utan, without.
förbi, by, past.
genom, through.
hos, at the house of.
i, inom, in, within.
jämte, near by, beside.
omkring, round.

å, på, on, upon.
åt, to, at, for.
sedan, after.
till, to, till, at.
undan, away, from.
mot, against.
nära, near.
ofvan, above.
om, about.
under, under.
utom, without.
ur, utur, out of.
vid, by, near.

CONJUNCTIONS. (*Bindeord.*)

The chief conjunctions are:—

Simple.

och, and.
men, but.
eller, or.
samt, with.
äfven, also.
ty, for.
om, in case.

då, then.
utan, unless.
när, when.
dertill, thereto.
derför, therefore.
ehuru, although.
att, that.

Compound.

ej heller, neither.
både och, also, as well as.
så som, as.
i fall, in case.
som om, as if.
emedan, since.
således, so.

INTERJECTIONS. (*Utropsord.*)

O! ah! ack! åh! hå! nå! hurra! O ve!

Some are imitative sounds of noises; as, *Kling klang! klatsch! kras! puff!* Some are merely elliptical renderings of invocations, oaths, etc.; as, *Gunås!* (*Gud nåde os*, 'God have mercy on us'); *Kors!* ('the Cross'); *Vassera tre!* (*Vår Herras trä*, 'our Lord's tree-cross'); *bevars!* (*bevare oss!* 'Preserve us!'), 'Oh dear!'

PART II.

ON THE USE AND CHARACTER OF THE DIFFERENT PARTS OF SPEECH.

THE INDEFINITE ARTICLE.

The Indefinite Article *en*, m., f., *ett*, n., 'a,' 'an,' is merely the unaccented form of the indefinite pronoun *en*, *ett*, ' one,' which is the same as the numeral *en, ett,* ' one.'

In Old Northern there is no trace of the use of a distinct indefinite article, the earliest representative of which was the indefinite pronoun *einn,* ' one,' *einhverr,* ' each one.' From these have been derived the modern Scandinavian *en, ett.*

The plural *ena,* 'ones,' ' some,' is used to express surprise or contempt; as, *det är ena obegripliga flickor,* ' they are incomprehensible girls!'

This article is in many respects governed by the same rules as in English. Thus it directly precedes the noun which it indicates; as, *en gosse,* ' a boy;' *en blomma,* ' a flower;' *ett hus,* ' a house;' while where the noun is qualified by an adjective, it precedes the latter; as, *en ädel fiende,* ' a noble foe;' *en god bok,* ' a good book;' *ett stort haf,* ' a great sea.'

It is not used, however, where a person's rank, profession,

or calling is indicated, unless the latter be qualified by an adjective; as, *han är general,* 'he is a general;' *min vän är* EN TAPPER *officer,* 'my friend is a brave officer;' *prestens son är läkare,* 'the clergyman's son is a doctor;' *gossen skall bli smed,* 'the boy is to be a smith.'

The Definite Articles.

In the Old Northern there was no distinct definite article till a comparatively late period, when its place was supplied by the use of the demonstrative pronoun—

hinn, m., hin, f., hint (hitt), n., singular, this, that;
hinir, ... hinar, ... hin,   ... plural, these, those;

which either followed the noun in an independent form, as *Sæmundr hinn frodi,* 'the wise Sæmund,' or was affixed to it with the *h* and final *n* dropped for euphony, as *hestr*IN, 'the horse.' In conformity with this process of adaptation, the modern Scandinavian tongues have used the demonstrative pronoun *den, det, de,* 'this,' 'that,' etc., as a definite independent article, pronounced without the vowel-stress that marks the former. In the earlier forms of Swedish this unaccented pronoun generally followed the noun which it defined, and came in process of time to be incorporated with it in the form of the suffixes -*en* or -*n,* m., f.; -*et* or -*t,* n. sing.; -*ne, -na, -en* or -*a,* pl., which now constitute one of the most distinctive characteristics of the language.

Swedish thus possesses two distinct forms of the definite article, the one independent, as *den blomma,* 'the flower,' and the other supplemental and affixed, as *blomman*, 'the flower.' The suffixes, which must accord in number and gender with the noun with which they are amalgamated, thus simply but completely represent the English definite article 'the;' as, *skald*en, 'the bard;' *blomm*an, f., 'the flower;' *namn*et, n., 'the name;' *rik*et, 'the kingdom;' *skald*erna, 'the bards;' *blommo*rna, 'the flowers;' *namn*en, 'the names;' *rik*ena, 'the kingdoms;' *skald*, *blomma*, etc., without such terminals, being indefinite, as 'bard,' 'flower,' etc.

Nouns used in an abstract sense take the article in Swedish where it is omitted in English; as, *lifv*et *är kort*, '(the) life is short;' *vin*et *pressas ur drufvor*, '(the) wine is extracted from grapes;' *hvad kostar smör*et *i dag?* 'what does (the) butter cost to-day?'

The affix is used with some names of countries and places; as for example: *Ital*ien, '(the) Italy;' *Alp*erna, 'the Alps;' *Scandinavi*en, 'Scandinavia;' and with certain titles; as, *Riksråd*et '(councillor)' *Lynberg*; *President*en *Wrangel*. But it is not used with *konung*, 'king;' *furste*, 'prince;' *grefve*, 'count;' *Herr*, 'Mr.;' *Löjtnant*, 'lieutenant;' nor with any feminine titles; as, *drottning*, 'queen;' *Fru*, 'Mrs.;' *Fröken*, *Jungfru*, 'Miss;' 'Madam,' etc.

When *Herr* precedes another title, the latter takes the terminal article; as, *har Herr grefv*en *varit i London?* 'have you been in London, count?

When a title or professional designation precedes the name of the person addressed, the former has the final article; as, *Docent*en *Almqvist*.

The article is omitted when the noun is preceded and governed by a genitive; as, *iqvnnans pligt är att älska sina barn,* 'a woman's duty (the duty of a woman) is to love her children.'

The affix-article is not used when the noun is preceded by a relative or interrogative pronoun; as, *hvilken pojke var det?* 'what boy was that?'

Swedish requires that the terminal article should be added to the noun, even when the latter is preceded by an adjective with the independent article, *den, det, de,* 'the;' as, *det behagede ej* DEN *lilla prinsessan,* 'this did not please the little princess.'

This pleonastic method of construction is also met with when the noun is preceded by the demonstrative pronoun, *den, det, de,* 'that,' 'those;' as, *den mannen skulle jag vilja lära känna,* 'that man I should like to know.'

In the older forms of the language the suffix-article was generally omitted in such modes of construction, as may be seen from certain familiar expressions still current; as, *i de äldsta tider,* 'in the olden times.'

The use of the definite article before a noun, where the latter is not qualified by an adjective, is regarded as a Germanism, and is of frequent occurrence in the Scriptures, which in many particulars reflect the German literary influences to which the earlier translators had been subjected; thus we find *de Romare,* 'the Romans;' *de Kolosser,* 'the Colossians,' instead of the more genuinely Northern construction '*Romarne,*' '*Kolosserne.*'

As a general rule it may be assumed that the terminal

suffix-article should be used wherever the English 'the' is required to define the noun; as, *jorden är rund*, the earth is round; *Såg du herrarne?* 'did you see the gentlemen?'

THE NOUN.

The noun agrees in gender and number with its predicate; as, *månen är klar*, 'the moon is bright;' *hästarne voro feta, men oxarne magra*, 'the horses were fat, but the oxen were lean.'

In simple sentences the subject noun precedes the verb; as, *jag ser flickan*, 'I see the girl.' But it follows the verb:—

1. In interrogatives; as, *hvarför ligger inte barnet?* 'why does not the child go to bed?'

2. In secondary sentences; as, *när flickan har något godt, så delar hon alltid med sig åt andra*, 'when the girl has anything good, she always shares it with others.'

3. When some assertion made by, or in reference to, the subject precedes the latter; as, *det är en öfversättning*, SER JAG, 'it is a translation, I see.'

4. When the subject follows the adverbial part of the sentence; as, *samma dag* UPPLÄSTE HAN *öfversättningen*, 'on the same day he read out the translation;' *förut* HADE HAN *hållit arbetet hemligt för dem*, 'before that, he had kept the work a secret from them.'

Elliptically the subject may be put into the accusative with an infinitive; as, *han* ANSÅGS VARA *en rik man*, 'he was regarded as a rich man;' *jag såg henne komma*, 'I saw her come.'

The genitive may be expressed by the use, not merely

of the inflectional *s*, as *qvinnans barn*, 'the woman's child,' but also by numerous prepositions, as *bland, till, af, efter*, etc.; as, *son till qvinnan*, 'the woman's son;' *hon är enka efter en prest*, 'she is a clergyman's widow;' *tre af oss*, 'three of us;' *den yngsta bland flickorna*, 'the youngest of the girls;' *kärleken till Gud*, 'the love of God.'

Where several nouns stand in apposition, the last only takes the genitive form; as, *kejsar Karl den Stores efterkommande*, 'the descendants of Charles the Great.'

After words expressing quantity the genitive is not used, although implied, such words being merely put in apposition with the nouns which they govern; as, *en hop soldater*, 'a number (of) soldiers;' *ett par handskar*, 'a pair (of) gloves;' *ett glas vin*, 'a glass (of) wine.'

The genitive is used after *hos*, 'at,' and in familiar parlance when a person's family or house is understood; as, *hon är hos prestens*, 'she is at the clergyman's;' *vi ha sett doktorns*, 'we saw the doctor's (family).' In some cases the genitive is used directly before the noun by which it is governed; as, *en* ÄRANS *man*, 'a man of honour;' *en sexton* ÅRS *flicka*, 'a girl of sixteen.'

The dative may be expressed simply by position; as, *Herren gaf* BONDEN *brefvet*, 'the gentleman gave (to) the peasant the letter;' *arbetet är oss nyttigt*, 'work is good for us.'

It may be expressed by *åt*, 'at;' *för*, 'for; as, *Smeden skrattade åt sitt eget infall*, 'the smith laughed at his own fancy;' *för hvem är arbetet nyttigt?* 'for (or to) whom is labour good?' *gif äpplet åt honom,* (or *gif honom äpplet,*) 'give him the apple.'

The objective may be used with an infinitive, as in Latin, in the place of a subjective with its predicate; as, *Jag anser* MIG UPPFYLLA *min skyldighet,* 'I consider that I am doing my duty.'

In regard to the five declensions of nouns adopted in modern Swedish, it may be well to draw attention to the following points:—

1. The *First Declension* includes all feminine nouns ending in *a*. Of these, some were masculines in the older forms of the language, and had in some of their cases the termination *u* (*o*,) which is still met with; as, *närvaro,* 'presence;' *frånvaro,* 'absence.' Some of these words may be used both with the present feminine and the older masculine termination; as, *ådra* or *åder,* 'vein.'

2. The *Second Declension,* which includes both masculines and feminines, has upwards of 600 of the former gender which are monosyllabic, and end in a consonant. Some have no plural; as, *gråt,* 'weeping;' *kål,* 'cabbage.' Most words in *sel* are without the plural; as, *känsel,* 'sense,' 'perception;' *trängsel,* 'crowd.' *Moder* and *dotter,* belonging to this declension, change the radical vowel in the plural, as, *mödrar,* 'mothers;' *döttrar,* 'daughters.' Here it may be remarked that many words belonging to the other declensions similarly make their plural in an *Umlaut,* or change of the radical vowel; as, *bonde,* pl. *bönder,* 'peasants;' *fader,* pl. *fäder,* 'fathers;' *broder,* pl. *bröder,* 'brothers;' etc.

3. The *Third Declension*, which includes nouns of all genders, contains a large proportion of foreign words. The termination *-er* in the plural, which is its distinctive character, is unknown in genuine Swedish words of the neuter gender, and is due to German or Danish influences.

4. The *Fourth Declension*, to which belong only neuter nouns ending in a vowel, includes the neuter nouns of the older form of the language ending in *a* and other vowels, which early in the eighteenth century began to acquire the plural termination *-n*, which is now the characteristic distinction of this declension.

5. The *Fifth Declension*, which includes masculine and neuter nouns, remains unchanged in the plural, although there is a tendency among modern writers to add *-er* or *-r* to express the plural; as, *svarander* instead of *svarande*, 'defendants.'

Many nouns vary in declension either from uncertainty of gender or from difference of meaning; as, *bolag*, n. sing., *bolag*, m. pl., 'partnership.'

Many nouns are of irregular declension; as, *sko*, m., *skor*, pl., 'shoe;' *fot*, m., *fötter*, pl., 'foot;' *öga*, n., *ögon*, pl., 'eye;' *öra*, n., *öron*, pl., 'ear.'

In these instances the apparent divergencies from the established rules are dependent on the declension originally followed by the word in the Old Northern.

Similar traces of the ancient construction are to be found in certain words and expressions which retain the termination of the original genitive, as, among many others, in *giftoman*, 'guardian' (giver in marriage);

kyrkogård, 'churchyard;' *i förmågo af,* 'in virtue of.' Thus, too, in the expression *i lagom tid,* 'in good time,' we have a survival of an old dative form.

The tendency of the spoken language is to disregard the older grammatical distinction of masculine, feminine and neuter, and to comprehend the two former under one *common* gender. Thus in speaking of inanimate objects, and even of animals, it is usual to refer to them as *den,* 'this, that,' instead of *han,* 'he,' and *hon,* 'she.'

Numerous divergencies between the written and the spoken language are observable in the tendency to lessen the number of declensions, by using the termination *-er* to mark the plural of many words for which grammatical rules demand a different ending. This is more especially the case in regard to neuters belonging to the fifth declension, but a similar practice prevails in reference to the plural of feminines belonging to the first declension, in which the terminal *-or* is frequently changed to *-er* in the spoken language.

Abstract nouns, or foreign words ending in *an* or *en,* do not take the affix-article; as, *början,* 'beginning,' 'the beginning;' *examen,* 'examination,' 'the examination.'

When an adjective is preceded by the independent article *den, det, de,* it may be used in the sense of a noun; as, *den flitige belönas,* 'the diligent (man, or individual, understood) is rewarded;' *den femtonde är snart inne,* 'the fifteenth (of the month) will soon be here.'

Adjectives.

The masculine singular and plural termination *-e* is generally changed to *-a* for the sake of euphony in speaking. It should, however, be retained when the adjective is used as a noun, or when it follows the latter as a distinctive cognomen, or is used as a vocative; as, *den gode*, 'the good (man);' *de vise*, 'the wise (men);' *Gustaf Adolf den store*, 'Gustavus Adolphus the Great;' *I ädle män!* 'ye noble men!' Where the adjective is used to express a noun, it takes *s* in the genitive; as, *de gamles son*, 'the old people's son.'

Some adjectives are defective or irregular in their mode of declension; as, *grå*, 'grey,' which may remain unchanged, or take an *a* in the plural; as, *grå ögon* or *gråa ögon*, 'grey eyes.' *Små*, although the plural of *liten, litet*, 'little,' may be used in the singular masculine and feminine in a collective sense; as, *små fisk*, 'small fish;' *småskog*, m., 'underwood.' As a noun or an adverb, *smått* is of common occurrence; as, *Jag har smått om tid*, 'I am pinched for time;' *det regnar smått*, 'it is (a small rain) drizzling.'

Survivals of older forms are to be found in such expressions as, *till fullo*, 'in full;' *på ljusan dag*, 'in broad daylight.'

Adjectives ending in *a, e, se*; as, *bra* (abbr. of *braf*), 'fine;' *lika*, 'like;' *öde*, 'desert; *'gängse,* 'current,' do not admit of being declined.

A similar rule applies to present participles and adverbs

used in the sense of adjectives; as, *ett leende barn*, 'a laughing child;' *inhyses hjon*, 'a dependant,' 'a person living free of cost in another person's house;' *inbördes krig*, 'intestine war.'

Certain superlatives are used only in prayer or invocation, and in epistolary and official communications; as, *den aller Högste*, 'the Most High;' *stormäktigst*, 'most mighty;' *allernådigst*, 'most gracious;' *tropligtigst*, 'most obedient;' *underdånigst*, 'most humbly.'

The comparative degree may be expressed by the help of the conjunction *än*, 'than;' as, *Adolf är äldre än sin syster Maria*, 'Adolphus is older than his sister Mary.'

A comparison between two persons or things is not expressed with the comparative but the superlative; as, *hvilken af de tränne qvinnorna är yngst?* 'which is the younger of the two women?'

As in English, a certain definite preposition must follow the adjective, to give it the special meaning required; as, *ledsen vid*, 'weary of;' *glad öfver*, 'glad of;' *kunnig i*, 'conversant with.'

The preposition may be omitted with some adjectives; as, *Albert är mäktig det svenska språket*, 'Albert is master (of) the Swedish language;' *min Moder blef henne qvitt*, 'my mother got rid (of) her.'

The Numerals. (*Räkneord.*)

The cardinal numbers (*grundtal*) are:—

1. *en, ett.*
2. *två (tu, tvänne).*
3. *tre (trenne).*
4. *fyra.*
5. *fem.*
6. *sex.*
7. *sju.*
8. *åtta.*
9. *nio.*
10. *tio.*
11. *elfva.*
12. *tolf.*
13. *tretton.*
14. *fjorton.*
15. *femton.*
16. *sexton.*
17. *sjutton.*
18. *aderton.*
19. *nitton.*
20. *tjugu.*
30. *trettio.*
40. *fyrtio (fyratio).*
50. *femtio.*
60. *sextio.*
70. *sjuttio.*
80. *åttio (åttatio).*
90. *nittio.*
100. *hundra.*
1000. *tusen.*

The cardinal numbers are indeclinable except *en, ett,* which may be used in the sense of an indefinite pronoun; as, *den ene,* 'the one;' *de ena,* 'the ones.' *Hundra* and *tusen* may be used as nouns. The old neuter *tu* may be used in some cases; as, *i tu,* 'in two;' *tu par,* 'two pairs.' The old masculine nominative *tver (tve)* occurs in compound words; as, *tvetydig,* 'ambiguous.'

The *o* in *nio* and *tio,* and the *u* in *tjugu,* are usually replaced in common parlance by *e*; as, *nie, tie, tjuge,* while *ti* similarly replaces the *tio* in the higher numerals; as, *tretti, fyrti, femti,* etc.

Between 20 and 100 the lesser number precedes the greater when *och,* 'and,' is used; as, *en och sextio,* 61, but when *och,* 'and,' is not used, the larger number precedes the smaller; as, *trettio fem,* 35.

The ordinal numbers (*ordingstal*) are:—

1st. *förste* (a).	16th. *sextonde.*
2nd. *andre* (a).	17th. *sjuttonde.*
3rd. *tredje.*	18th. *adertonde.*
4th. *fjerde.*	19th. *nittonde.*
5th. *femte.*	20th. *tjugonde.*
6th. *sjette.*	30th. *trettionde.*
7th. *sjunde.*	40th. *fyrtionde.*
8th. *åttonde.*	50th. *femtionde.*
9th. *nionde.*	60th. *sextionde.*
10th. *tionde.*	70th. *sjuttionde.*
11th. *elfte.*	80th. *åttionde.*
12th. *tolfte.*	90th. *nittionde.*
13th. *trettonde.*	100th. *hundrade.*
14th. *fjortonde.*	1000th. *tusende.*
15th. *femtonde.*	

Excepting *förste* (a) and *andre* (a), the ordinal numbers are indeclinable. In regard to order of precedence, they follow the same rule as the cardinal numbers; as, *han är på första och femtionde året,* 'he is in his fifty-first year;' *hon kom den tjugu-första,* 'she came on the twenty-first.'

A fractional amount is made to refer to the greater, and not the lesser number; as, *klockan är tre qrarter på fyra,* 'it is a quarter (three-quarters on) to four;' *klockan half fem,* 'half-past four;' *half annan,* 'one and a half.' Where *och,* 'and,' is used, the position of the fractional part is altered in such sentences; as, *tre och en half mil,* 'three miles and a half;' *fem och ett halft pund kött,* 'five and a half pounds of meat.'

The ordinal numbers may take *s* in the genitive; as, *Karl den tolftes död,* 'Charles the XIIth's death.'

In common parlance the word *stycken,* 'pieces,' is often added to the numeral in defining persons as well as things; as, *de voro tio, tolf stycken,* 'there were ten or twelve of them.'

'The former,' 'latter,' 'last,' are expressed by *den förre, senare, siste;* while certain fractional and multiple terms, such as, 'a third,' 'a fourth,' are rendered by *en tredjedel, en fjerdedel;* 'twofold,' 'threefold,' etc., by *tvåfaldig, trefaldig,* etc.

Pronouns.

The use of the proper pronoun in addressing others presents considerable difficulty in Swedish, which may be said to be passing through a transition period in regard to the ceremonial formulæ of speech. The obsequious deference to rank and social standing enforced in past times, seems, however, to be so far giving way in Sweden, as to warrant the hope that one uniform mode of address may soon be adopted among Swedes of all classes.

The second person *du*, while used in prayer, and between the nearest relatives much the same in Swedish as in German, is not unfrequently superseded between parents and children and near relatives by the name or designation of the individual addressed ; as, *Vil Anna ha rosen ?* 'Will you have the rose, Anna ?' *Har Pappa sin pibe ?* 'Have you got your pipe, papa ?'

Ni is commonly used in narratives, novels, etc., to express the term 'you' in conversations between two persons, and it is used in correspondence between acquaintances, but it has not been very generally accepted as a mode of social address. *Er, eder*, are still more commonly used than *ni* in epistolary and social intercourse. More frequently than either of these simple forms of the personal pronoun, the title or name of the individual addressed is used with the third person of the verb ; as, *Grefven befinner sig icke väl i dag ?* 'Are you not well to-day, Count ?' *Fruen såg mig i går ?* 'Did you not see me yesterday, madam (or Mrs. —) ?' *Ja visst, jag såg herren*, 'Yes, certainly I saw you, sir (or Mr. —); *Har doktoren varit i Stockholm ?* 'Have you been in Stockholm, Doctor ?'

The pronouns *han*, 'he,' *hon*, 'she,' are still occasionally used in addressing inferiors, but *ni* is more frequently used by masters and employers to those in their service.

Ni has been derived from the terminal letter *n* of the second person plural of verbs, and the pronoun *i*, 'you' or 'ye;' as *tron i*, 'believe ye,' corrupted into *tro ni*.

Min herr is used as 'sir,' *mine herrar*, as 'gentlemen.' *Herrskapet*,' 'master and mistress,' is often used to include

E

persons of both sexes, in addressing equals no less than superiors; as, *Hur många personer är herrskapet?* 'How many of you are there?'

Fru, Fröken, Mrs., Madam, Miss, are respectively used with the third person in addressing a married or unmarried lady. Ladies take the rank of their husbands and share in their social designations; as, *Generalinna,* 'Mrs. General;' *Prestinna,* 'the clergyman's wife (Mrs. Pastor).'

The reflective pronoun *sig* may be used to refer to the third person in the plural, as well as the singular; as, *gossarne öfva sig,* 'the boys are practising (themselves):' *hon närmade sig presten,* 'she drew (herself) near the clergyman.'

The possessive pronoun *sin, sitt, sine,* 'his,' 'hers,' 'its,' can only be used in the subjective reflective sense, while *hans, hennes, dess,* have an objective significance; as, *han går hem till de sina,* 'he is going home to his own children (or family);' *jag visste ej hans son var död,* 'I did not know that his son was dead.'

The possessive is sometimes used in the place of the personal pronoun in interjections and familiar expressions of endearment, lament, etc.; as, DIN *söda lilla ängel,* 'thou sweet little angel!' MIN *stackare!* 'poor me!'

The demonstrative pronouns *den, det, de,* when combined with *här,* 'here,' and *der,* 'there,' indicate respectively 'this' and 'that;' as, *det* HÄR *träd är högre än det* DER, 'this tree is higher than that one.' *Det* is used impersonally in the sense of 'there;' as, *det har varit en tiggare här,* 'there has been a beggar here.'

Denne and *den samme*, 'that one,' 'the same,' have a more demonstrative character than *den*.

Ho, 'who,' is chiefly used in biblical or poetical language; *hvem* in common parlance.

Hvilken, hvad för, hvilken som, are all used as relatives; as, *jag vet ej hvilken som kommer, eller hvad som vore bäst att göra*, 'I do not know who is coming, or what would be best to do.'

The prefix *e* gives the same significance to relatives as is derived in English from the addition of 'ever;' as, *eho*, 'whoever;' *ehvad*, 'whatever;' *ehurudan*, 'who or whatever;' *hvilken än, hvem än*, etc., have much the same significance.

The relative *som* is indeclinable, and may be used for all genders; as, *här är mannen* SOM *önskar tala med Er*, 'here is the man, who wishes to speak to you;' *min broder har sålt det huset som han köpte i Juni*, 'my brother has sold the house which he bought last June.'

The Old Northern demonstrative form *y* (*ty*), 'that,' is traceable in *dylik*, 'the like' (such), and occurs in such expressions as, *efter ty som säges*, 'according to what is said;' *i ty fall*, 'in that case.' The Old Northern gen. pl. *þeirra* is traceable in such words as *endera*, 'one of them;' *bäggedera*, 'both of them;' *någondera*, 'some of them,' etc.

The pronoun must agree in gender and number with the noun which it represents; as, *Hvar är flickan? Hon är i trädgården*, 'Where is the girl? She is in the orchard.' In some cases, however, the pronoun follows the natural rather than the grammatical gender; as, *Har du set statsrådet?*

Nej, HAN *är sjuk,* 'Have you seen the councillor? No, he is ill.'

Verbs.

In a simple affirmative sentence the verb follows its subject, with which it agrees in number and person; as, *min moder gaf tjenaren brefvet,* 'my mother gave the servant the letter;' *hans fader och broder hafva (ha) afrest,* 'his father and brother have gone away.'

In secondary and interrogative sentences, the verb precedes its subject; as, *De sista åren af Gustafs regering förflöto i ro,* UNDERTAGER MAN *ett krig med Ryssland,* 'The last years of the reign of Gustavus passed in peace, if we except a war with Russia.' *Kommer icke soldaten här?* 'Is the soldier not coming here?'

Where the sentence begins with an adverb, the verb precedes its subject; as, *derpå begaf han sig till generalen,* 'thereupon he betook himself to the general.'

The indicative present is used to express a certain or conditional future as well as a mere present; as, *min son kommer i afton,* 'my son will come this evening;' *kommer han, så går jag icke,* 'if he should come, I will not go.'

This tense is also used instead of the preterite or imperfect, to express a continued action at a past period; as, *jag bor i Stockholm sedan min ungdom,* 'I have lived in Stockholm from my youth upwards.'

On the other hand, the preterite is sometimes used in cases where in English the indicative present is employed; as, *det var lustig!* 'that's a good joke!'

The compound tenses are sometimes used instead of the future; as, *jag har strax slutat*, 'I shall have done immediately.'

This use of the compound instead of the simple tenses is regarded as a Germanism which should be avoided; thus the sentence *Konungen* HAR *i går* HÅLLIT *statsråd*, would be more correctly rendered *Konungen* HÖLL *statsråd i går*, 'the king held a council of state yesterday.'

The conjunctive is not much used in modern Swedish, its place being often taken by the various defective auxiliaries, which constitute a striking characteristic of the language; as, *må, månne, måste*, 'may;' *må det gå dig väl!* 'good betide thee!' *månne någon gifver mig det!* 'perhaps some one may give it to me!'

It is used in an optative sense in a few forms of expression; as, *Gud välsigne dig*, 'may God bless thee!' *länge lefve konungen*, 'long live the king!'

The imperative is often expressed by the help of the auxiliary *få*, 'to get,' 'must;' as, *du får ej gå*, 'you must not go!' 'do not go!'

The auxiliary *att hafva* is often omitted before the past participle in compound tenses; as, *sedan solen (har) gått ned, inträder mörkret*, 'when the sun has gone down, darkness comes on;' *skräddaren skulle sytt gossen en rock*, 'the tailor should have made the boy a coat.'

The infinitive is often used in the place of a gerund; as, *han läser för att lära*, 'he reads for the sake of learning;' *konsten att måla*, 'the art of painting.' *Att*, 'to,' may be omitted before the infinitive when it constitutes the thing-object of a personal object; as, *min broder lärde mig simma,* 'my brother taught me to swim.'

The participle present is sometimes changed to the passive form in such sentences as, *han kom ridandes,* 'he came riding.'

It may also be used adverbially or as a preposition; as, *luften är tryckande het,* 'the air is oppressively hot;' ANGÅENDE *denna vigtiga sak,* 'concerning this important matter.'

This participle, which always ends in *ande* or *ende,* is very commonly used in the sense of an adjective; as, *en svinlande höjd,* 'a dizzy height.'

The past participle, which ends in *d, t,* or *en,* may be used similarly; as, *en förtjent man,* 'a deserving man;' *den älskade qvinnan,* 'the beloved woman;' *en erfaren läkare,* 'an experienced doctor.'

The supine, which always ends in *t,* and has been derived from the neuter of the perfect participle, is always used in conjunction with the verb *hafva,* 'to have;' as, *han har tänkt på henne,* 'he has thought of her.'

An impersonal passive or deponent is used in the following manner: *det dansades hela natten,* 'dancing was going on all night;' *ännu mer förvånades han,* 'he was still more surprised.'

Transitive verbs generally admit of being used in the passive as well as the active form, as, *älska, älskas,* 'to love,' 'to be loved;' but intransitive verbs can usually only be employed in an impersonal form in the passive, when they acquire a significance peculiar to the Scandinavian languages; as, *det dansas här i afton*, 'there will be dancing here this evening.' They may, however, be used with *är* and *var* in an active sense; as, *konungen* ÄR AFREST *till Norge*, ' the king has gone to Norway.'

In Old Swedish the passive was expressed by the use of the auxiliaries *verda* (*varða*), ' to be,' as it may still be rendered by *vara*, or more generally by *blifva*, ' to be;' as, *han har blifvit sårad*, ' he has been wounded,' instead of *han har sårats*.

Some verbs can only be used reflectively; as, *att beflita sig*, ' to strive;' many verbs admit of being used both reflectively and actively; as, *att inbilla sig*, ' to imagine;' *man bör icke inbilla en annan sådan något*, ' one ought not to make any one believe such a thing.'

Compound verbs are generally declined like the corresponding verbs from which they have been derived; as, *håller*, *höll*, and *anhåller*, *anhöll*, etc., 'hold,' and 'detain.' But where they have been derived from German, or other foreign sources, they do not follow the inflection of the corresponding Swedish verb; as, *hushålla*, ' to keep house,' which is not derived directly from *hus*, ' house,' and *hålla*, ' to hold,' but from the German ' *haushalten*,' and makes *husholdte*.

Verbs which can be used both transitively and intransitively generally follow the second conjugation in the former and the fourth conjugation in the latter case; as, *han hjelpte andra och stjelpte sig sjelf*, ' he helped others and ruined himself;' *det halp icke, han stalp*, 'there was no help for it, he was ruined.'

Some verbs can be used both as intransitives and impersonal reflectives; as, *det får han ångra,* 'he will repent of that;' *det ångrar mig,* 'I regret.'

The irregularities of Swedish verbs scarcely admit of being reduced to any definite classification, but are dependent on various conditions, such as a foreign origin; mere disregard of grammatical construction; or retention of some only of the characteristics of the Old Northern, as may be seen from the following examples:

att bringa,	to bring,	*bragte,*	*bragt.*
,, *förgäta,*	,, forget,	*förgat,*	*förgätit.*
,, *dö,*	,, die,	*dog,*	*dött.*
,, *gå,*	,, go,	*gick,*	*gått.*
,, *ligga,*	,, lie,	*låg.*	*legat.*
,, *qväda,*	,, sing,	*qvad,*	*qrädit.*
,, *se,*	,, see,	*såg,*	*sett.*
,, *sofva,*	,, sleep,	*sof,*	*sofvit.*
,, *tälja,*	,, count,	*talde,*	*talt.*
,, *veta,*	,, know,	*visste,*	*vetat.*
,, *äta,*	,, eat,	*åt,*	*ätit.*

Compound verbs are either separable or inseparable; as, *att tillhöra,* or *att höra till,* 'to belong to,' and *att beklage,* 'to complain.' To the former class belong verbs composed of a preposition, adjective, or other independent part of speech; as, *att genomborra,* 'to bore through,' *att frigöra,* 'to free;' while to the latter belong generally all verbs compounded of a particle and another verb; as, *att erkänna,* 'to acknowledge.'

The first conjugation, which includes five-sixths of all the

Swedish verbs, embraces nearly all weak verbs having *a, o, u*, or *å* as their radical vowel, followed by a consonant; as, *fråga*, 'to ask.' To this conjugation belong also generally verbs compounded of particles, or having two or more syllables; as, *afskeda*, 'to dismiss;' *arbeta*, 'to labour.'

To the second conjugation belong many verbs having a soft radical vowel, as *e, i, y, ä*, or *ö*; as, *leda*, 'to lead;' *spilla*, 'to spill;' *pryda*, 'to adorn;' *svälla*, 'to swell;' *föda*, 'to give birth to.'

The third conjugation, which now is without the final *a* in the infinitive, is of comparatively modern origin, that characteristic termination having been present in the Old Swedish; as, *att bo*a, instead of *bo*, 'to dwell;' *att tro*a, instead of *tro*, 'to believe.'

The fourth, or *strong* mode of conjugation, which is the most ancient and most flexible of any, comprises five distinct classes of verbs; as, (1) verbs in which the imperf. indicative ends in short *a*; (2) in long *a*; (3) in *o*; (4) in *e*; (5) in *ö*. As—

	Imp. Indic.	Past. Part.
binda, to bind,	*band*,	*bundit*.
gifva, to give,	*gaf*,	*gifvit*.
taga, to take,	*tog*,	*tagit*.
skrifva, to write,	*skref*,	*skrifvit*.
klyfva, to cleave,	*klöf*,	*klufvit*.

Some verbs may be declined according both to the first and the second form of conjugation; as, (*att*) *dela*, 'to share,' which may be written imperf. *del*ade or *del*te, participle past *del*at or *delt*.

Other verbs vary between the other conjugations, as—

	Imperfect.	Supine.
(*att*) *duga*, to be fit for,	*dugde* or *dög*,	*dugat* or *dugt.*
,, *heta*, to be called,	*hette* or *het*,	*hetat.*
,, *lefva*, to live,	*lefde* or *leftc*,	*lefvat* or *left.*

There is a tendency in modern Swedish to transfer verbs of the fourth or strong form of conjugation to the first or second weak form. Similarly, modern usage tends to reject the harder radical vowels in favour of their softer derivatives, taking *ä* for *å*, *ö* for *u*, etc.; while for the same considerations of euphony the *j* is frequently dropped, as in *böd*, originally *bjöd*, imperf. indicative of *bjuda*, 'to bid;' *söng*, originally *sjöng*, imp. ind. of *sjunga*, 'to sing.'

Contractions are of frequent occurrence even among the best speakers and writers; as, *bli, ta, dra, gi,* for *blifva, taga, draga, gifva; blir, tar, drar,* for *blifver, tager, drager, gifver;* and *vi, de bli, ta, dra, I blin, tan, dran,* for *vi, de blifva, taga, draga, I blifven, tagen, dragen.*

The personal termination *er* is always dropped in *gala*, 'to crow;' *mala*, 'to grind;' *fara, befara*, 'to go, travel;' *skära*, 'to cut;' *stjäla*, 'to steal,' etc.

ADVERBS. (*Omständighetsord.*)

The place of the adverb in Swedish is in many cases identical with that which it occupies in English; as, *den unga flickan taler väl*, 'the young girl speaks well;' *dagen derpå, gik han bort*, 'the day after, he went away;' *glädjen är förbi*, 'the pleasure is over;' *der du är, der vil jag vara!* 'where you are, there I will be!'

The affirmative *ja* is used where no negative is involved, *jo* where the question is put in a negative form; as, *Var soldaten här i går?* 'Was the soldier here yesterday?' *Ja,* 'Yes.' *Var icke soldaten der?* 'Was not the soldier there?' *Jo,* 'Yes.' The word *ju* gives a confirmative or more emphatic significance to the sentence; as, *du var ju der i går?* 'you (surely) were there yesterday?' It is used in connection with comparative modes of expression, and may be rendered by 'the,' as, *ju för ju hellere,* 'the sooner the better.'

The negative *icke*, 'not,' is a modification of the Old Northern *gi* which also appears in *aldrig (aldrige),* 'never.' This and *ej, inte,* 'not,' often follow the verb both in questions and affirmatives; as, *Sjunger icke foglen?* 'Is not the bird singing?' *Lärkan sjunger icke,* 'The lark is not singing;' *Känner du inte igen doktorn här?* 'Do you not know the doctor again?' *Nej, jag kan inte erinra mig,* 'No, I cannot remember (him).'

Certain adverbs, may be used in Swedish in the same attributive sense as in English; as, *endast Gud är allvetande,* 'only God is omniscient.'

Others may be used with a preposition in the sense of a noun; as, *jag har ej sett honom* PÅ LÄNGE, 'I have not seen him for a long time;' *du har fällt nog af tårar,* 'you have shed enough tears.'

Some adverbs are used as relative or demonstrative pronouns; as, *det tidehvarf* HVARI *Luther framstod var en af de stora verldshistoriska epoker,* 'the age in which Luther appeared marked one of the great historical epochs of the world;' HVAREST *vinet går in, der går vettet ut,* 'where wine enters in, sense goes out.'

Prepositions. (*Förord*).

A preposition in Swedish generally precedes directly the noun which it governs; as, *nu blifver det en stor glädje på gården och i hela huset,* ' now there will be great joy on the estate, and in the house.'

Some prepositions may follow the noun or pronoun; as, *det kan ske honom förutan,* 'that may happen without him;' *oss emellan sagdt, älskar jag henne icke,* ' between ourselves, I do not care for her;' *att gå om,* 'to pass by;' *systeren gjorde det mig emot,* ' my sister did it against my wishes;' *ni med,* ' you and all.'

Many prepositions govern the genitive in accordance with the Old Northern construction; as, *till lands,* ' by land;' *till bords,* 'to (table) dinner.' This older form is also traceable in such expressions as, *tillhanda,* 'to hand;' *i somras,* ' last summer;' *i sommar,* 'this summer;' *om sommaren,* ' in the summer;' *i höstas,* 'last autumn;' *i höst,* ' this autumn.'

The correct use of the prepositions presents considerable difficulty in Swedish. Thus, for instance, in rendering the English 'of,' a number of different prepositions are needed in accordance with the special nature of the relations or conditions referred to; as, *herren* I *huset,* 'the master of the house;' *släppen* PÅ *rocken,* ' the train of the dress;' *skälet* TILL, 'the reason of;' *enkaman* EFTER *min syster,* 'widower of my sister;' *tjenaren* HOS *generalen*, 'the servant of the general;' *full* MED, 'full of;' AF *gammal familj*, 'of an old family;' *en man* AF *snille*, 'a man of genius.'

Till still governs a genitive as in Old Swedish; as, *till fots*, 'on foot;' but the Swedish prepositions generally govern the dative or the accusative.

CONJUNCTIONS. (*Bindeord.*)

The conjunction *samt*, 'with,' 'also,' is frequently used in the place of 'and;' as, *Generalen kom med grefven samt presten*, 'the general came with the count and the clergyman.

Ej heller, 'nor,' is used after a negative; as, *min fader vet det icke, ej heller min broder*, 'neither my father nor my brother knows it.'

Ej, or *icke blott*, 'not only,' is used in combination with *men*, 'but,' or *utan afven*, 'but also,' 'but even;' as, *ej blott min fader, men min broder vet det*, 'my brother knows it as well as my father;' *icke blott fadren, utan äfven brodren trodde det*, 'not only the father, but the brother even believed it.'

Att, 'that,' often requires to be preceded by *än*, 'than,' or *för*, 'for;' as, *barnet är yngre* ÄN ATT *det kunna resa allena*, 'the child is too young to be able to travel alone;' *hon var alt för mycket nedslagen, för* ATT *hon skulle gå i sällskap*, 'she was much too depressed to go into society;' *Svenskarne uppreste sig mot Kristian II. af Danmark*, DERFÖR ATT *han var en tyrann*, 'the Swedes rose against Christian II. of Denmark because he was a tyrant.'

Så sant som, hvar om icke, 'if not,' may be used in an elliptical sense; as, *jag är oskyldig, så sant mig Gud hjelpe,* 'I am innocent, so help me God.' *Om jag vinner spelet blir jag glad,* HVAR OM ICKE, *tröstar jag mig,* 'I shall be glad if I win the game, but if I do not, I shall console myself.' *Så* is often used at the beginning of a secondary sentence, to connect it with the primary sentence; as, *när min vän kommer så är jag väl tillfreds,* 'when my friend comes, I am well pleased;' *om vädret blir vackert, så kommer min syster i afton,* 'if the weather should be good, my sister will come this evening.'

Såsom, 'as,' is often used in the sense of 'namely;' as, *från Ostindien erhållas allahande kryddor,* SÅSOM *peppar kanel,* etc., 'from the East Indies we obtain various spices, namely, pepper, cinnamon,' etc. *Nämligen,* 'namely,' is, on the other hand, used in the sense of 'for,' 'because;' as, *hans beteende är oförklarligt; han har* NÄMLIGEN *alltid ansetts vara en hederlig man,* 'his conduct is inexplicable because he has always been regarded as an honest man.' *Ty,* may be similarly used; as, *Åskan är nyttig, ty hon rensar luften,* 'thunder is of use because it clears the air.'

Antingen—eller are used in the sense of 'whether'—'or;' as, *han har änu ej bestämt sig* ANTINGEN *han skall bli läkare* ELLER *jurist,* 'he has not yet decided if he will be a doctor or a lawyer.' The elliptical expression *vare sig,* 'be it,' may be similarly employed; as, VARE SIG *rik,* VARE SIG *fattig, så bör man njuta skydd af lagen,* 'whether it be rich, or poor, all ought to enjoy the protection of the law.'

The conversion of adverbs and prepositions into conjunctions, and the post-position of prepositions, of both of which we subjoin a few additional examples, constitute peculiar features of Swedish, specially worthy of attention owing to the light which they throw on the origin of various idiomatic expressions in English.

Icke mannen, UTAN *qvinnan förde ordet.*
It was the woman and not the man who spoke.

Han sprang, ELLER *snarare flög.*
He sprang, or rather flew.

Han är för dem hvad han fordom varit.
He is the same to them as he formerly was.

Han är fegare, ÄN ATT *han skulle våga försöket.*
He is too cowardly to make the attempt.

Bäst jåg språng, horde jag ett rop bakom mig.
As I ran (as I best could) I heard a cry behind me.

DET FÖRSTA *han kommer hem, skall han köra Er på dörren.*
As soon as he comes home, he will drive you out of doors.

ÄN *regnar det,* ÄN *skiner solen.*
It either rains, or the sun shines.

Gossen tar jag vård OM.
I will take charge of the boy.

Oss EMELLAN *sagdt, gjorde han mig* EMOT.
Between ourselves, he acted against me.

Linné blef en furste i den vetenskap han egnade sig ÅT.
Linnæus was a prince in the science to which he devoted himself.

Han var frisk UTOM ATT *han haltade något.*
He was fresh and cool, although he had not stopped on the way.

HURU *lärd han* ÄN *är, förstår han icke detta.*
However learned he may be, he does not understand that.

Luften är icke varm, OAKTADT *solen skiner.*
The air is not warm, although (notwithstanding that) the sun shines.

Hon såg mig AN.
She looked at me.

HVAD ÄN *må inträffa.*
Whatever (then) may happen.

Dagen FÖR ÄN *han for.*
The day before (than) he started.

At tage sig bra UT.
To look well.

Han tar rocken PÅ.
He puts on his coat.

Hvem tar ni mig FÖR?
Who do you take me for?

Här tar vägen AF.
Here the road turns off.

Det är ingenting at tale OM.
It is not worth speaking of.

BARA *jag viste sanheten !*
If I only knew the truth !
Man gör framsteg DERIGENOM ATT *man är flitig.*
One makes progress by being diligent.

OLDER SWEDISH MODES OF INFLECTION.

We give the following examples of the manner in which nouns, adjectives, pronouns and nouns were inflected in the *Forn-Svenskan* (Ancient Swedish), in order to show the leading characteristic differences between that earlier form of the language and Modern Swedish.

As has already been noticed in the Introduction, the so-called *Forn-Svenskan*, which was spoken by Goths as well as Swedes, and which was almost identical with the *Dönsk Tunga* (Danish Tongue), and *Forn-Norskan* (Ancient Norse) of the early Northmen, continued with slight modifications to be the spoken speech of the Swedish people till about the time of the Reformation. At that period, under Gustaf Vasa, the language passed to that middle stage of its development which is characterized as that of *Gammal-Svenskan*, or Old Swedish, in contradistinction to its latest and still existing phase *Ny-Svenskan*, or Modern Swedish.

In *Forn-Svenskan* we have, therefore, the earliest intermediate link between the Swedish of our own times and the Old Northern, which was the common tongue of all the Scandinavian peoples before their separation into distinct nations as Swedes, Norwegians, and Danes. This remnant of ancient Scandinavian consequently possesses an

F

interest second only to that of its sister-form of speech the Icelandic, or *Forn-Norskan* of the ninth century, whose earliest literary remains are admitted to be the most perfect representatives extant of the so-called *Old Northern*. And if *Forn-Svenskan* has comparatively little importance from a merely literary point of view, a study of its grammatical structure, and of numerous survivals in the later forms of Swedish, will be found to throw considerable light on the process of development through which many English as well as Scandinavian words have passed, showing that notwithstanding their actual differences they have had one common origin.

Nouns.

Strong mode of declension without the Article.

	Masculine.	Feminine.	Neuter.
Sing.: N.	*brander*, fire.	*sak*, thing.	*land*, country.
G.	*brands*	*sakar*	*lands*
D.	*brandi(e)*	*saku(sak)*	*landi(e)*
A.	*brand*	*sak*	*land*
Plur.: N.	*brandar*	*sakar(ir, er)*	*land*
G.	*branda*	*saka*	*landa*
D.	*brandum(om)*	*sakum(om)*	*landum(om)*
A.	*branda*	*sakar*	*land*.

With the Article.

Sing.: N.	*brandrin(en)*	*sakin(en)*	*landit(et)*
G.	*brandsins*	*sakinnar*	*landsins*

OLD SWEDISH. 67

Masculine.	Feminine.	Neuter.
D. *brand*inum	*sak*inni	*land*inu
A. *brand*in	*sak*ina	*land*it
Plur.: N. *brand*anir(*ni, ne*)	*sak*anar(*na*)	*land*in(*en*)
G. *brand*anna	*sak*anna	*land*anna
D. *brand*umin	*sak*umin	*land*umin
A. *brand*ana	*sak*anar	*land*in.

STRONG MODE OF DECLENSION OF ADJECTIVES.

Sing.: N. *goðer*, good.	*goð*	*got*
G. *goðs*	*goðrar*	*goðs*
D. *goðum*(*om*)	*goðri*	*goðu*(*o*)
A. *goðan*	*goða*	*got*
Plur.: N. *goðir*	*goðar*	*goð*
G. *goðra*	*goðra*	*goðra*
D. *goðum*(*om*)	*goðum*(*om*)	*goðum*(*om*)
A. *goða*	*goðar*	*goð*.

Comparative, *bœtri, bœtra*; Superlative, *bœsti, bœsta*.

PERSONAL PRONOUNS.

Sing.: N. *ik*(*iak*), I.	*ðu*, thou.	*han*, he.	*hun* (*hon*),she.
G. *min*	*ðin*	*hans*	*hœnnar*
D. *mer*	*ðer*	*hanum*	*hœnni*
A. *mik*	*ðik*	*han*	*hana* (*hona*).
Plur.: N. *vir*, we.	*ir*, ye.		
G. *var*	*iðar*		
D. & A. *os*	*iðer*		

Demonstrative Pronouns.

	Masc.	Fem.	Neut.
Sing. N.	sar (sa)	su	ðat, 'that.'
G.	ðes	ðeirrar	ðes
D.	ðeim	ðeirri	ðy
A.	ðan (ðæn)	ða	ðat
Plur. N.	ðeir	ðær	ðau, 'those.'
G.	ðeirra	ðeirra	ðeirra
D.	ðeim	ðeim	ðeim
A.	ða	ðær	ðau
Sing. N.	ðessi	ðessi	ðetta, 'this.'
G.	ðessa	ðessar	ðessa
D.	ðessum	ðessi	ðessu
A.	ðenna	ðessa	ðetta
Plur. N.	ðessir	ðessar	ðessi, 'these.'
G.	ðessa	ðessa	ðessa
D.	ðessum	ðessum	ðessum
A.	ðessa	ðessar	ðessi.

The third demonstrative pronoun in Old Swedish *hin*, *hin*, *hint*, from which the modern definite and terminal affix-articles have been derived were declined like the possessive pronouns *min*, 'my;' *ðin*, 'thy,' &c.

	Masc.	Fem.	Neut.
Sing. N.	hin	hin	hint (hit), 'this,' 'that.'
G.	hins	hinnar	hins
D.	hinum	hinni	hinu,
A.	hin	hina	hint (hit)
Plur. N.	hinir	hinar	hin, 'these,' 'those.'
G.	hinna	hinna	hinna
D.	hinum	hinum	hinum
A.	hina	hinar	hin

It will be observed that the modern Swedish demonstrative pronouns, *den, denne,* which appeared early in the language in their present form, have been directly derived from the older accusatives ðan, ðæn, ðenna.

VERBS.

Weak mode of Conjugation.   *Strong mode of Conjugation.*
Infinitive, *kalla,* 'to call.'   *brinna,* ' to burn.'
Pres. Part. *kallandi*   *brinnandi.*
Perf. Part. *kallaðer*   *brunnin.*

The supine does not appear in the Old Swedish.

Indicative.

Present.

Sing. 1, 2, 3 Pers. *kallar*   *brinder*
Plur. 1.   ,,   *kallum(om)*   *brinnum(om)*
2.   ,,   *kallin(en)*   *brinnin(en)*
3.   ,,   *kalla*   *brinna.*

Imperfect.

Sing. 1, 2, 3 Pers. *kallaði*   1, 3, Pers. *bran*
                                 2 Pers. *brant*
Plur. 1.   ,,   *kallaðum*   *brunnum*
2.   ,,   *kallaðin*   *brunnin*
3.   ,,   *kallaðu*   *brunnu(o).*

Imperative.

Sing. 2nd Pers. *kalla*   *brin*
Plur. 1.   ,,   *kallum*   *brinnum*
2.   ,,   *kallin*   *brinnin.*

A CATALOGUE OF IMPORTANT WORKS,

PUBLISHED BY

TRÜBNER & CO.

57 AND 59 LUDGATE HILL.

ABEL.—LINGUISTIC ESSAYS. By Carl Abel. CONTENTS: Language as the Expression of National Modes of Thought—The Conception of Love in some Ancient and Modern Languages—The English Verbs of Command—The Discrimination of Synonyms—Philological Methods—The Connection between Dictionary and Grammar—The Possibility of a Common Literary Language for the Slav Nations—Coptic Intensification—The Origin of Language—The Order and Position of Words in the Latin Sentence. Post 8vo, pp. xii. and 282, cloth. 1882. 9s.

ABEL.—SLAVIC AND LATIN. Ilchester Lectures on Comparative Lexicography. Delivered at the Taylor Institution, Oxford. By Carl Abel, Ph.D. Post 8vo, pp. vi.-124, cloth. 1883. 5s.

ABRAHAMS.—A MANUAL OF SCRIPTURE HISTORY FOR USE IN JEWISH SCHOOLS AND FAMILIES. By L. B. Abrahams, B.A., Principal Assistant Master, Jews' Free School. With Map and Appendices. Third Edition. Crown 8vo, pp. viii. and 152, cloth. 1883. 1s. 6d.

AGASSIZ.—AN ESSAY ON CLASSIFICATION. By Louis Agassiz. 8vo, pp. vii. and 381, cloth. 1859. 12s.

AHLWARDT.—THE DIVANS OF THE SIX ANCIENT ARABIC POETS, ENNÁBIGA, 'ANTARA, THARAFA, ZUHAIR, 'ALQUAMA, and IMRUULQUAIS; chiefly according to the MSS. of Paris, Gotha, and Leyden, and the Collection of their Fragments, with a List of the various Readings of the Text. Edited by W. Ahlwardt, Professor of Oriental Languages at the University of Greifswald. Demy 8vo, pp. xxx. and 340, cloth. 1870. 12s.

AHN.—PRACTICAL GRAMMAR OF THE GERMAN LANGUAGE. By Dr. F. Ahn. A New Edition. By Dr. Dawson Turner, and Prof. F. L. Weinmann. Crown 8vo, pp. cxii. and 430, cloth. 1878. 3s. 6d.

AHN.—NEW, PRACTICAL, AND EASY METHOD OF LEARNING THE GERMAN LANGUAGE. By Dr. F. Ahn. First and Second Course. Bound in 1 vol. 12mo, pp. 86 and 120, cloth. 1866. 3s.

AHN.—KEY to Ditto. 12mo, pp. 40, sewed. 8d.

AHN.—MANUAL OF GERMAN AND ENGLISH CONVERSATIONS, or Vade Mecum for English Travellers. 12mo, pp. x. and 137, cloth. 1875. 1s. 6d.

A

AHN.—New, Practical, and Easy Method of Learning the French Language. By Dr. F. Ahn. First Course and Second Course. 12mo, cloth. Each 1s. 6d. The Two Courses in 1 vol. 12mo, pp. 114 and 170, cloth. 1865. 3s.

AHN.—New, Practical, and Easy Method of Learning the French Language. Third Course, containing a French Reader, with Notes and Vocabulary. By H. W. Ehrlich. 12mo, pp. viii. and 125, cloth. 1866. 1s. 6d.

AHN.—Manual of French and English Conversations, for the use of Schools and Travellers. By Dr. F. Ahn. 12mo, pp. viii. and 200, cloth. 1862. 2s. 6d.

AHN.—New, Practical, and Easy Method of Learning the Italian Language. By Dr. F. Ahn. First and Second Course. 12mo, pp. 198, cloth. 1872. 3s. 6d.

AHN.—New, Practical, and Easy Method of Learning the Dutch Language, being a complete Grammar, with Selections. By Dr. F. Ahn. 12mo, pp. viii. and 166, cloth. 1862. 3s. 6d.

AHN.—Ahn's Course. Latin Grammar for Beginners. By W. Ihne, Ph.D. 12mo, pp. vi. and 184, cloth. 1864. 3s.

ALABASTER.—The Wheel of the Law: Buddhism illustrated from Siamese Sources by the Modern Buddhist, a Life of Buddha, and an Account of the Phra Bat. By Henry Alabaster, Esq., Interpreter of Her Majesty's Consulate-General in Siam. Demy 8vo, pp. lviii. and 324, cloth. 1871. 14s.

ALI.—The Proposed Political, Legal, and Social Reforms in the Ottoman Empire and other Mohammedan States. By Moulaví Cherágh Ali, H.H. the Nizam's Civil Service. Demy 8vo, pp. liv. and 184, cloth. 1883. 8s.

ALLAN-FRASER.—Christianity and Churchism. By Patrick Allan-Fraser. 2d (revised and enlarged) Edition. Crown 8vo, pp. 52, cloth. 1884. 1s.

ALLEN.—The Colour Sense. See English and Foreign Philosophical Library, Vol. X.

ALLIBONE.—A Critical Dictionary of English Literature and British and American Authors (Living and Deceased). From the Earliest Accounts to the latter half of the 19th century. Containing over 46,000 Articles (Authors), with 40 Indexes of subjects. By S. A. Allibone. In 3 vols. royal 8vo, cloth. £5, 8s.

ALTHAUS.—The Spas of Europe. By Julius Althaus, M.D. 8vo, pp. 516, cloth. 1862. 7s. 6d.

AMATEUR Mechanic's Workshop (The). A Treatise containing Plain and Concise Directions for the Manipulation of Wood and Metals; including Casting, Forging, Brazing, Soldering, and Carpentry. By the Author of "The Lathe and its Uses." Sixth Edition. Demy 8vo, pp. vi. and 148, with Two Full-Page Illustrations, on toned paper and numerous Woodcuts, cloth. 1880. 6s.

AMATEUR MECHANICAL SOCIETY.—Journal of the Amateur Mechanical Society. 8vo. Vol. i. pp. 344 cloth. 1871-72. 12s. Vol. ii. pp. vi. and 290, cloth. 1873-77. 12s. Vol. iii. pp. iv. and 246, cloth. 1878-79. 12s. 6d.

AMERICAN Almanac and Treasury of Facts, Statistical, Financial, and Political. Edited by Ainsworth R. Spofford, Librarian of Congress. Crown 8vo, cloth. Published yearly. 1878-1884. 7s. 6d. each.

AMERY.—Notes on Forestry. By C. F. Amery, Deputy Conservator N. W. Provinces, India. Crown 8vo, pp. viii. and 120, cloth. 1875. 5s.

AMBERLEY.—An Analysis of Religious Belief. By Viscount Amberley. 2 vols. demy 8vo, pp. xvi. and 496 and 512, cloth. 1876. 30s.

AMONGST MACHINES. A Description of Various Mechanical Appliances used in the Manufacture of Wood, Metal, and other Substances. A Book for Boys, copiously Illustrated. By the Author of "The Young Mechanic." Second Edition. Imperial 16mo, pp. viii. and 336, cloth. 1878. 7s. 6d.

ANDERSON.—PRACTICAL MERCANTILE CORRESPONDENCE. A Collection of Modern Letters of Business, with Notes, Critical and Explanatory, and an Appendix, containing a Dictionary of Commercial Technicalities, pro forma Invoices, Account Sales, Bills of Lading, and Bills of Exchange; also an Explanation of the German Chain Rule. 24th Edition, revised and enlarged. By William Anderson. 12mo, pp. 288, cloth. 5s.

ANDERSON and TUGMAN.—MERCANTILE CORRESPONDENCE, containing a Collection of Commercial Letters in Portuguese and English, with their translation on opposite pages, for the use of Business Men and of Students in either of the Languages, treating in modern style of the system of Business in the principal Commercial Cities of the World. Accompanied by pro forma Accounts, Sales, Invoices, Bills of Lading, Drafts, &c. With an Introduction and copious Notes. By William Anderson and James E. Tugman. 12mo, pp. xi. and 193, cloth. 1867. 6s.

APEL.—PROSE SPECIMENS FOR TRANSLATION INTO GERMAN, with copious Vocabularies and Explanations. By H. Apel. 12mo, pp. viii. and 246, cloth. 1862. 4s. 6d.

APPLETON (Dr.)—LIFE AND LITERARY RELICS. See English and Foreign Philosophical Library, Vol. XIII.

ARAGO.—LES ARISTOCRATIES. A Comedy in Verse. By Etienne Arago. Edited, with English Notes and Notice on Etienne Arago, by the Rev. E. P. H. Brette, B.D., Head Master of the French School, Christ's Hospital, Examiner in the University of London. Fcap. 8vo, pp. 244, cloth. 1868. 4s.

ARMITAGE.—LECTURES ON PAINTING : Delivered to the Students of the Royal Academy. By Edward Armitage, R.A. Crown 8vo, pp. 256, with 29 Illustrations, cloth. 1883. 7s. 6d.

ARNOLD.—INDIAN IDYLLS. From the Sanskrit of the Mahâbhârata. By Edwin Arnold, C.S.I., &c. Crown 8vo, pp. xii. and 282, cloth. 1883. 7s. 6d.

ARNOLD.—PEARLS OF THE FAITH; or, Islam's Rosary : being the Ninety-nine beautiful names of Allah. With Comments in Verse from various Oriental sources as made by an Indian Mussulman. By Edwin Arnold, M.A., C.S.I., &c. Third Edition. Crown 8vo, pp. xvi. and 320, cloth. 1884. 7s. 6d.

ARNOLD.—THE LIGHT OF ASIA; or, THE GREAT RENUNCIATION (Mahâbhinishkramana). Being the Life and Teaching of Gautama, Prince of India, and Founder of Buddhism (as told in verse by an Indian Buddhist). By Edwin Arnold, C.S.I., &c. Crown 8vo, pp. xiii. and 238, limp parchment. 1884. 2s. 6d. Library Edition. 1883. 7s. 6d.

ARNOLD.—THE ILIAD AND ODYSSEY OF INDIA. By Edwin Arnold, M.A., F.R.G.S., &c., &c. Fcap. 8vo, pp. 24, sewed. 1s.

ARNOLD.—A SIMPLE TRANSLITERAL GRAMMAR OF THE TURKISH LANGUAGE. Compiled from Various Sources. With Dialogues and Vocabulary. By Edwin Arnold, M.A., C.S.I., F.R.G.S. Post 8vo, pp. 80, cloth. 1877. 2s. 6d.

ARNOLD.—INDIAN POETRY. See Trübner's Oriental Series.

ARTOM.—SERMONS. By the Rev. B. Artom, Chief Rabbi of the Spanish and Portuguese Congregations of England. First Series. Second Edition. Crown 8vo, pp. viii. and 314, cloth. 1876. 6s.

ASHER.—ON THE STUDY OF MODERN LANGUAGES in general, and of the English Language in particular. An Essay. By David Asher, Ph.D. 12mo, pp. viii. and 80, cloth. 1859. 2s.

ASIATIC SOCIETY OF BENGAL. List of Publications on application.

ASIATIC SOCIETY.—JOURNAL OF THE ROYAL ASIATIC SOCIETY OF GREAT BRITAIN AND IRELAND, from the Commencement to 1863. First Series, complete in 20 Vols. 8vo, with many Plates. £10, or in parts from 4s. to 6s. each.

ASIATIC SOCIETY.—JOURNAL OF THE ROYAL ASIATIC SOCIETY OF GREAT BRITAIN AND IRELAND. New Series. 8vo. Stitched in wrapper. 1864-84.

Vol. I., 2 Parts, pp. iv. and 490, 16s.—Vol. II., 2 Parts, pp. 522, 16s.—Vol. III., 2 Parts, pp. 516, with Photograph, 22s.—Vol. IV., 2 Parts, pp. 521, 16s.—Vol. V., 2 Parts, pp. 463, with 10 full-page and folding Plates, 18s. 6d.—Vol. VI., Part 1, pp. 212, with 2 Plates and a Map, 8s.—Vol. VI. Part 2, pp. 272, with Plate and Map, 8s.—Vol. VII., Part 1, pp. 194, with a Plate. 8s.—Vol. VII., Part 2, pp. 204, with 7 Plates and a Map, 8s.—Vol. VIII., Part 1, pp. 156, with 3 Plates and a Plan, 8s.—Vol. VIII., Part 2, pp. 152, 8s.—Vol. IX., Part 1, pp. 154, with a Plate, 8s.—Vol. IX., Part 2, pp. 292, with 3 Plates, 10s. 6d.—Vol. X., Part 1, pp. 156, with 2 Plates and a Map, 8s.—Vol. X., Part 2, pp. 146, 6s.—Vol. X., Part 3, pp. 204, 8s.—Vol. XI., Part 1, pp. 128, 5s.—Vol. XI., Part 2, pp. 158, with 2 Plates, 7s. 6d.—Vol. XI., Part 3, pp. 250, 8s.—Vol. XII., Part 1, pp. 152, 5s.—Vol. XII., Part 2, pp. 182, with 2 Plates and Map, 6s.—Vol. XII., Part 3, pp. 100, 4s.—Vol. XII., Part 4, pp. x., 152., cxx , 16, 8s.—Vol. XIII., Part 1, pp. 120, 5s.—Vol. XIII., Part 2, pp. 170, with a Map, 8s.—Vol. XIII., Part 3, pp. 178, with a Table, 7s. 6d.—Vol. XIII., Part 4, pp. 282, with a Plate and Table, 10s. 6d.—Vol. XIV., Part 1, pp. 124, with a Table and 2 Plates, 5s.—Vol. XIV., Part 2, pp. 164, with 1 Table, 7s. 6d.—Vol. XIV., Part 3, pp. 206, with 6 Plates, 8s.—Vol. XIV., Part 4, pp. 492, with 1 Plate, 14s.—Vol. XV., Part 1, pp. 136, 6s. ; Part 2, pp. 158, with 3 Tables, 5s. ; Part 3, pp. 192, 6s. ; Part 4, pp. 140, 5s.—Vol. XVI., Part 1, pp. 138, with 2 Plates, 7s. Part 2, pp. 184, with 1 Plate, 9s. Part 3, July 1884, pp.

ASPLET.—THE COMPLETE FRENCH COURSE. Part II. Containing all the Rules of French Syntax, &c., &c. By Georges C. Asplet, French Master, Frome. Fcap. 8vo, pp. xx. and 276, cloth. 1880. 2s. 6d.

ASTON.—A Short Grammar of the Japanese Spoken Language. By W. G. Aston, M.A. Third Edition. Crown 8vo, pp. 96, cloth. 1873. 12s.

ASTON.—A GRAMMAR OF THE JAPANESE WRITTEN LANGUAGE. By W. G. Aston, M.A., Assistant Japanese Secretary H.B.M.'s Legation, Yedo, Japan. Second Edition. 8vo, pp. 306, cloth. 1877. 28s.

ASTONISHED AT AMERICA. BEING CURSORY DEDUCTIONS, &c., &c. By Zigzag. Fcap. 8vo, pp. xvi.-108, boards. 1880. 1s.

AUCTORES SANSCRITI.

Vol. I. THE JAIMINÎYA-NYÂYA-MÂLÂ-VISTARA. Edited for the Sanskrit Text Society, under the supervision of Theodor Goldstücker. Large 4to, pp. 582, cloth. £3, 13s. 6d.

Vol. II. THE INSTITUTES OF GAUTAMA. Edited, with an Index of Words, by A. F. Stenzler, Ph.D., Prof. of Oriental Languages in the University of Breslau. 8vo, pp. iv. and 78, cloth. 1876. 4s. 6d. Stitched, 3s. 6d.

Vol. III. VAITÂNA SUTRA : THE RITUAL OF THE ATHARVA VEDA. Edited, with Critical Notes and Indices, by Dr. R. Garbe. 8vo, pp. viii. and 120, sewed. 1878. 5s.

Vols. IV. and V.—VARDHAMANA'S GANARATNAMAHODADHI, with the Author's Commentary. Edited, with Critical Notes and Indices, by Julius Eggeling, Ph.D. 8vo. Part I., pp. xii. and 240, wrapper. 1879. 6s. Part II., pp. 240, wrapper. 1881. 6s.

AUGIER.—DIANE. A Drama in Verse. By Émile Augier. Edited with English Notes and Notice on Augier. By Theodore Karcher, LL.B., of the Royal Military Academy and the University of London. 12mo, pp. xiii. and 146, cloth. 1867. 2s. 6d.

AUSTIN.—A PRACTICAL TREATISE on the Preparation, Combination, and Application of Calcareous and Hydraulic Limes and Cements. To which is added many useful Recipes for various Scientific, Mercantile, and Domestic Purposes. By James G. Austin, Architect. 12mo, pp. 192, cloth. 1862. 5s.

AXON.—THE MECHANIC'S FRIEND. A Collection of Receipts and Practical Suggestions relating to Aquaria, Bronzing, Cements, Drawing, Dyes, Electricity, Gilding, Glass-working, &c. Numerous Woodcuts. Edited by W. E. A. Axon, M.R.S.L , F.S.S. Crown 8vo, pp. xii. and 339, cloth. 1875. 4s. 6d.

BABA.—An Elementary Grammar of the Japanese Language, with Easy Progressive Exercises. By Tatui Baba. Crown 8vo, pp. xiv, and 92, cloth. 1873. 5s.

BACON.—THE LIFE AND TIMES OF FRANCIS BACON. Extracted from the Edition of his Occasional Writings by James Spedding. 2 vols. post 8vo, pp. xx., 710, and xiv., 708, cloth. 1878. 21s.

BADEN-POWELL.—PROTECTION AND BAD TIMES, with Special Reference to the Political Economy of English Colonisation. By George Baden-Powell, M.A., F.R.A.S., F.S.S., Author of "New Homes for the Old Country," &c., &c. 8vo, pp. xii.-376, cloth. 1879. 6s. 6d.

BADER.—THE NATURAL AND MORBID CHANGES OF THE HUMAN EYE, AND THEIR TREATMENT. By C. Bader. Medium 8vo, pp. viii. and 506, cloth. 1868. 16s.

BADER.—PLATES ILLUSTRATING THE NATURAL AND MORBID CHANGES OF THE HUMAN EYE. By C. Bader. Six chromo-lithographic Plates, each containing the figures of six Eyes, and four lithographed Plates, with figures of Instruments. With an Explanatory Text of 32 pages. Medium 8vo, in a portfolio. 21s. Price for Text and Atlas taken together, £1, 12s.

BADLEY.—INDIAN MISSIONARY RECORD AND MEMORIAL VOLUME. By the Rev. B. H. Badley, of the American Methodist Mission. 8vo, pp. xii. and 280, cloth. 1876. 10s. 6d.

BALFOUR.—WAIFS AND STRAYS FROM THE FAR EAST; being a Series of Disconnected Essays on Matters relating to China. By Frederick Henry Balfour. 1 vol. demy 8vo, pp. 224, cloth. 1876. 10s. 6d.

BALFOUR.—THE DIVINE CLASSIC OF NAN-HUA; being the Works of Chuang Tsze, Taoist Philosopher. With an Excursus, and Copious Annotations in English and Chinese. By F. H. Balfour, F.R.G.S., Author of "Waifs and Strays from the Far East," &c. Demy 8vo, pp. xlviii. and 426, cloth. 1881. 14s.

BALL.—THE DIAMONDS, COAL, AND GOLD OF INDIA; their Mode of Occurrence and Distribution. By V. Ball, M.A., F.G.S., of the Geological Survey of. India. Fcap. 8vo, pp. viii. and 136, cloth. 1881. 5s.

BALL.—A MANUAL OF THE GEOLOGY OF INDIA. Part III. Economic Geology. By V. Ball, M.A., F.G.S. Royal 8vo, pp. xx. and 640, with 6 Maps and 10 Plates, cloth. 1881. 10s. (For Parts I. and II. see MEDLICOTT.)

BALLAD SOCIETY—Subscriptions, small paper, one guinea; large paper, two guineas per annum. List of publications on application.

BALLANTYNE.—ELEMENTS OF HINDI AND BRAJ BHAKHA GRAMMAR. Compiled for the use of the East India College at Haileybury. By James R. Ballantyne. Second Edition. Crown 8vo, pp. 38, cloth. 1868. 5s.

BALLANTYNE.—FIRST LESSONS IN SANSKRIT GRAMMAR; together with an Introduction to the Hitopadesa. New Edition. By James R. Ballantyne, LL.D., Librarian of the India Office. 8vo, pp. viii. and 110, cloth. 1873. 3s. 6d.

BARANOWSKI.—VADE MECUM DE LA LANGUE FRANÇAISE, rédigé d'après les Dictionnaires classiques avec les Exemples de Bonnes Locutions que donne l'Académie Française, on qu'on trouve dans les ouvrages des plus célèbres auteurs. Par J. J. Baranowski, avec l'approbation de M. E. Littré, Sénateur, &c. 32mo, pp. 224. 1879. Cloth, 2s. 6d.; morocco, 3s. 6d.; morocco tuck, 4s.

BARANOWSKI.—ANGLO-POLISH LEXICON. By J. J. Baranowski, formerly Under-Secretary to the Bank of Poland, in Warsaw. Fcap. 8vo, pp. viii. and 492, cloth. 1884. 12s.

BARENTS' RELICS.—Recovered in the summer of 1876 by Charles L. W. Gardiner, Esq., and presented to the Dutch Government. Described and explained by J. K. J. de Jonge, Deputy Royal Architect at the Hague. Published by command of His Excellency, W. F. Van F.R.P. Taelman Kip, Minister of Marine. Translated, with a Preface, by S. R. Van Campen. With a Map, Illustrations, and a fac-simile of the Scroll. 8vo, pp. 70, cloth. 1877. 5s.

BARRIERE and CAPENDU.—LES FAUX BONSHOMMES, a Comedy. By Théodore Barrière and Ernest Capendu. Edited, with English Notes and Notice on Barrière, by Professor Ch. Cassal, LL.D., of University College, London. 12mo, pp. xvi. and 304, cloth. 1863. 4s.

BARTH.—THE RELIGIONS OF INDIA. See Trübner's Oriental Series.

BARTLETT.—DICTIONARY OF AMERICANISMS. A Glossary of Words and Phrases colloquially used in the United States. By John Russell Bartlett. Fourth Edition, considerably enlarged and improved. 8vo, pp. xlvi. and 814, cloth. 1877. 20s.

BATTYE.—WHAT IS VITAL FORCE? or, a Short and Comprehensive Sketch, including Vital Physics, Animal Morphology, and Epidemics; to which is added an Appendix upon Geology, IS THE DENTRITAL THEORY OF GEOLOGY TENABLE? By Richard Fawcett Battye. 8vo, pp. iv. and 336, cloth. 1877. 7s. 6d.

BAZLEY.—NOTES ON THE EPICYCLODIAL CUTTING FRAME of Messrs. Holtzapffel & Co. With special reference to its Compensation Adjustment, and with numerous Illustrations of its Capabilities. By Thomas Sebastian Bazley, M.A. 8vo, pp. xvi. and 192, cloth. Illustrated. 1872. 10s. 6d.

BAZLEY.—THE STARS IN THEIR COURSES: A Twofold Series of Maps, with a Catalogue, showing how to identify, at any time of the year, all stars down to the 5.6 magnitude, inclusive of Heis, which are clearly visible in English latitudes. By T. S. Bazley, M.A., Author of "Notes on the Epicycloidal Cutting Frame." Atlas folio, pp. 46 and 24, Folding Plates, cloth. 1878. 15s.

BEAL.—TRAVELS OF FAH-HIAN AND SUNG-YUN, Buddhist Pilgrims, from China to India (400 A.D. and 518 A.D.) Translated from the Chinese. By Samuel Beal, B.A., Trin. Coll., Cam., &c. Crown 8vo, pp. lxxiii. and 210, with a coloured Map, cloth, ornamental. 1869. 10s. 6d.

BEAL.—A CATENA OF BUDDHIST SCRIPTURES FROM THE CHINESE. By S. Beal, B.A., Trinity College, Cambridge; a Chaplain in Her Majesty's Fleet, &c. 8vo, pp. xiv. and 436, cloth. 1871. 15s.

BEAL.—THE ROMANTIC LEGEND OF SAKYA BUDDHA. From the Chinese-Sanskrit. By the Rev. Samuel Beal. Crown 8vo, pp. 408, cloth. 1875. 12s.

BEAL.—DHAMMAPADA. See Trübner's Oriental Series.

BEAL.—BUDDHIST LITERATURE IN CHINA: Abstract of Four Lectures, Delivered by Samuel Beal, B.A., Professor of Chinese at University College, London. Demy 8vo, pp. xx. and 186, cloth. 1882. 10s. 6d.

BEAMES.—OUTLINES OF INDIAN PHILOLOGY. With a Map showing the Distribution of Indian Languages. By John Beames, M.R.A.S., Bengal Civil Service, Member of the Asiatic Society of Bengal, the Philological Society of London, and the Société Asiatique of Paris. Second enlarged and revised Edition. Crown 8vo, pp. viii. and 96, cloth. 1868. 5s.

BEAMES.—A COMPARATIVE GRAMMAR OF THE MODERN ARYAN LANGUAGES OF INDIA, to wit, Hindi, Panjabi, Sindhi, Gujarati, Marathi, Oriya, and Bengali. By John Beames, Bengal Civil Service, M.R.A.S., &c , &c. Demy 8vo. Vol. I. On Sounds. Pp. xvi. and 360, cloth. 1872. 16s.—Vol. II. The Noun and the Pronoun. Pp. xii. and 348, cloth. 1875. 16s.—Vol. III. The Verb. Pp. xii. and 316, cloth. 1879. 16s.

BELLEW.—FROM THE INDUS TO THE TIGRIS. A Narrative of a Journey through the Countries of Balochistan, Afghanistan, Khorassan, and Iran in 1872; together with a complete Synoptical Grammar and Vocabulary of the Brahoe Language, and a Record of the Meteorological Observations and Altitudes on the March from the Indus to the Tigris. By Henry Walter Bellew, C S.I., Surgeon, Bengal Staff Corps. Demy 8vo, pp. viii. and 496, cloth. 1874. 14s.

BELLEW.—KASHMIR AND KASHGHAR; a Narrative of the Journey of the Embassy to Kashghar in 1873-74. By H. W. Bellew, C.S.I. Demy 8vo, pp. xxxii. and 420, cloth. 1875. 16s.

BELLEW.—THE RACES OF AFGHANISTAN. Being a Brief Account of the Principal Nations Inhabiting that Country. By Surgeon-Major H. W. Bellew, C.S.I., late on Special Political Duty at Kabul. 8vo, pp. 124, cloth. 1880. 7s. 6d.

BELLOWS.—ENGLISH OUTLINE VOCABULARY for the use of Students of the Chinese, Japanese, and other Languages. Arranged by John Bellows. With Notes on the Writing of Chinese with Roman Letters, by Professor Summers, King's College, London. Crown 8vo, pp. vi. and 368, cloth. 1867. 6s.

BELLOWS.—OUTLINE DICTIONARY FOR THE USE OF MISSIONARIES, EXPLORERS, AND STUDENTS OF LANGUAGE. By Max Müller, M.A., Taylorian Professor in the University of Oxford. With an Introduction on the proper use of the ordinary English Alphabet in transcribing Foreign Languages. The Vocabulary compiled by John Bellows. Crown 8vo, pp. xxxi. and 368, limp morocco. 1867. 7s. 6d.

BELLOWS.—TOUS LES VERBES. Conjugations of all the Verbs in the French and English Languages. By John Bellows. Revised by Professor Beljame, B.A., LL.B., of the University of Paris, and Official Interpreter to the Imperial Court, and George B. Strickland, late Assistant French Master, Royal Naval School, London. Also a New Table of Equivalent Values of French and English Money, Weights, and Measures. 32mo, 76 Tables, sewed. 1867. 1s.

BELLOWS.—FRENCH AND ENGLISH DICTIONARY FOR THE POCKET. By John Bellows. Containing the French-English and English-French divisions on the same page; conjugating all the verbs; distinguishing the genders by different types; giving numerous aids to pronunciation; indicating the *liaison* or *non-liaison* of terminal consonants; and translating units of weight, measure, and value, by a series of tables differing entirely from any hitherto published. The new edition, which is but six ounces in weight, has been remodelled, and contains many thousands of additional words and renderings. Miniature maps of France, the British Isles, Paris, and London, are added to the Geographical Section. Second Edition. 32mo, pp. 608, roan tuck, or persian without tuck. 1877. 10s. 6d.; morocco tuck, 12s. 6d.

BENEDIX.—DER VETTER. Comedy in Three Acts. By Roderich Benedix. With Grammatical and Explanatory Notes by F. Weinmann, German Master at the Royal Institution School, Liverpool, and G. Zimmermann, Teacher of Modern Languages. 12mo, pp. 128, cloth. 1863. 2s. 6d.

BENFEY.—A PRACTICAL GRAMMAR OF THE SANSKRIT LANGUAGE, for the use of Early Students. By Theodor Benfey, Professor of Sanskrit in the University of Göttingen. Second, revised, and enlarged Edition. Royal 8vo, pp. viii. and 296, cloth. 1868. 10s. 6d.

BENTHAM.—THEORY OF LEGISLATION. By Jeremy Bentham. Translated from the French of Etienne Dumont by R. Hildreth. Fourth Edition. Post 8vo, pp. xv. and 472, cloth. 1882. 7s. 6d.

BETTS.—*See* VALDES.

BEVERIDGE.—THE DISTRICT OF BAKARGANJ. Its History and Statistics. By H. Beveridge, B.C.S., Magistrate and Collector of Bakarganj. 8vo, pp. xx. and 460, cloth. 1876. 21s.

BICKNELL.—*See* HAFIZ.

BIERBAUM.—HISTORY OF THE ENGLISH LANGUAGE AND LITERATURE.—By F. J. Bierbaum, Ph.D. Crown 8vo, pp. viii. and 270, cloth. 1883. 3s.

BIGANDET.—THE LIFE OF GAUDAMA. See Trübner's Oriental Series.

BILLINGS.—THE PRINCIPLES OF VENTILATION AND HEATING, and their Practical Application. By John S. Billings, M.D., LL.D. (Edinb.), Surgeon U.S. Army. Demy 8vo, pp. x. and 216, cloth. 1884. 15s.

BIRCH.—FASTI MONASTICI AEVI SAXONICI; or, An Alphabetical List of the Heads of Religious Houses in England previous to the Norman Conquest, to which is prefixed a Chronological Catalogue of Contemporary Foundations. By Walter de Gray Birch. 8vo, pp. vii. and 114, cloth. 1873. 5s.

BIRD.—PHYSIOLOGICAL ESSAYS. Drink Craving, Differences in Men, Idiosyncrasy, and the Origin of Disease. By Robert Bird, M.D. Demy 8vo, pp. 246, cloth. 1870. 7s. 6d.

BIZYENOS.—ΑΤΘΙΔΕΣ ΑΥΡΑΙ. Poems. By George M. Bizyenos. With Frontispiece Etched by Prof. A. Legros. Royal 8vo, pp. viii.-312, printed on hand-made paper, and richly bound. 1883. £1, 11s. 6d.

BLACK.—YOUNG JAPAN, YOKOHAMA AND YEDO. A Narrative of the Settlement and the City, from the Signing of the Treaties in 1858 to the Close of the Year 1879; with a Glance at the Progress of Japan during a Period of Twenty-one Years. By John R. Black, formerly Editor of the "Japan Herald" and the "Japan Gazette." Editor of the "Far East." 2 vols. demy 8vo, pp. xviii. and 418; xiv. and 522, cloth. 1881. £2, 2s.

BLACKET.—RESEARCHES INTO THE LOST HISTORIES OF AMERICA; or, The Zodiac shown to be an Old Terrestrial Map, in which the Atlantic Isle is delineated; so that Light can be thrown upon the Obscure Histories of the Earthworks and Ruined Cities of America. By W. S. Blacket. Illustrated by numerous Engravings. 8vo, pp. 336, cloth. 1883. 10s. 6d.

BLADES.—SHAKSPERE AND TYPOGRAPHY. Being an Attempt to show Shakspere's Personal Connection with, and Technical Knowledge of, the Art of Printing; also Remarks upon some common Typographical Errors, with especial reference to the Text of Shakspere. By William Blades. 8vo, pp. viii. and 78, with an Illustration, cloth. 1872. 3s.

BLADES.—THE BIOGRAPHY AND TYPOGRAPHY OF WILLIAM CAXTON, England's First Printer. By William Blades. Founded to a great extent upon the Author's "Life and Typography of William Caxton." Brought up to the Present Date, and including all Discoveries since made. Elegantly and appropriately printed in demy 8vo, on hand-made paper, imitation old bevelled binding. 1877. £1, 1s. Cheap Edition. Crown 8vo, cloth. 1881. 5s.

BLADES.—THE ENEMIES OF BOOKS. By William Blades, Typograph. Crown 8vo, pp. xvi. and 112, parchment wrapper. 1880.

BLAKEY.—MEMOIRS OF DR. ROBERT BLAKEY, Professor of Logic and Metaphysics, Queen's College, Belfast. Edited by the Rev. Henry Miller. Crown 8vo, pp. xii. and 252, cloth. 1879. 5s.

BLEEK.—REYNARD THE FOX IN SOUTH AFRICA; or, Hottentot Fables and Tales, chiefly Translated from Original Manuscripts in the Library of His Excellency Sir George Grey, K.C.B. By W. H. I. Bleek, Ph.D. Post 8vo, pp. xxvi. and 94, cloth. 1864. 3s. 6d.

BLEEK.—A BRIEF ACCOUNT OF BUSHMAN FOLK LORE, and other Texts. By W. H. I. Bleek. Ph.D. Folio, pp. 21, paper. 2s. 6d.

BLUMHARDT.—See CHARITABALI.

BOEHMER.—*See* VALDES, and SPANISH REFORMERS.

BOJESEN.—A GUIDE TO THE DANISH LANGUAGE. Designed for English Students. By Mrs. Maria Bojesen. 12mo, pp. 250, cloth. 1863. 5s.

BOLIA.—THE GERMAN CALIGRAPHIST: Copies for German Handwriting. By C. Bolia. Oblong 4to, sewed. 1s.

BOOLE.—MESSAGE OF PSYCHIC SCIENCE TO MOTHERS AND NURSES. By Mary Boole. Crown 8vo, pp. xiv. and 266, cloth. 1883. 5s.

BOY ENGINEERS.—See under LUKIN.

BOYD.—NÁGÁNANDA; or, the Joy of the Snake World. A Buddhist Drama in Five Acts. Translated into English Prose, with Explanatory Notes, from the Sanskrit of Sá-Harsha-Deva. By Palmer Boyd, B.A., Sanskrit Scholar of Trinity College, Cambridge. With an Introduction by Professor Cowell. Crown 8vo, pp. xvi. and 100, cloth. 1872. 4s. 6d.

BRADSHAW.—B. BRADSHAW'S DICTIONARY OF BATHING PLACES AND CLIMATIC HEALTH RESORTS. Much Revised and Considerably Enlarged. With a Map in Eleven Colours. Second Edition. Small Crown 8vo, pp. lxxviii. and 364, cloth. 1883. 2s. 6d.

BRENTANO.—ON THE HISTORY AND DEVELOPMENT OF GILDS, AND THE ORIGIN OF TRADE-UNIONS. By Lujo Brentano, of Aschaffenburg, Bavaria, Doctor Juris Utriusque et Philosophiæ. 1. The Origin of Gilds. 2. Religious (or Social) Gilds. 3. Town-Gilds or Gild-Merchants. 4. Craft-Gilds. 5. Trade-Unions. 8vo, pp. xvi. and 136, cloth. 1870. 3s. 6d.

BRETSCHNEIDER.—EARLY EUROPEAN RESEARCHES INTO THE FLORA OF CHINA. By E. Bretschneider, M.D., Physician of the Russian Legation at Peking. Demy 8vo, pp. iv. and 194, sewed. 1881. 7s. 6d.

BRETSCHNEIDER.—BOTANICON SINICUM. Notes on Chinese Botany, from Native and Western Sources. By E. Bretschneider, M.D. Crown 8vo, pp. 228, wrapper. 1882. 10s. 6d.

BRETTE.—FRENCH EXAMINATION PAPERS SET AT THE UNIVERSITY OF LONDON FROM 1839 TO 1871. Arranged and edited by the Rev. P. H. Ernest Brette, B.D. Crown 8vo, pp. viii. and 278, cloth. 3s. 6d.; interleaved, 4s. 6d.

BRITISH MUSEUM.—LIST OF PUBLICATIONS OF THE TRUSTEES OF THE BRITISH MUSEUM, on application.

BROWN.—THE DERVISHES; OR, ORIENTAL SPIRITUALISM. By John P. Brown, Secretary and Dragoman of the Legation of the United States of America at Constantinople. Crown 8vo, pp. viii. and 416, cloth, with 24 Illustrations. 1868. 14s.

BROWN.—SANSKRIT PROSODY AND NUMERICAL SYMBOLS EXPLAINED. By Charles Philip Brown, M.R.A.S., Author of a Telugu Dictionary, Grammar, &c., Professor of Telugu in the University of London. 8vo, pp. viii. and 56, cloth. 1869. 3s. 6d.

BROWNE.—HOW TO USE THE OPHTHALMOSCOPE; being Elementary Instruction in Ophthalmoscopy. Arranged for the use of Students. By Edgar A. Browne, Surgeon to the Liverpool Eye and Ear Infirmary, &c. Second Edition. Crown 8vo, pp. xi. and 108, with 35 Figures, cloth. 1883. 3s. 6d.

BROWNE.—A BÁNGÁLI PRIMER, in Roman Character. By J. F. Browne, B.C.S. Crown 8vo, pp. 32, cloth. 1881. 2s.

BROWNE.—A HINDI PRIMER IN ROMAN CHARACTER. By J. F. Browne, B.C.S. Crown 8vo, pp. 36, cloth. 1882. 2s. 6d.

BROWNE.—AN URIYÁ PRIMER IN ROMAN CHARACTER. By J. F. Browne, B.C.S. Crown 8vo, pp. 32, cloth. 1882. 2s. 6d.

BROWNING SOCIETY'S PAPERS.—Demy 8vo, wrappers. 1881-84. Part I., pp. 116. 10s. Bibliography of Robert Browning from 1833-81. Part II., pp. 142. 10s. Part III., pp. 168. 10s. Part IV., pp. 148. 10s.

BROWNING'S POEMS, ILLUSTRATIONS TO. 4to, boards. Parts I. and II. 10s. each.

BRUNNOW.—See SCHEFFEL.

BRUNTON.—MAP OF JAPAN. See under JAPAN.

BUDGE.—ARCHAIC CLASSICS. Assyrian Texts; being Extracts from the Annals of Shalmaneser II., Sennacherib, and Assur-Bani-Pal. With Philological Notes. By Ernest A. Budge, B.A., M.R.A.S., Assyrian Exhibitioner, Christ's College, Cambridge. Small 4to, pp. viii. and 44, cloth. 1880. 7s. 6d.

BUDGE.—HISTORY OF ESARHADDON. See Trübner's Oriental Series.

BUNYAN.—SCENES FROM THE PILGRIM'S PROGRESS. By. R. B. Rutter. 4to, pp. 142, boards, leather back. 1882. 5s.

A Catalogue of Important Works,

BURGESS :—
ARCHÆOLOGICAL SURVEY OF WESTERN INDIA :—
REPORT OF THE FIRST SEASON'S OPERATIONS IN THE. BELGÂM AND KALADI DISTRICTS. January to May 1874. By James Burgess, F.R.G.S. With 56 Photographs and Lithographic Plates. Royal 4to, pp. viii. and 45; half bound. 1875. £2, 2s.
REPORT ON THE ANTIQUITIES OF KÂTHIÂWÂD AND KACHH, being the result of the Second Season's Operations of the Archæological Survey of Western India, 1874-75. By James Burgess, F.R.G.S. Royal 4to, pp. x. and 242, with 74 Plates; half bound. 1876. £3, 3s.
REPORT ON THE ANTIQUITIES IN THE BIDAR AND AURANGABAD DISTRICTS, in the Territories of His Highness the Nizam of Haiderabad, being the result of the Third Season's Operations of the Archæological Survey of Western India, 1875-76. By James Burgess, F.R.G.S., M.R.A.S., Archæological Surveyor and Reporter to Government, Western India. Royal 4to, pp. viii. and 138, with 63 Photographic Plates ; half bound. 1878. £2, 2s.
REPORT ON THE BUDDHIST CAVE TEMPLES AND THEIR INSCRIPTIONS ; containing Views, Plans, Sections, and Elevation of Façades of Cave Temples ; Drawings of Architectural and Mythological Sculptures ; Facsimiles of Inscriptions, &c. ; with Descriptive and Explanatory Text, and Translations of Inscriptions, &c., &c. By James Burgess, LL.D., F.R.G.S., &c. Royal 4to, pp. x. and 140, with 86 Plates and Woodcuts ; half-bound.
REPORT ON ELURA CAVE TEMPLES, AND THE BRAHMANICAL AND JAINA CAVES IN WESTERN INDIA. By James Burgess, LL.D., F.R.G.S., &c. Royal 4to, pp. viii. and 90, with 66 Plates and Woodcuts ; half-bound.
} 2 Vols. 1883. £6, 6s.

BURMA.—THE BRITISH BURMA GAZETTEER. Compiled by Major H. R. Spearman, under the direction of the Government of India. 2 vols. 8vo, pp. 764 and 878, with 11 Photographs, cloth. 1880. £2, 10s.

BURMA.—HISTORY OF. See Trübner's Oriental Series, page 70.

BURNE.—SHROPSHIRE FOLK-LORE. A Sheaf of Gleanings. Edited by Charlotte S. Burne. from the Collections of Georgina F. Jackson. Part I. Demy 8vo, pp. xvi.-176, wrapper. 1883. 7s. 6d.

BURNELL.—ELEMENTS OF SOUTH INDIAN PALÆOGRAPHY, from the Fourth to the Seventeenth Century A.D., being an Introduction to the Study of South Indian Inscriptions and MSS. By A. C. Burnell. Second enlarged and improved Edition. 4to, pp. xiv. and 148, Map and 35 Plates, cloth. 1878. £2, 12s. 6d.

BURNELL.—A CLASSIFIED INDEX TO THE SANSKRIT MSS. IN THE PALACE AT TANJORE. Prepared for the Madras Government. By A. C. Burnell, Ph.D., &c., &c. 4to, stiff wrapper. Part I., pp. iv.-80, Vedic and Technical Literature. Part II., pp. iv.-80, Philosophy and Law. Part III., Drama, Epics, Purânas, and Zantras ; Indices. 1879. 10s. each.

BURNEY.—THE BOYS' MANUAL OF SEAMANSHIP AND GUNNERY, compiled for the use of the Training-Ships of the Royal Navy. By Commander C. Burney, R.N., F.R.G.S., Superintendent of Greenwich Hospital School. Seventh Edition. Approved by the Lords Commissioners of the Admiralty to be used in the Training-Ships of the Royal Navy. Crown 8vo, pp. xxii. and 352, with numerous Illustrations, cloth. 1879. 6s.

BURNEY.—THE YOUNG SEAMAN'S MANUAL AND RIGGER'S GUIDE. By Commander C. Burney, R.N., F.R.G.S. Sixth Edition. Revised and corrected. Approved by the Lords Commissioners of the Admiralty. Crown 8vo. pp. xxxviii. and 592, cloth. With 200 Illustrations and 16 Sheets of Signals. 1878. 7s. 6d.

BURTON.—CAPTAIN RICHARD F. BURTON'S HANDBOOK FOR OVERLAND EXPEDITIONS; being an English Edition of the "Prairie Traveller," a Handbook for Overland Expeditions. With Illustrations and Itineraries of the Principal Routes between the Mississippi and the Pacific, and a Map. By Captain Randolph B. Marcy (now General and Chief of the Staff, Army of the Potomac). Edited, with Notes, by Captain Richard F. Burton. Crown 8vo, pp. 270, numerous Woodcuts, Itineraries, and Map, cloth. 1863. 6s. 6d.

BUTLER.—EREWHON; or, Over the Range. By Samuel Butler. Seventh Edition. Crown 8vo, pp. xii. and 244, cloth. 1884. 5s.

BUTLER.—THE FAIR HAVEN. A Work in Defence of the Miraculous Element in Our Lord's Ministry upon Earth, both as against Rationalistic Impugners and certain Orthodox Defenders. By the late John Pickard Owen. With a Memoir of the Author by William Bickersteth Owen. By Samuel Butler. Second Edition. Demy 8vo, pp. x. and 248, cloth. 1873. 7s. 6d.

BUTLER.—LIFE AND HABIT. By Samuel Butler. Second Edition. Crown 8vo, pp. x. and 308, cloth. 1878. 7s. 6d.

BUTLER.—EVOLUTION, OLD AND NEW; or, The Theories of Buffon, Dr. Erasmus Darwin, and Lamarck, as compared with that of Mr. Charles Darwin. By Samuel Butler. Second Edition, with an Appendix and Index. Crown 8vo, pp. xii. and 430, cloth. 1882. 10s. 6d.

BUTLER.—UNCONSCIOUS MEMORY: A Comparison between the Theory of Dr. Ewald Hering, Professor of Physiology at the University of Prague, and the "Philosophy of the Unconscious" of Dr. Edward von Hartmann. With Translations from these Authors, and Preliminary Chapters bearing on "Life and Habit," "Evolution, New and Old," and Mr. Charles Darwin's edition of Dr. Krause's "Erasmus Darwin." By Samuel Butler. Crown 8vo, pp. viii. and 288, cloth. 1880. 7s. 6d.

BUTLER.—ALPS AND SANCTUARIES OF PIEDMONT AND THE CANTON TICINO. Profusely Illustrated by Charles Gogin, H. F. Jones, and the Author. By Samuel Butler. Foolscap 4to, pp. viii. and 376, cloth. 1882. 21s.

BUTLER.—SELECTIONS FROM HIS PREVIOUS WORKS, with Remarks on Mr. G. J. Romanes' recent work, "Mental Evolution in Animals," and "A Psalm of Montreal." By Samuel Butler. Crown 8vo, pp. viii. and 326, cloth. 1884. 7s. 6d.

BUTLER.—THE SPANISH TEACHER AND COLLOQUIAL PHRASE-BOOK. An Easy and Agreeable Method of acquiring a Speaking Knowledge of the Spanish Language. By Francis Butler. Fcap. 8vo, pp. xviii. and 240, half-roan. 2s. 6d.

BUTLER.—HUNGARIAN POEMS AND FABLES FOR ENGLISH READERS. Selected and Translated by E. D. Butler, of the British Museum; with Illustrations by A. G. Butler. Foolscap, pp. vi. and 88, limp cloth. 1877. 2s.

BUTLER.—THE LEGEND OF THE WONDROUS HUNT. By John Arany. With a few Miscellaneous Pieces and Folk-Songs. Translated from the Magyar by E. D. Butler, F.R.G.S. Crown 8vo, pp. viii. and 70. Limp cloth. 2s. 6d.

CAITHNESS.—SERIOUS LETTERS TO SERIOUS FRIENDS. By the Countess of Caithness, Authoress of "Old Truths in a New Light." Crown 8vo, pp. viii. and 352, cloth. 1877. 7s. 6d.

CAITHNESS.—LECTURES ON POPULAR AND SCIENTIFIC SUBJECTS. By the Earl of Caithness, F.R.S. Delivered at various times and places. Second enlarged Edition. Crown 8vo, pp. 174, cloth. 1879. 2s. 6d.

CALCUTTA REVIEW.—SELECTIONS FROM Nos. I.-XXXVII. 5s. each.

CALDER.—THE COMING ERA. By A. Calder, Officer of the Legion of Honour, and Author of "The Man of the Future." 8vo, pp. 422, cloth. 1879. 10s. 6d.

CALDWELL.—A COMPARATIVE GRAMMAR OF THE DRAVIDIAN OR SOUTH INDIAN FAMILY OF LANGUAGES. By the Rev. R. Caldwell, LL.D. A second, corrected, and enlarged Edition. Demy 8vo, pp. 804, cloth. 1875. 28s.

CALENDARS OF STATE PAPERS. List on application.

CALL.—REVERBERATIONS. Revised. With a chapter from My Autobiography. By W. M. W. Call, M.A., Cambridge, Author of "Lyra Hellenica" and "Golden Histories." Crown 8vo, pp. viii. and 200, cloth. 1875. 4s. 6d.

CALLAWAY.—NURSERY TALES, TRADITIONS, AND HISTORIES OF THE ZULUS. In their own words, with a Translation into English, and Notes. By the Rev. Canon Callaway, M.D. Vol. I., 8vo, pp. xiv. and 378, cloth. 1868. 16s.

CALLAWAY.—THE RELIGIOUS SYSTEM OF THE AMAZULU.

Part I.—Unkulunkulu ; or, The Tradition of Creation as existing among the Amazulu and other Tribes of South Africa, in their own words, with a Translation into English, and Notes. By the Rev. Canon Callaway, M.D. 8vo, pp. 128, sewed. 1868. 4s.

Part II.—Amatongo ; or, Ancestor-Worship as existing among the Amazulu, in their own words, with a Translation into English, and Notes. By the Rev. Canon Callaway, M.D. 8vo, pp. 127, sewed. 1869. 4s.

Part III.—Izinyanga Zokubula ; or, Divination, as existing among the Amazulu, in their own words, with a Translation into English, and Notes. By the Rev. Canon Callaway, M.D. 8vo, pp. 150, sewed. 1870. 4s.

Part IV.—On Medical Magic and Witchcraft. 8vo, pp. 40, sewed, 1s. 6d.

CAMBRIDGE PHILOLOGICAL SOCIETY (TRANSACTIONS). Vol. I., from 1872-1880. 8vo, pp. xvi.-420, wrapper. 1881. 15s. Vol. II., for 1881 and 1882. 8vo, pp. viii.-286, wrapper. 1883. 12s.

CAMERINI.—L'ECO ITALIANO ; a Practical Guide to Italian Conversation. By E. Camerini. With a Vocabulary. 12mo, pp. 98, cloth. 1860. 4s. 6d.

CAMPBELL.—THE GOSPEL OF THE WORLD'S DIVINE ORDER. By Douglas Campbell. New Edition. Revised. Crown 8vo, pp. viii. and 364, cloth. 1877. 4s. 6d.

CANDID EXAMINATION OF THEISM. By Physicus. Post 8vo, pp. xviii. and 198, cloth. 1878. 7s. 6d.

CANTICUM CANTICORUM, reproduced in facsimile, from the Scriverius copy in the British Museum. With an Historical and Bibliographical Introduction by I. Ph. Berjeau. Folio, pp. 36, with 16 Tables of Illustrations, vellum. 1860. £2, 2s.

CAREY.—THE PAST, THE PRESENT, AND THE FUTURE. By H. C. Carey. Second Edition. 8vo, pp. 474, cloth. 1856. 10s. 6d.

CARLETTI.—HISTORY OF THE CONQUEST OF TUNIS. Translated by J. T. Carletti. Crown 8vo, pp. 40, cloth. 1883. 2s. 6d.

CARNEGY.—NOTES ON THE LAND TENURES AND REVENUE ASSESSMENTS OF UPPER INDIA. By P. Carnegy. Crown 8vo, pp. viii. and 136, and forms, cloth. 1874. 6s.

CATHERINE II., MEMOIRS OF THE EMPRESS. Written by herself. With a Preface by A. Herzen. Trans. from the French. 12mo, pp. xvi. and 352, bds. 1859. 7s. 6d.

CATLIN.—O-KEE-PA. A Religious Ceremony ; and other Customs of the Mandans. By George Catlin. With 13 coloured Illustrations. Small 4to, pp. vi. and 52, cloth. 1867. 14s.

CATLIN.—THE LIFTED AND SUBSIDED ROCKS OF AMERICA, with their Influence on the Oceanic, Atmospheric, and Land Currents, and the Distribution of Races. By George Catlin. With 2 Maps. Cr. 8vo, pp. xii. and 238, cloth. 1870. 6s. 6d.

CATLIN.—SHUT YOUR MOUTH AND SAVE YOUR LIFE. By George Catlin, Author of "Notes of Travels amongst the North American Indians," &c., &c. With 29 Illustrations from Drawings by the Author. Eighth Edition, considerably enlarged. Crown 8vo, pp. 106, cloth. 1882. 2s. 6d.

CAXTON.—THE BIOGRAPHY AND TYPOGRAPHY OF. See BLADES.

Published by Trübner & Co. 13

CAXTON CELEBRATION, 1877.—CATALOGUE OF THE LOAN COLLECTION OF ANTIQUITIES, CURIOSITIES, AND APPLIANCES CONNECTED WITH THE ART OF PRINTING. Edited by G. Bullen, F.S.A. Post 8vo, pp. xx. and 472, cloth, 3s. 6d.

CAZELLES.—OUTLINE OF THE EVOLUTION-PHILOSOPHY. By Dr. W. E. Cazelles. Translated from the French by the Rev. O. B. Frothingham. Crown 8vo, pp. 156, cloth. 1875. 3s. 6d.

CESNOLA.—SALAMINIA (Cyprus). The History, Treasures, and Antiquities of Salamis in the Island of Cyprus. By A. Palma di Cesnola, F.S.A., &c. With an Introduction by S. Birch, Esq., D.C.L., LL.D., Keeper of the Egyptian and Oriental Antiquities in the British Museum. Royal 8vo, pp. xlviii. and 325, with upwards of 700 Illustrations and Map of Ancient Cyprus, cloth. 1882. 31s. 6d.

CHALMERS.—STRUCTURE OF CHINESE CHARACTERS, under 300 Primary Forms after the Shwoh-wan, 100 A.D., and the Phouetic Shwoh-wan, 1833. By J. Chalmers, M.A., LL.D., A.B. Demy 8vo, pp. x. and 200, with two plates, limp cloth. 1882. 12s. 6d.

CHAMBERLAIN.—THE CLASSICAL POETRY OF THE JAPANESE. By Basil Hall Chamberlain, Author of "Yeigo Henkaku, Ichirañ." Post 8vo, pp. xii. and 228, cloth. 1880. 7s. 6d.

CHAPMAN.—CHLOROFORM AND OTHER ANÆSTHETICS : Their History and Use during Childbirth. By John Chapman, M.D. 8vo, pp. 51, sewed. 1859. 1s.

CHAPMAN.—DIARRHŒA AND CHOLERA : Their Nature, Origin, and Treatment through the Agency of the Nervous System. By John Chapman, M.D., M.R.C.P., M.R.C.S. 8vo, pp. xix. and 248, cloth. 7s. 6d.

CHAPMAN.—MEDICAL CHARITY : its Abuses, and how to Remedy them. By John Chapman, M.D. 8vo, pp. viii. and 108, cloth. 1874. 2s. 6d.

CHAPMAN.—SEA-SICKNESS, AND HOW TO PREVENT IT. An Explanation of its Nature and Successful Treatment, through the Agency of the Nervous System, by means of the Spinal Ice Bag; with an Introduction on the General Principles of Neuro-Therapeutics. By John Chapman, M.D., M.R.C.P., M.R.C.S. Second Edition. 8vo, pp. viii. and 112, cloth. 1868. 3s.

CHAPTERS ON CHRISTIAN CATHOLICITY. By a Clergyman. 8vo, pp. 282, cloth. 1878. 5s.

CHARITABALI (THE), or, Instructive Biography. By Isvarnchandra Vidyasagara. With a Vocabulary of all the Words occurring in the Text. By J. F. Blumhardt, Bengal Lecturer at the University College, London ; and Teacher of Bengali for the Cambridge University. 12mo, pp. 174, cloth. 1884. 5s. The Vocabulary only, 2s. 6d.

CHARNOCK.—A GLOSSARY OF THE ESSEX DIALECT. By Richard Stephen Charnock, Ph.D., F.S.A. Fcap., pp. xii. and 64, cloth. 1880. 3s. 6d.

CHARNOCK.—PRŒNOMINA ; or, The Etymology of the Principal Christian Names of Great Britain and Ireland. By R. S. Charnock, Ph.D., F.S.A. Crown 8vo, pp. xvi. and 128, cloth. 1882. 6s.

CHATTOPADHYAYA.—THE YÀTRÂS ; or, The Popular Dramas of Bengal. By N. Chattopadhyaya. Post 8vo, pp. 50, wrapper. 1882. 2s.

CHAUCER SOCIETY.—Subscription, two guineas per annum. List of Publications on application.

CHILDERS.—A PALI-ENGLISH DICTIONARY, with Sanskrit Equivalents, and with numerous Quotations, Extracts, and References. Compiled by Robert Cæsar Childers, late of the Ceylon Civil Service. Imperial 8vo, double columns, pp. 648, cloth. 1875. £3, 3s.

CHILDERS.—THE MAHAPARINIBBANASUTTA OF THE SUTTA PITAKA. The Pali Text. Edited by the late Professor R. C. Childers. 8vo, pp. 72, limp cloth. 1878. 5s.

A Catalogue of Important Works,

CHINTAMON.—A COMMENTARY ON THE TEXT OF THE BHAGAVAD-GITÁ; or, The Discourse between Khrishna and Arjuna of Divine Matters A Sanskrit Philosophical Poem. With a few Introductory Papers. By Hurrychund Chintamon, Political Agent to H. H. the Guicowar Mulhar Rao Maharajah of Baroda. Post 8vo, pp. 118, cloth. 1874. 6s.

CHRONICLES AND MEMORIALS OF GREAT BRITAIN AND IRELAND DURING THE MIDDLE AGES. List on application.

CLARK.—MEGHADUTA, THE CLOUD MESSENGER. Poem of Kalidasa. Translated by the late Rev. T. Clark, M.A. Fcap. 8vo, pp. 64, wrapper. 1882. 1s.

CLARK.—A FORECAST OF THE RELIGION OF THE FUTURE. Being Short Essays on some important Questions in Religious Philosophy. By W. W. Clark. Post 8vo, pp. xii. and 238, cloth. 1879. 3s. 6d.

CLARKE.—TEN GREAT RELIGIONS: An Essay in Comparative Theology. By James Freeman Clarke. Demy 8vo, pp. x. and 528, cloth. 1871. 15s.

CLARKE.—TEN GREAT RELIGIONS. Part II., A Comparison of all Religions. By J. F. Clarke. Demy 8vo, pp. xxviii.- 414, cloth. 1883. 10s. 6d.

CLARKE.—THE EARLY HISTORY OF THE MEDITERRANEAN POPULATIONS, &c., in their Migrations and Settlements. Illustrated from Autonomous Coins, Gems, Inscriptions, &c. By Hyde Clarke. 8vo, pp. 80, cloth. 1882. 5s.

CLAUSEWITZ.—ON WAR. By General Carl von Clausewitz. Translated by Colonel J. J. Graham, from the third German Edition. Three volumes complete in one. Fcap 4to, double columns, pp. xx. and 564, with Portrait of the author, cloth. 1873. 10s. 6d.

COKE.—CREEDS OF THE DAY: or, Collated Opinions of Reputable Thinkers. By Henry Coke. In Three Series of Letters. 2 vols. Demy 8vo, pp. 302-324, cloth. 1883. 21s.

COLEBROOKE.—THE LIFE AND MISCELLANEOUS ESSAYS OF HENRY THOMAS COLEBROOKE. The Biography by his Son, Sir T. E. Colebrooke, Bart., M.P. 3 vols. Vol. I. The Life. Demy 8vo, pp. xii. and 492, with Portrait and Map, cloth. 1873. 14s. Vols. II. and III. The Essays. A new Edition, with Notes by E. B. Cowell, Professor of Sanskrit in the University of Cambridge. Demy 8vo, pp. xvi. and 544, and x. and 520, cloth. 1873. 28s.

COLENSO.—NATAL SERMONS. A Series of Discourses Preached in the Cathedral Church of St Peter's, Maritzburg. By the Right Rev. John William Colenso, D.D., Bishop of Natal. 8vo, pp. viii. and 373, cloth. 1866. 7s. 6d. The Second Series. Crown 8vo, cloth. 1868. 5s.

COLLINS.—A GRAMMAR AND LEXICON OF THE HEBREW LANGUAGE, Entitled Sefer Hassoham. By Rabbi Moseh Ben Yitshak, of England. Edited from a MS. in the Bodleian Library of Oxford, and collated with a MS. in the Imperial Library of St. Petersburg, with Additions and Corrections, by G. W. Collins, M.A. Demy 4to, pp. 112, wrapper. 1882. 7s. 6d.

COLYMBIA.—Crown 8vo, pp. 260, cloth. 1873. 5s.

"The book is amusing as well as clever."—*Athenæum.*   "Many exceedingly humorous passages."—*Public Opinion.*   "Deserves to be read."—*Scotsman.*   "Neatly done."—*Graphic.*   "Very amusing."—*Examiner.*

COMTE.—A GENERAL VIEW OF POSITIVISM. By Auguste Comte. Translated by Dr. J. H. Bridges. 12mo, pp. xi. and 426, cloth. 1865. 8s. 6d.

COMTE.—THE CATECHISM OF POSITIVE RELIGION: Translated from the French of Auguste Comte. By Richard Congreve. Second Edition. Revised and Corrected, and conformed to the Second French Edition of 1874. Crown 8vo, pp. 316, cloth, 1883. 2s. 6d.

COMTE.—THE EIGHT CIRCULARS OF AUGUSTE COMTE. Translated from the French, under the auspices of R. Congreve. Fcap. 8vo, pp. iv. and 90, cloth. 1882. 1s. 6d.

COMTE.—PRELIMINARY DISCOURSE ON THE POSITIVE SPIRIT. Prefixed to the "Traité Philosophique d'Astronomie Populaire." By M. Auguste Comte. Translated by W. M. W. Call, M.A., Camb. Crown 8vo, pp. 154, cloth. 1883. 2s. 6d.

COMTE.—THE POSITIVE PHILOSOPHY OF AUGUSTE COMTE. Translated and condensed by Harriet Martineau. 2 vols. Second Edition. 8vo, cloth. Vol. I., pp. xxiv. and 400; Vol. II., pp. xiv. and 468. 1875. 25s.

CONGREVE.—THE ROMAN EMPIRE OF THE WEST. Four Lectures delivered at the Philosophical Institution, Edinburgh, February 1855, by Richard Congreve, M.A. 8vo, pp. 176, cloth. 1855. 4s.

CONGREVE.—ELIZABETH OF ENGLAND. Two Lectures delivered at the Philosophical Institution, Edinburgh, January 1862. By Richard Congreve. 18mo, pp. 114, sewed. 1862. 2s. 6d.

CONTOPOULOS.—A LEXICON OF MODERN GREEK-ENGLISH AND ENGLISH MODERN GREEK. By N. Contopoulos. Part I. Modern Greek-English. Part II. English Modern Greek. 8vo, pp. 460 and 582, cloth. 1877. 27s.

CONWAY.—THE SACRED ANTHOLOGY: A Book of Ethnical Scriptures. Collected and Edited by Moncure D. Conway. Fifth Edition. Demy 8vo, pp. viii. and 480, cloth. 1876. 12s.

CONWAY.—IDOLS AND IDEALS. With an Essay on Christianity. By Moncure D. Conway, M.A., Author of "The Eastern Pilgrimage," &c. Crown 8vo, pp. 352, cloth. 1877. 5s.

CONWAY.—EMERSON AT HOME AND ABROAD. See English and Foreign Philosophical Library.

CONWAY.—TRAVELS IN SOUTH KENSINGTON. By M. D. Conway. Illustrated. 8vo, pp. 234, cloth. 1882. 12s.
CONTENTS.—The South Kensington Museum—Decorative Art and Architecture in England—Bedford Park.

COOMARA SWAMY.—THE DATHAVANSA; or, The History of the Tooth Relic of Gotama Buddha, in Pali verse. Edited, with an English Translation, by Mutu Coomara Swamy, F.R.A.S. Demy 8vo, pp. 174, cloth. 1874. 10s. 6d. English Translation. With Notes. pp. 100. 6s.

COOMARA SWAMY.—SUTTA NIPATA; or, Dialogues and Discourses of Gotama Buddha (2500 years old). Translated from the original Pali. With Notes and Introduction. By Mutu Coomara Swamy, F.R.A.S. Crown 8vo, pp. xxxvi. and 160, cloth. 1874. 6s.

CORNELIA. A Novel. Post 8vo, pp. 250, boards. 1863. 1s. 6d.

COTTA.—GEOLOGY AND HISTORY. A Popular Exposition of all that is known of the Earth and its Inhabitants in Pre-historic Times. By Bernhard Von Cotta, Professor of Geology at the Academy of Mining, Freiberg, in Saxony. 12mo, pp. iv. and 84, cloth. 1865. 2s.

COUSIN.—THE PHILOSOPHY OF KANT. Lectures by Victor Cousin. Translated from the French. To which is added a Biographical and Critical Sketch of Kant's Life and Writings. By A. G. Henderson. Large post 8vo, pp. xciv. and 194, cloth. 1864. 6s.

COUSIN.—ELEMENTS OF PSYCHOLOGY: included in a Critical Examination of Locke's Essay on the Human Understanding, and in additional pieces. Translated from the French of Victor Cousin, with an Introduction and Notes. By Caleb S. Henry, D.D. Fourth improved Edition, revised according to the Author's last corrections. Crown 8vo, pp. 568, cloth. 1871. 8s.

COWELL.—A SHORT INTRODUCTION TO THE ORDINARY PRAKRIT OF THE SANSKRIT DRAMAS. With a List of Common Irregular Prâkrit Words. By E. B. Cowell, Professor of Sanskrit in the University of Cambridge, and Hon. LL.D. of the University of Edinburgh. Crown 8vo, pp. 40, limp cloth. 1875. 3s. 6d.

COWELL.—Prakrita-Prakasa; or, The Prakrit Grammar of Vararuchi, with the Commentary (Manorama) of Bhamaha; the first complete Edition of the Original Text, with various Readings from a collection of Six MSS. in the Bodleian Library at Oxford, and the Libraries of the Royal Asiatic Society and the East India House; with Copious Notes, an English Translation, and Index of Prakrit Words, to which is prefixed an Easy Introduction to Prakrit Grammar. By Edward Byles Cowell, of Magdalen Hall, Oxford, Professor of Sanskrit at Cambridge. New Edition, with New Preface, Additions, and Corrections. Second Issue. 8vo, pp. xxxi. and 204, cloth. 1868. 14s.

COWELL.—The Sarvadarsana Samgraha. See Trübner's Oriental Series.

COWLEY.—Poems. By Percy Tunnicliff Cowley. Demy 8vo, pp. 104, cloth. 1881. 5s.

CRAIG.—The Irish Land Labour Question, Illustrated in the History of Ralahine and Co-operative Farming. By E. T. Craig. Crown 8vo, pp. xii. and 202, cloth. 1882. 2s. 6d. Wrappers, 2s.

CRANBROOK.—Credibilia; or, Discourses on Questions of Christian Faith. By the Rev. James Cranbrook, Edinburgh. Reissue. Post 8vo, pp. iv. and 190, cloth. 1868. 3s. 6d.

CRANBROOK.—The Founders of Christianity; or, Discourses upon the Origin of the Christian Religion. By the Rev. James Cranbrook, Edinburgh. Post 8vo, pp. xii. and 324. 1868. 6s.

CRAVEN.—The Popular Dictionary in English and Hindustani, and Hindustani and English. With a Number of Useful Tables. Compiled by the Rev. T. Craven, M.A. 18mo, pp. 430, cloth. 1881. 3s. 6d.

CRAWFORD.—Recollections of Travel in New Zealand and Australia. By James Coutts Crawford, F.G.S., Resident Magistrate, Wellington, &c., &c. With Maps and Illustrations. 8vo, pp. xvi. and 468, cloth. 1880. 18s.

CROSLAND.—Apparitions; An Essay explanatory of Old Facts and a New Theory. To which are added Sketches and Adventures. By Newton Crosland. Crown 8vo, pp. viii. and 166, cloth. 1873. 2s. 6d.

CROSLAND.—Pith: Essays and Sketches Grave and Gay, with some Verses and Illustrations. By Newton Crosland. Crown 8vo, pp. 310, cloth. 1881. 5s.

CROSLAND.—The New Principia; or, The Astronomy of the Future. An Essay Explanatory of a Rational System of the Universe. By N. Crosland, Author of "Pith," &c. Foolscap 8vo, pp. 88, cloth limp elegant, gilt edges. 1884. 2s. 6d.

CROSS.—Hesperides. The Occupations, Relaxations, and Aspirations of a Life. By Launcelot Cross, Author of "Characteristics of Leigh Hunt," "Brandon Tower," "Business," &c. Demy 8vo, pp. iv.-486, cloth. 1883. 10s. 6d.

CUMMINS.—A Grammar of the Old Friesic Language. By A. H. Cummins, A.M. Crown 8vo, pp. x. and 76, cloth. 1881. 3s. 6d.

CUNNINGHAM.—The Ancient Geography of India. I. The Buddhist Period, including the Campaigns of Alexander and the Travels of Hwen-Thsaug. By Alexander Cunningham, Major-General, Royal Engineers (Bengal Retired). With 13 Maps. 8vo, pp. xx. and 590, cloth. 1870. £1, 8s.

CUNNINGHAM.—The Stupa of Bharhut: A Buddhist Monument ornamented with numerous Sculptures illustrative of Buddhist Legend and History in the Third Century B.C. By Alexander Cunningham, C.S.I., C.I.E., Maj.-Gen., R.E. (B.R.), Dir.-Gen. Archæol. Survey of India. Royal 8vo, pp. viii. and 144, with 57 Plates, cloth. 1879. £3, 3s.

CUNNINGHAM.—Archæological Survey of India, Reports from 1862-80. By A. Cunningham, C.S.I., C.I.E., Major-General, R.E. (Bengal Retired), Director-General, Archæological Survey of India. With numerous Plates, cloth, Vols. I.-XI. 10s. each. (Except Vols. VII., VIII., and IX., and also Vols. XII., XIII., XIV., XV. and XVI., which are 12s. each.)

CUSHMAN.—CHARLOTTE CUSHMAN: Her Letters and Memories of her Life. Edited by her friend, Emma Stebbins. Square 8vo, pp. viii. and 308, cloth. With Portrait and Illustrations. 1879. 12s. 6d.

CUST.—LANGUAGES OF THE EAST INDIES. See Trübner's Oriental Series.

CUST.—LINGUISTIC AND ORIENTAL ESSAYS. See Trübner's Oriental Series.

CUST.—LANGUAGES OF AFRICA. See Trübner's Oriental Series.

CUST.—PICTURES OF INDIAN LIFE, Sketched with the Pen from 1852 to 1881. By R. N. Cust, late I.C.S., Hon. Sec. Royal Asiatic Society. Crown 8vo, pp. x. and 346, cloth. With Maps. 1881. 7s. 6d.

DANA.—A TEXT-BOOK OF GEOLOGY, designed for Schools and Academies. By James D. Dana, LL.D., Professor of Geology, &c., at Yale College. Illustrated. Crown 8vo, pp. vi. and 354, cloth. 1876. 10s.

DANA.—MANUAL OF GEOLOGY, treating of the Principles of the Science, with special Reference to American Geological History; for the use of Colleges, Academies, and Schools of Science. By James D. Dana, LL.D. Illustrated by a Chart of the World, and over One Thousand Figures. 8vo, pp. xvi. and 800, and Chart, cl. 21s.

DANA.—THE GEOLOGICAL STORY BRIEFLY TOLD. An Introduction to Geology for the General Reader and for Beginners in the Science. By J. D. Dana, LL.D. Illustrated. 12mo, pp. xii. and 264, cloth. 7s. 6d.

DANA.—A SYSTEM OF MINERALOGY. Descriptive Mineralogy. comprising the most Recent Discoveries. By J. D. Dana, aided by G. J. Brush. Fifth Edition, re-written and enlarged, and illustrated with upwards of 600 Woodcuts, with three Appendixes and Corrections. Royal 8vo, pp. xlviii. and 892, cloth. £2, 2s.

DANA.—A TEXT BOOK OF MINERALOGY. With an Extended Treatise on Crystallography and Physical Mineralogy. By E. S. Dana, on the Plan and with the Co-operation of Professor J. D. Dana. Third Edition, revised. Over 800 Woodcuts and 1 Coloured Plate. 8vo, pp. viii. and 486, cloth. 1879. 18s.

DANA.—MANUAL OF MINERALOGY AND LITHOLOGY; Containing the Elements of the Science of Minerals and Rocks, for the Use of the Practical Mineralogist and Geologist, and for Instruction in Schools and Colleges. By J. D. Dana. Fourth Edition, rearranged and rewritten. Illustrated by numerous Woodcuts. Crown 8vo, pp. viii. and 474, cloth. 1882. 7s. 6d.

DATES AND DATA RELATING TO RELIGIOUS ANTHROPOLOGY AND BIBLICAL ARCHÆOLOGY. (Primæval Period.) 8vo, pp. viii. and 106, cloth. 1876. 5s.

DAUDET.—LETTERS FROM MY MILL. From the French of Alphonse Daudet, by Mary Corey. Fcap. 8vo, pp. 160. 1880. Cloth, 3s.; boards, 2s.

DAVIDS.—BUDDHIST BIRTH STORIES. See Trübner's Oriental Series.

DAVIES.—HINDU PHILOSOPHY. 2 vols. See Trübner's Oriental Series.

DAVIS.—NARRATIVE OF THE NORTH POLAR EXPEDITION, U.S. SHIP Polaris, Captain Charles Francis Hall Commanding. Edited under the direction of the Hon. G. M. Robeson, Secretary of the Navy, by Rear-Admiral C. H. Davis, U.S.N. Third Edition. With numerous Steel and Wood Engravings, Photolithographs, and Maps. 4to, pp. 696, cloth. 1881. £1, 8s.

DAY.—THE PREHISTORIC USE OF IRON AND STEEL; with Observations on certain matter ancillary thereto. By St. John V. Day, C.E., F.R.S.E., &c. 8vo, pp. xxiv. and 278, cloth. 1877. 12s.

DE FLANDRE.—MONOGRAMS OF THREE OR MORE LETTERS, DESIGNED AND DRAWN ON STONE. By C. De Flandre, F.S.A. Scot., Edinburgh. With Indices, showing the place and style or period of every Monogram, and of each individual Letter. 4to, 42 Plates, cloth. 1880. Large paper, £7, 7s.; small paper, £3, 3s.

DELBRÜCK.—INTRODUCTION TO THE STUDY OF LANGUAGE: A Critical Survey of the History and Methods of Comparative Philology of the Indo-European Languages. By B. Delbrück. Authorised Translation, with a Preface by the Author. 8vo, pp. 156, cloth. 1882. 5s. Sewed, 4s.

DELEPIERRE.—Histoire Litteraire des Fous. Par Octave Delepierre. Crown 8vo, pp. 184, cloth. 1860. 5s.

DELEPIERRE.—Macaroneana Andra; overum Nouveaux Mélanges de Litterature Macaronique. Par Octave Delepierre. Small 4to, pp. 180, printed by Whittingham, and handsomely bound in the Roxburghe style. 1862. 10s. 6d.

DELEPIERRE.—Analyse des Travaux de la Societe des Philobiblon de Londres. Par Octave Delepierre. Small 4to, pp. viii. and 134, bound in the Roxburghe style. 1862. 10s. 6d.

DELEPIERRE.—Revue Analytique des Ouvrages Écrits en Centons, depuis les Temps Anciens, jusqu'au xixième Siècle. Par un Bibliophile Belge. Small 4to, pp. 508, stiff covers. 1868. £1, 10s.

DELEPIERRE.—Tableau de la Littérature du Centon, chez les Anciens et chez les Modernes. Par Octave Delepierre. 2 vols, small 4to, pp. 324 and 318. Paper cover. 1875. £1, 1s.

DELEPIERRE.—L'Enfer: Essai Philosophique et Historique sur les Légendes de la Vie Future. Par Octave Delepierre. Crown 8vo, pp. 160, paper wrapper. 1876. 6s. Only 250 copies printed.

DENNYS.—A Handbook of the Canton Vernacular of the Chinese Language. Being a Series of Introductory Lessons for Domestic and Business Purposes. By N. B. Dennys, M.R.A.S., &c. Royal 8vo, pp. iv. and 228, cloth. 1874. 30s.

DENNYS.—A Handbook of Malay Colloquial, as spoken in Singapore, being a Series of Introductory Lessons for Domestic and Business Purposes. By N. B. Dennys, Ph.D., F.R.G.S., M.R.A.S. Impl. 8vo, pp. vi. and 204, cloth. 1878. 21s.

DENNYS.—The Folk-Lore of China, and its Affinities with that of the Aryan and Semitic Races. By N. B. Dennys, Ph.D., F.R.G.S., M.R.A.S. 8vo, pp. 166, cloth. 1876. 10s. 6d.

DE VALDES.—See Valdes.

DE VINNE.—The Invention of Printing: A Collection of Texts and Opinions. Description of Early Prints and Playing Cards, the Block-Books of the Fifteenth Century, the Legend of Lourens Janszoon Coster of Haarlem, and the Works of John Gutenberg and his Associates. Illustrated with Fac-similes of Early Types and Woodcuts. By Theo. L. De Vinne. Second Edition. In royal 8vo, elegantly printed, and bound in cloth, with embossed portraits, and a multitude of Fac-similes and Illustrations. 1877. £1, 1s.

DICKSON.—Who was Scotland's First Printer? Ane Compendious and breue Tractate, in Commendation of Andrew Myllar. Compylit be Robert Dickson, F.S.A. Scot. Fcap. 8vo, pp. 24, parchment wrapper. 1881. 1s.

DOBSON.—Monograph of the Asiatic Chiroptera, and Catalogue of the Species of Bats in the Collection of the Indian Museum, Calcutta. By G. E. Dobson, M.A., M.B., F.L.S., &c. 8vo, pp. viii. and 228, cloth. 1876. 12s.

D'ORSEY.—A Practical Grammar of Portuguese and English, exhibiting in a Series of Exercises, in Double Translation, the Idiomatic Structure of both Languages, as now written and spoken. Adapted to Ollendorff's System by the Rev. Alexander J. D. D'Orsey, of Corpus Christi College, Cambridge, and Lecturer on Public Reading and Speaking at King's College, London. Third Edition. 12mo, pp. viii. and 298, cloth. 1868. 7s.

DOUGLAS.—Chinese-English Dictionary of the Vernacular or Spoken Language of Amoy, with the principal variations of the Chang-Chew and Chin-Chew Dialects. By the Rev. Carstairs Douglas, M.A., LL.D., Glasg., Missionary of the Presbyterian Church in England. High quarto, double columns, pp. 632, cloth. 1873. £3, 3s.

DOUGLAS.—Chinese Language and Literature. Two Lectures delivered at the Royal Institution, by R. K. Douglas, of the British Museum, and Professor of Chinese at King's College. Crown 8vo, pp. 118, cloth. 1875. 5s.

DOUGLAS.—THE LIFE OF JENGHIZ KHAN. Translated from the Chinese. With an Introduction. By Robert K. Douglas, of the British Museum, and Professor of Chinese at King's College. Crown 8vo, pp. xxxvi. and 106, cloth. 1877. 5s.

DOUSE.—GRIMM'S LAW. A Study; or, Hints towards an Explanation of the so-called "Lautverschiebung;" to which are added some Remarks on the Primitive Indo-European K, and several Appendices. By T. Le Marchant Douse. 8vo, pp. xvi. and 232, cloth. 1876. 10s. 6d.

DOWSON.—DICTIONARY OF HINDU MYTHOLOGY, &c. See Trübner's Oriental Series.

DOWSON.—A GRAMMAR OF THE URDŪ OR HINDŪSTĀNĪ LANGUAGE. By John Dowson, M.R.A.S., Professor of Hindūstānī, Staff College, Sandhurst. Crown 8vo, pp. xvi. and 264, with 8 Plates, cloth. 1872. 10s. 6d.

DOWSON.—A HINDŪSTĀNĪ EXERCISE BOOK; containing a Series of Passages and Extracts adapted for Translation into Hindūstānī. By John Dowson, M.R.A.S., Professor of Hindūstānī, Staff College, Sandhurst. Crown 8vo, pp. 100, limp cloth. 1872. 2s. 6d.

DUNCAN.—GEOGRAPHY OF INDIA, comprising a Descriptive Outline of all India, and a Detailed Geographical, Commercial, Social, and Political Account of each of its Provinces. With Historical Notes. By George Duncan. Tenth Edition (Revised and Corrected to date from the latest Official Information). 18mo, pp. viii. and 182, limp cloth. 1880. 1s. 6d.

DUSAR.—A GRAMMAR OF THE GERMAN LANGUAGE; with Exercises. By P. Friedrich Dusar, First German Master in the Military Department of Cheltenham College. Second Edition. Crown 8vo, pp. viii. and 208, cloth. 1879. 4s. 6d.

DUSAR.—A GRAMMATICAL COURSE OF THE GERMAN LANGUAGE. By P. Friedrich Dusar. Third Edition. Crown 8vo, pp. x. and 134, cloth. 1883. 3s. 6d.

DYMOCK.—THE VEGETABLE MATERIA MEDICA OF WESTERN INDIA. By W. Dymock, Surgeon-Major Bombay Army, &c. &c. To be completed in four parts. 8vo, Part I., pp. 160; Part II., pp. 168; wrappers, 4s. each.

EARLY ENGLISH TEXT SOCIETY.—Subscription, one guinea per annum. *Extra Series.* Subscriptions—Small paper, one guinea; large paper, two guineas, per annum. List of publications on application.

EASTWICK.—KHIRAD AFROZ (the Illuminator of the Understanding). By Maulaví Hafízu'd-dín. A New Edition of the Hindūstānī Text, carefully revised, with Notes, Critical and Explanatory. By Edward B. Eastwick, F.R.S., F.S.A., M.R.A.S., Professor of Hindūstānī at Haileybury College. Imperial 8vo, pp. xiv. and 319, cloth. Reissue, 1867. 18s.

EASTWICK.—THE GULISTAN. See Trübner's Oriental Series.

EBERS.—THE EMPEROR. A Romance. By Georg Ebers. Translated from the German by Clara Bell. In two volumes, 16mo, pp. iv. 319 and 322, cloth. 1881. 7s. 6d.

EBERS.—A QUESTION: The Idyl of a Picture by his friend, Alma Tadema. Related by Georg Ebers. From the German, by Mary J. SAFFORD. 16mo, pp. 125, with Frontispiece, cloth. 1881. 4s.

ECHO (DEUTSCHES). THE GERMAN ECHO. A Faithful Mirror of German Conversation. By Ludwig Wolfram. With a Vocabulary. By Henry P. Skelton. Post 8vo, pp. 130 and 70, cloth. 1863. 3s.

ECHO FRANÇAIS. A PRACTICAL GUIDE TO CONVERSATION. By Fr. de la Fruston. With a complete Vocabulary. By Anthony Maw Border. Post 8vo, pp. 120 and 72, cloth. 1860. 3s.

ECO ITALIANO (L'). A PRACTICAL GUIDE TO ITALIAN CONVERSATION. By Eugene Camerini. With a complete Vocabulary. By Henry P. Skelton. Post 8vo, pp. vi., 128, and 98, cloth. 1860. 4s. 6d.

A Catalogue of Important Works,

ECO DE MADRID. THE ECHO OF MADRID. A Practical Guide to Spanish Conversation. By J. E. Hartzenbusch and Henry Lemming. With a complete Vocabulary, containing copious Explanatory Remarks. By Henry Lemming. Post 8vo, pp. xii., 144, and 83, cloth. 1860. 5s.

ECKSTEIN.—PRUSIAS: A Romance of Ancient Rome under the Republic. By Ernst Eckstein. From the German by Clara Bell. Two vols., 16mo, pp. 356 and 336, cloth. 1884. 7s. 6d.; paper, 5s.

EDDA SÆMUNDAR HINNS FRODA. The Edda of Sæmund the Learned. Translated from the Old Norse, by Benjamin Thorpe. Complete in 1 vol. fcap. 8vo, pp. viii. and 152, and pp. viii. and 170, cloth. 1866. 7s. 6d.

EDKINS.—CHINA'S PLACE IN PHILOLOGY. An attempt to show that the Languages of Europe and Asia have a common origin. By the Rev. Joseph Edkins. Crown 8vo, pp. xxiii. and 403, cloth. 1871. 10s. 6d.

EDKINS.—INTRODUCTION TO THE STUDY OF THE CHINESE CHARACTERS. By J. Edkins, D.D., Peking, China. Royal 8vo, pp. 340, paper boards. 1876. 18s.

EDKINS.—RELIGION IN CHINA. See English and Foreign Philosophical Library, Vol. VIII., or Trübner's Oriental Series.

EDKINS.—CHINESE BUDDHISM. See Trübner's Oriental Series.

EDWARDS.—MEMOIRS OF LIBRARIES, together with a Practical Handbook of Library Economy. By Edward Edwards. Numerous Illustrations. 2 vols. royal 8vo, cloth. Vol. i. pp. xxviii. and 841; Vol. ii. pp. xxxvi. and 1104. 1859. £2, 8s.
DITTO, large paper, imperial 8vo, cloth. £4, 4s.

EDWARDS.—CHAPTERS OF THE BIOGRAPHICAL HISTORY OF THE FRENCH ACADEMY. 1629-1863. With an Appendix relating to the Unpublished Chronicle "Liber de Hyda." By Edward Edwards. 8vo, pp. 180, cloth. 1864. 6s.
DITTO, large paper, royal 8vo. 10s. 6d.

EDWARDS.—LIBRARIES AND FOUNDERS OF LIBRARIES. By Edward Edwards. 8vo. pp. xix. and 506, cloth. 1865. 18s.
DITTO, large paper, imperial 8vo, cloth. £1, 10s.

EDWARDS.—FREE TOWN LIBRARIES, their Formation, Management, and History in Britain, France, Germany, and America. Together with Brief Notices of Book Collectors, and of the respective Places of Deposit of their Surviving Collections. By Edward Edwards. 8vo, pp. xvi. and 634, cloth. 1869. 21s.

EDWARDS.—LIVES OF THE FOUNDERS OF THE BRITISH MUSEUM, with Notices of its Chief Augmentors and other Benefactors. 1570-1870. By Edward Edwards. With Illustrations and Plans. 2 vols. 8vo, pp. xii. and 780, cloth. 1870. 30s.

EDWARDES.—See ENGLISH AND FOREIGN PHILOSOPHICAL LIBRARY, Vol. XVII.

EGER AND GRIME.—An Early English Romance. Edited from Bishop Percy's Folio Manuscripts, about 1650 A.D. By John W. Hales, M.A., Fellow and late Assistant Tutor of Christ's College, Cambridge, and Frederick J. Furnivall, M.A., of Trinity Hall, Cambridge. 4to, large paper, half bound, Roxburghe style, pp. 64. 1867. 10s. 6d.

EGERTON.—SUSSEX FOLK AND SUSSEX WAYS. Stray Studies in the Wealden Formation of Human Nature. By the Rev. J. Coker Egerton, M.A., Rector of Burwash. Crown 8vo, pp. 140, cloth. 1884. 2s.

EGGELING.—See AUCTORES SANSKRITI, Vols. IV. and V.

EGYPTIAN GENERAL STAFF PUBLICATIONS:—

PROVINCES OF THE EQUATOR: Summary of Letters and Reports of the Governor-General. Part 1. 1874. Royal 8vo, pp. viii. and 90, stitched, with Map. 1877. 5s.

GENERAL REPORT ON THE PROVINCE OF KORDOFAN. Submitted to General C. P. Stone, Chief of the General Staff Egyptian Army. By Major H. G. Prout, Corps of Engineers, Commanding Expedition of Reconnaissance. Made at El-Obeiyad (Kordofan), March 12th, 1876. Royal 8vo, pp. 232, stitched, with 6 Maps. 1877. 10s. 6d.

EGYPTIAN GENERAL STAFF PUBLICATIONS—*continued*.
REPORT ON THE SEIZURE BY THE ABYSSINIANS of the Geological and Mineralogical Reconnaissance Expedition attached to the General Staff of the Egyptian Army. By L. H. Mitchell, Chief of the Expedition. Containing an Account of the subsequent Treatment of the Prisoners and Final Release of the Commander. Royal 8vo, pp. xii. and 126, stitched, with a Map. 1878. 7s. 6d.

EGYPTIAN CALENDAR for the year 1295 A.H. (1878 A.D.) : Corresponding with the years 1594, 1595 of the Koptic Era. 8vo, pp. 98, sewed. 1878. 2s. 6d.

EHRLICH.—FRENCH READER : With Notes and Vocabulary. By H. W. Ehrlich. 12mo, pp. viii. and 125, limp cloth. 1877. 1s. 6d.

EITEL.—BUDDHISM : Its Historical, Theoretical, and Popular Aspects. In Three Lectures. By E. J. Eitel, M.A., Ph.D. Second Edition. Demy 8vo, pp. 130. 1873. 5s.

EITEL.—FENG-SHUI ; or, The Rudiments of Natural Science in China. By E. J. Eitel, M.A., Ph.D. Royal 8vo, pp. vi. and 84, sewed. 1873. 6s.

EITEL.—HANDBOOK FOR THE STUDENT OF CHINESE BUDDHISM. By the Rev. E. J. Eitel, of the London Missionary Society. Crown 8vo, pp. viii. and 224, cloth. 1870. 18s.

ELLIOT.—MEMOIRS ON THE HISTORY, FOLK-LORE, AND DISTRIBUTION OF THE RACES OF THE NORTH-WESTERN PROVINCES OF INDIA. By the late Sir Henry M. Elliot, K.C.B. Edited, revised, and rearranged by John Beames, M.R.A.S., &c., &c. In 2 vols. demy 8vo, pp. xx., 370, and 396, with 3 large coloured folding Maps, cloth. 1869. £1, 16s.

ELLIOT.—THE HISTORY OF INDIA, as told by its own Historians. The Muhammadan Period. Edited from the Posthumous Papers of the late Sir H. M. Elliot, K.C.B., East India Company's Bengal Civil Service. Revised and continued by Professor John Dowson, M.R.A.S., Staff College, Sandhurst. 8vo. Vol. I.—Vol. II., pp. x. and 580, cloth. Vol. III., pp. xii. and 627, cloth. 21s.—Vol. IV., pp. xii. and 564, cloth. 1872. 21s.—Vol. V., pp. x. and 576, cloth. 1873. 21s.—Vol. VI., pp. viii. 574, cloth. 21s.—Vol. VII., pp. viii.-574. 1877. 21s. Vol. VIII., pp. xxxii.–444. With Biographical, Geographical, and General Index. 1877. 24s. Complete sets, £8, 8s. Vols. I. and II. not sold separately.

ELLIS.—ETRUSCAN NUMERALS. By Robert Ellis, B.D., late Fellow of St. John's College, Cambridge. 8vo, pp. 52, sewed. 1876. 2s. 6d.

ELY.—FRENCH AND GERMAN SOCIALISM IN MODERN TIMES. By R. T. Ely, Ph.D., Associate Professor of Political Economy in the Johns Hopkins University, Baltimore ; and Lecturer on Political Economy in Cornell University, Ithaca, N. Y. Crown 8vo, pp. viii.-274, cloth. 1884. 3s. 6d.

EMERSON AT HOME AND ABROAD. See English and Foreign Philosophical Library, Vol. XIX.

EMERSON.—INDIAN MYTHS ; or, Legends, Traditions, and Symbols of the Aborigines of America, compared with those of other Countries, including Hindostan, Egypt, Persia, Assyria, and China. By Ellen Russell Emerson. Illustrated. Post 8vo, pp. viii.-678, cloth. 1884. £1, 1s.

ENGLISH DIALECT SOCIETY.—Subscription, 10s. 6d. per annum. List of publications on application.

ENGLISH AND FOREIGN PHILOSOPHICAL LIBRARY (THE).
Post 8vo, cloth, uniformly bound.
I. to III.—A HISTORY OF MATERIALISM, and Criticism of its present Importance. By Professor F. A. Lange. Authorised Translation from the German by Ernest C. Thomas. In three volumes. Vol. I. Second Edition. pp. 350. 1878. 10s. 6d.—Vol. II., pp. viii. and 398. 1880. 10s. 6d. —Vol. III., pp. viii. and 376. 1881. 10s. 6d.

ENGLISH AND FOREIGN PHILOSOPHICAL LIBRARY—*continued.*

IV.—NATURAL LAW: an Essay in Ethics. By Edith Simcox. Second Edition. Pp. 366. 1878. 10s. 6d.

V. and VI.—THE CREED OF CHRISTENDOM; its Foundations contrasted with Superstructure. By W. R. Greg. Eighth Edition, with a New Introduction. In two volumes, pp. cxiv.-154 and vi.-282. 1883. 15s.

VII.—OUTLINES OF THE HISTORY OF RELIGION TO THE SPREAD OF THE UNIVERSAL RELIGIONS. By Prof. C. P. Tiele. Translated from the Dutch by J. Estlin Carpenter, M.A., with the author's assistance. Third Edition. Pp. xx. and 250. 1884. 7s. 6d.

VIII.—RELIGION IN CHINA; containing a brief Account of the Three Religions of the Chinese; with Observations on the Prospects of Christian Conversion amongst that People. By Joseph Edkins, D.D., Peking. Third Edition. Pp. xvi. and 260. 1884. 7s. 6d.

IX.—A CANDID EXAMINATION OF THEISM. By Physicus. Pp. 216. 1878. 7s. 6d.

X.—THE COLOUR-SENSE; its Origin and Development; an Essay in Comparative Psychology. By Grant Allen, B.A., author of "Physiological Æsthetics." Pp. xii. and 282. 1879. 10s. 6d

XI.—THE PHILOSOPHY OF MUSIC; being the substance of a Course of Lectures delivered at the Royal Institution of Great Britain in February and March 1877. By William Pole, F.R.S., F.R.S.E., Mus. Doc., Oxon. Pp. 336. 1879. 10s. 6d.

XII.—CONTRIBUTIONS TO THE HISTORY OF THE DEVELOPMENT OF THE HUMAN RACE: Lectures and Dissertations, by Lazarus Geiger. Translated from the German by D. Asher, Ph.D. Pp. x. and 156. 1880. 6s.

XIII.—DR. APPLETON: his Life and Literary Relics. By J. H. Appleton, M.A., and A. H. Sayce, M.A. Pp. 350. 1881. 10s. 6d.

XIV.—EDGAR QUINET: His Early Life and Writings. By Richard Heath. With Portraits, Illustrations, and an Autograph Letter. Pp. xxiii. and 370. 1881. 12s. 6d.

XV.—THE ESSENCE OF CHRISTIANITY. By Ludwig Feuerbach. Translated from the German by Marian Evans, translator of Strauss's "Life of Jesus." Second Edition. Pp. xx. and 340. 1881. 7s. 6d.

XVI.—AUGUSTE COMTE AND POSITIVISM. By the late John Stuart Mill, M.P. Third Edition. Pp. 200. 1882. 3s. 6d.

XVII.—ESSAYS AND DIALOGUES OF GIACOMO LEOPARDI. Translated by Charles Edwardes. With Biographical Sketch. Pp. xliv. and 216. 1882. 7s. 6d.

XVIII.—RELIGION AND PHILOSOPHY IN GERMANY: A Fragment. By Heinrich Heine. Translated by J. Snodgrass. Pp. xii. and 178, cloth. 1882. 6s.

XIX.—EMERSON AT HOME AND ABROAD. By M. D. Conway. Pp. viii. and 310. With Portrait. 1883. 10s. 6d.

XX.—ENIGMAS OF LIFE. By W. R. Greg. Fifteenth Edition, with a Postscript. CONTENTS: Realisable Ideals—Malthus Notwithstanding—Non-Survival of the Fittest—Limits and Directions of Human Development—The Significance of Life—De Profundis—Elsewhere—Appendix. Pp. xx. and 314, cloth. 1883. 10s. 6d.

XXI.—ETHIC DEMONSTRATED IN GEOMETRICAL ORDER AND DIVIDED INTO FIVE PARTS, which treat (1) Of God, (2) Of the Nature and Origin of the Mind, (3) Of the Origin and Nature of the Affects, (4) Of Human Bondage, or of the Strength of the Affects, (5) Of the Power of the Intellect, or of Human Liberty. By Benedict de Spinoza. Translated from the Latin by William Hale White. Pp. 328. 1883. 10s. 6d.

XXII.—THE WORLD AS WILL AND IDEA. By Arthur Schopenhauer. Translated from the German by R. B. Haldane, M.A., and John Kemp, M.A. 3 vols. Vol. I., pp. xxxii.-532. 1883. 18s.

ENGLISH AND FOREIGN PHILOSOPHICAL LIBRARY—*continued*.

XXV. to XXVII.—THE PHILOSOPHY OF THE UNCONSCIOUS. By Eduard Von Hartmann. Speculative Results, according to the Inductive Method of Physical Science. Authorised Translation, by William C. Coupland, M.A. 3 vols. pp. xxxii.-372; vi.-368; viii.-360. 1884. 31s. 6d.

Extra Series.

I. and II.—LESSING : His Life and Writings. By James Sime, M.A. Second Edition. 2 vols., pp. xxii. and 328, and xvi. and 358, with portraits. 1879. 21s.

III. and VI.—AN ACCOUNT OF THE POLYNESIAN RACE: its Origin and Migrations, and the Ancient History of the Hawaiian People to the Times of Kamehameha I. By Abraham Fornander, Circuit Judge of the Island of Maui, H.I. Vol. I., pp. xvi. and 248. 1877. 7s. 6d. Vol. II., pp. viii. and 400, cloth. 1880. 10s. 6d.

IV. and V.—ORIENTAL RELIGIONS, and their Relation to Universal Religion—India. By Samuel Johnson. In 2 vols., pp. viii. and 408; viii. and 402. 1879. 21s.

VI.—AN ACCOUNT OF THE POLYNESIAN RACE. By A. Fornander. Vol. II., pp. viii. and 400, cloth. 1880. 10s. 6d.

ER SIE ES.—FACSIMILE OF A MANUSCRIPT supposed to have been found in an Egyptian Tomb by the English soldiers last year. Royal 8vo, in ragged canvas covers, with string binding, with dilapidated edges (? just as discovered). 1884. 6s. 6d.

ETHERINGTON.—THE STUDENT'S GRAMMAR OF THE HINDÍ LANGUAGE. By the Rev. W. Etherington, Missionary, Benares. Second Edition. Crown 8vo, pp. xiv., 255, and xiii., cloth. 1873. 12s.

EYTON.—DOMESDAY STUDIES : AN ANALYSIS AND DIGEST OF THE STAFFORDSHIRE SURVEY. Treating of the Method of Domesday in its Relation to Staffordshire, &c. By the Rev. R. W. Eyton. 4to, pp. vii. and 135, cloth. 1881. £1, 1s.

FABER.—THE MIND OF MENCIUS. See Trübner's Oriental Series.

FALKE.—ART IN THE HOUSE. Historical, Critical, and Æsthetical Studies on the Decoration and Furnishing of the Dwelling. By J. von Falke, Vice-Director of the Austrian Museum of Art and Industry at Vienna. Translated from the German. Edited, with Notes, by C. C. Perkins, M.A. Royal 8vo, pp. xxx. 356, cloth. With Coloured Frontispiece, 60 Plates, and over 150 Illustrations. 1878. £3.

FARLEY.—EGYPT, CYPRUS, AND ASIATIC TURKEY. By J. L. Farley, author of "The Resources of Turkey," &c. 8vo, pp. xvi. and 270, cloth gilt. 1878. 10s. 6d.

FEATHERMAN.—THE SOCIAL HISTORY OF THE RACES OF MANKIND. Vol. V. THE ARAMÆANS. By A. Featherman. Demy 8vo, pp. xvii. and 664, cloth. 1881. £1, 1s.

FENTON.—EARLY HEBREW LIFE: a Study in Sociology. By John Fenton. 8vo, pp. xxiv. and 102, cloth. 1880. 5s.

FERGUSSON.—ARCHÆOLOGY IN INDIA. With especial reference to the works of Babu Rajendralala Mitra. By James Fergusson, C.I.E., F.R.S., D.C.L., LL.D., V.-P.R.A.S., &c. Demy 8vo, pp. 116, with Illustrations, sewed. 1884. 5s.

FERGUSSON.—THE TEMPLE OF DIANA AT EPHESUS. With Especial Reference to Mr. Wood's Discoveries of its Remains. By James Fergusson, C.I.E., D.C.L., LL.D., F.R.S., &c. From the Transactions of the Royal Institute of British Architects. Demy 4to, pp. 24, with Plan, cloth. 1883. 5s.

FERGUSSON AND BURGESS.—THE CAVE TEMPLES OF INDIA. By James Fergusson, D.C.L., F.R.S., and James Burgess, F.R.G.S. Impl. 8vo, pp. xx. and 536, with 98 Plates, half bound. 1880. £2, 2s.

FERGUSSON.—CHINESE RESEARCHES. First Part. Chinese Chronology and Cycles. By Thomas Fergusson, Member of the North China Branch of the Royal Asiatic Society. Crown 8vo, pp. viii. and 274, sewed. 1881. 10s. 6d.

FEUERBACH.—The Essence of Christianity. See English and Foreign Philosophical Library, vol. XV.

FICHTE.—J. G. Fichte's Popular Works: The Nature of the Scholar—The Vocation of Man—The Doctrine of Religion. With a Memoir by William Smith, LL.D. Demy 8vo, pp. viii. and 564, cloth. 1873. 15s.

FICHTE.—Characteristics of the Present Age. By J. G. Fichte. Translated from the German by W. Smith. Post 8vo, pp. xi. and 271, cloth. 1847. 6s.

FICHTE.—Memoir of Johann Gottlieb Fichte. By William Smith. Second Edition. Post 8vo, pp. 168, cloth. 1848. 4s.

FICHTE.—On the Nature of the Scholar, and its Manifestations. By Johann Gottlieb Fichte. Translated from the German by William Smith. Second Edition. Post 8vo, pp. vii. and 131. cloth. 1848. 3s.

FICHTE.—New Exposition of the Science of Knowledge. By J. G. Fichte. Translated from the German by A. E. Kroeger. 8vo, pp. vi. and 182, cloth. 1869. 6s.

FIELD.—Outlines of an International Code. By David Dudley Field. Second Edition. Royal 8vo, pp. iii. and 712, sheep. 1876. £2, 2s.

FIGANIERE.—Elva: A Story of the Dark Ages. By Viscount de Figanière, G.C. St. Anne, &c. Crown 8vo, pp. viii. and 194, cloth. 1878. 5s.

FISCHEL.—Specimens of Modern German Prose and Poetry; with Notes, Grammatical, Historical, and Idiomatical. To which is added a Short Sketch of the History of German Literature. By Dr. M. M. Fischel, formerly of Queen's College, Harley Street, and late German Master to the Stockwell Grammar School. Crown 8vo, pp. viii. and 280, cloth. 1880. 4s.

FISKE.—The Unseen World, and other Essays. By John Fiske, M.A., LL.B. Crown 8vo, pp. 350. 1876. 10s.

FISKE.—Myths and Myth-Makers; Old Tales and Superstitions, interpreted by Comparative Mythology. By John Fiske, M.A., LL.B., Assistant Librarian, and late Lecturer on Philosophy at Harvard University. Crown 8vo, pp. 260, cloth. 1873. 10s.

FITZGERALD.—Australian Orchids. By R. D. Fitzgerald, F.L.S. Folio.—Part I. 7 Plates.—Part II. 10 Plates.—Part III. 10 Plates.—Part IV. 10 Plates.—Part V. 10 Plates.—Part VI. 10 Plates. Each Part, Coloured 21s.; Plain, 10s. 6d.

FITZGERALD.—An Essay on the Philosophy of Self-Consciousness. Comprising an Analysis of Reason and the Rationale of Love. By P. F. Fitzgerald. Demy 8vo, pp. xvi. and 196, cloth. 1882. 5s.

FORJETT.—External Evidences of Christianity. By E. H. Forjett. 8vo, pp. 114, cloth. 1874. 2s. 6d.

FORNANDER.—The Polynesian Race. See English and Foreign Philosophical Library, Extra Series, Vols. III. and VI.

FORSTER.—Political Presentments.—By William Forster, Agent-General for New South Wales. Crown 8vo, pp. 122, cloth. 1878. 4s. 6d.

FOULKES.—The Daya Bhaga, the Law of Inheritance of the Sarasvati Vilasa. The Original Sanskrit Text, with Translation by the Rev. Thos. Foulkes, F.L.S., M.R.A.S., F.R.G.S., Fellow of the University of Madras, &c. Demy 8vo, pp. xxvi. and 194-162, cloth. 1881. 10s. 6d.

FOX.—Memorial Edition of Collected Works, by W. J. Fox. 12 vols. 8vo, cloth. £3.

FRANKLYN.—Outlines of Military Law, and the Laws of Evidence. By H. B. Franklyn, LL.B. Crown 16mo, pp. viii. and 152, cloth. 1874. 3s. 6d.

FREEMAN.—Lectures to American Audiences. By E. A. Freeman, D.C.L., LL.D., Honorary Fellow of Trinity College, Oxford. I. The English People in its Three Homes. II. The Practical Bearings of General European History. Post 8vo, pp. viii.-454, cloth. 1883. 8s. 6d.

FRIEDRICH.—PROGRESSIVE GERMAN READER, with Copious Notes to the First Part. By P. Friedrich. Crown 8vo, pp. 166, cloth. 1868. 4s. 6d.

FRIEDRICH.—A GRAMMATICAL COURSE OF THE GERMAN LANGUAGE. See under DUSAR.

FRIEDRICH.—A GRAMMAR OF THE GERMAN LANGUAGE, WITH EXERCISES. See under DUSAR.

FRIEDERICI.—BIBLIOTHECA ORIENTALIS, or a Complete List of Books, Papers, Serials, and Essays, published in England and the Colonies, Germany and France; on the History, Geography, Religions, Antiquities, Literature, and Languages of the East. Compiled by Charles Friederici. 8vo, boards. 1876, pp. 86, 2s. 6d. 1877, pp. 100, 3s. 1878, pp. 112, 3s. 6d. 1879, 3s. 1880, 3s.

FRŒMBLING.—GRADUATED GERMAN READER. Consisting of a Selection from the most Popular Writers, arranged progressively; with a complete Vocabulary for the first part. By Friedrich Otto Frœmbling. Eighth Edition. 12mo, pp. viii. and 306, cloth. 1883. 3s. 6d.

FRŒMBLING.—GRADUATED EXERCISES FOR TRANSLATION INTO GERMAN. Consisting of Extracts from the best English Authors, arranged progressively; with an Appendix, containing Idiomatic Notes. By Friedrich Otto Frœmbling, Ph.D., Principal German Master at the City of London School. Crown 8vo, pp. xiv. and 322, cloth. With Notes, pp. 66. 1867. 4s. 6d. Without Notes, 4s.

FROUDE.—THE BOOK OF JOB. By J. A. Froude, M.A., late Fellow of Exeter College, Oxford. Reprinted from the *Westminster Review*. 8vo, pp. 38, cloth. 1s.

FRUSTON.—ECHO FRANÇAIS. A Practical Guide to French Conversation. By F. de la Fruston. With a Vocabulary. 12mo, pp. vi. and 192, cloth. 3s.

FRYER.—THE KHYENG PEOPLE OF THE SANDOWAY DISTRICT, ARAKAN. By G. E. Fryer, Major, M.S.C., Deputy Commissioner, Sandoway. With 2 Plates. 8vo, pp. 44, cloth. 1875. 3s. 6d.

FRYER.—PÁLI STUDIES. No. I. Analysis, and Páli Text of the Subodhálankarn, or Easy Rhetoric, by Sangharakkhita Thera. 8vo, pp. 35, cloth. 1875. 3s. 6d.

FURNIVALL.—EDUCATION IN EARLY ENGLAND. Some Notes used as forewords to a Collection of Treatises on "Manners and Meals in Olden Times," for the Early English Text Society. By Frederick J. Furnivall, M.A. 8vo, pp. 4 and lxxiv., sewed. 1867. 1s.

GALDOS.—TRAFALGAR: A Tale. By B. Perez Galdos. From the Spanish by Clara Bell. 16mo, pp. 256, cloth. 1884. 4s. Paper, 2s. 6d.

GALDOS.—MARIANELA. By B. Perez Galdos. From the Spanish, by Clara Bell. 16mo, pp. 264, cloth. 1883. 4s.

GALDOS.—GLORIA: A Novel. By B. Perez Galdos. From the Spanish, by Clara Bell. Two volumes, 16mo, pp. vi. and 318, iv. and 362, cloth. 1883. 7s. 6d.

GALLOWAY.—A TREATISE ON FUEL. Scientific and Practical. By Robert Galloway, M.R.I.A., F.C.S., &c. With Illustrations. Post 8vo, pp. x. and 136, cloth. 1880. 6s.

GALLOWAY.—EDUCATION: SCIENTIFIC AND TECHNICAL; or, How the Inductive Sciences are Taught, and How they Ought to be Taught. By Robert Galloway, M.R.I.A., F.C.S. 8vo, pp. xvi. and 462, cloth. 1881. 10s. 6d.

GAMBLE.—A MANUAL OF INDIAN TIMBERS: An Account of the Structure, Growth, Distribution, and Qualities of Indian Woods. By J. C. Gamble, M.A., F.L.S. 8vo, pp. xxx. and 522, with a Map, cloth. 1881. 10s.

GARBE.—See AUCTORES SANSKRITI, Vol. III.

GARFIELD.—THE LIFE AND PUBLIC SERVICE OF JAMES A. GARFIELD, Twentieth President of the United States. A Biographical Sketch. By Captain F. H. Mason, late of the 42d Regiment, U.S.A. With a Preface by Bret Harte. Crown 8vo, pp. vi. and 134, cloth. With Portrait. 1881. 2s. 6d.

GARRETT.—A CLASSICAL DICTIONARY OF INDIA : Illustrative of the Mythology, Philosophy, Literature, Antiquities, Arts, Manners, Customs, &c., of the Hindus. By John Garrett, Director of Public Instruction in Mysore. 8vo, pp. x. and 794, cloth. With Supplement, pp. 160. 1871 and 1873. £1, 16s.

GAUTAMA.—THE INSTITUTES OF. See AUCTORES SANSKRITI, Vol. II.

GAZETTEER OF THE CENTRAL PROVINCES OF INDIA. Edited by Charles Grant, Secretary to the Chief Commissioner of the Central Provinces. Second Edition. With a very large folding Map of the Central Provinces of India. Demy 8vo, pp. clvii. and 582, cloth. 1870. £1, 4s.

GEIGER.—A PEEP AT MEXICO ; Narrative of a Journey across the Republic from the Pacific to the Gulf, in December 1873 and January 1874. By J. L. Geiger, F.R.G.S. Demy 8vo, pp. 368, with Maps and 45 Original Photographs. Cloth, 24s.

GEIGER.—CONTRIBUTIONS TO THE HISTORY OF THE DEVELOPMENT OF THE HUMAN RACE : Lectures and Dissertations, by Lazarus Geiger. Translated from the Second German Edition, by David Asher, Ph.D. Post 8vo, pp. x.-156, cloth. 1880. 6s.

GELDART.—FAITH AND FREEDOM. Fourteen Sermons. By E. M. Geldart, M.A. Crown 8vo, pp. vi. and 168, cloth. 1881. 4s. 6d.

GELDART.—A GUIDE TO MODERN GREEK. By E. M. Geldart, M.A. Post 8vo, pp. xii. and 274, cloth. 1883. 7s. 6d. Key, pp. 28, cloth. 1883. 2s. 6d.

GELDART.—GREEK GRAMMAR. See Trübner's Collection.

GEOLOGICAL MAGAZINE (THE) : OR, MONTHLY JOURNAL OF GEOLOGY. With which is incorporated "The Geologist." Edited by Henry Woodward, LL.D., F.R.S., F.G.S., &c., of the British Museum. Assisted by Professor John Morris, M.A., F.G.S., &c., and Robert Etheridge, F.R.S., L. & E., F.G.S., &c., of the Museum of Practical Geology. 8vo, cloth. 1866 to 1883. 20s. each.

GHOSE.—THE MODERN HISTORY OF THE INDIAN CHIEFS, RAJAS, ZAMINDARS, &c. By Loke Nath Ghose. 2 vols. post 8vo, pp. xii. and 218, and xviii. and 612, cloth. 1883. 21s.

GILES.—CHINESE SKETCHES.—By Herbert A. Giles, of H.B.M.'s China Consular Service. 8vo, pp. 204, cloth. 1875. 10s. 6d.

GILES.—A DICTIONARY OF COLLOQUIAL IDIOMS IN THE MANDARIN DIALECT. By Herbert A. Giles. 4to, pp. 65, half bound. 1873. 28s.

GILES.—SYNOPTICAL STUDIES IN CHINESE CHARACTER. By Herbert A. Giles. 8vo, pp. 118, half bound. 1874. 15s.

GILES.—CHINESE WITHOUT A TEACHER. Being a Collection of Easy and Useful Sentences in the Mandarin Dialect. With a Vocabulary. By Herbert A. Giles. 12mo, pp. 60, half bound. 1872. 5s.

GILES.—THE SAN TZU CHING ; or, Three Character Classic ; and the Ch'Jen Tsu Wen ; or, Thousand Character Essay. Metrically Translated by Herbert A. Giles. 12mo, pp. 28, half bound. 1873. 2s. 6d.

GLASS.—ADVANCE THOUGHT. By Charles E. Glass. Crown 8vo, pp. xxxvi. and 188, cloth. 1876. 6s.

GOETHE'S FAUST.—See SCOONES and WYSARD.

GOETHE'S MINOR POEMS.—See SELSS.

GOLDSTÜCKER.—A DICTIONARY, SANSKRIT AND ENGLISH, extended and improved from the Second Edition of the Dictionary of Professor H. H. Wilson, with his sanction and concurrence. Together with a Supplement, Grammatical Appendices, and an Index, serving as a Sanskrit-English Vocabulary. By Theodore Goldstücker. Parts I. to VI. 4to, pp. 400. 1856-63. 6s. each.

GOLDSTÜCKER.—See AUCTORES SANSKRITI, Vol. I.

GOOROO SIMPLE. Strange Surprising Adventures of the Venerable G. S. and his Five Disciples, Noodle, Doodle, Wiseacre, Zany, and Foozle; adorned with Fifty Illustrations, drawn on wood, by Alfred Crowquill. A companion Volume to "Münchhausen" and "Owlglass," based upon the famous Tamul tale of the Gooroo Paramartan, and exhibiting, in the form of a skilfully-constructed consecutive narrative, some of the finest specimens of Eastern wit and humour. Elegantly printed on tinted paper, in crown 8vo, pp. 223, richly gilt ornamental cover, gilt edges. 1861. 10s. 6d.

GORKOM.—HANDBOOK OF CINCHONA CULTURE. By K. W. Van Gorkom, formerly Director of the Government Cinchona Plantations in Java. Translated by B. D. Jackson, Secretary of the Linnæan Society of London. With a Coloured Illustration. Imperial 8vo, pp. xii. and 292, cloth. 1882. £2.

GOUGH.—The SARVA-DARSANA-SAMGRAHA. See Trübner's Oriental Series.

GOUGH.—PHILOSOPHY OF THE UPANISHADS. See Trübner's Oriental Series.

GOVER.—THE FOLK-SONGS OF SOUTHERN INDIA. By C. E. Gover, Madras. Contents: Canarese Songs; Badaga Songs; Coorg Songs; Tamil Songs; The Cural; Malayalam Songs; Telugu Songs. 8vo, pp. xxviii. and 300, cloth. 1872. 10s. 6d.

GRAY.—DARWINIANA: Essays and Reviews pertaining to Darwinism. By Asa Gray. Crown 8vo, pp. xii. and 396, cloth. 1877. 10s.

GRAY.—NATURAL SCIENCE AND RELIGION: Two Lectures Delivered to the Theological School of Yale College. By Asa Gray. Crown 8vo, pp. 112, cloth. 1880. 5s.

GREEN.—SHAKESPEARE AND THE EMBLEM-WRITERS: An Exposition of their Similarities of Thought and Expression. Preceded by a View of the Emblem-Book Literature down to A.D. 1616. By Henry Green, M.A. In one volume, pp. xvi. 572, profusely illustrated with Woodcuts and Photolith. Plates, elegantly bound in cloth gilt. 1870. Large medium 8vo, £1, 11s. 6d.; large imperial 8vo, £2, 12s. 6d.

GREEN.—ANDREA ALCIATI, and his Books of Emblems: A Biographical and Bibliographical Study. By Henry Green, M.A. With Ornamental Title, Portraits, and other Illustrations. Dedicated to Sir William Stirling-Maxwell, Bart., Rector of the University of Edinburgh. Only 250 copies printed. Demy 8vo, pp. 360, handsomely bound. 1872. £1, 1s.

GREENE.—A NEW METHOD OF LEARNING TO READ, WRITE, AND SPEAK THE FRENCH LANGUAGE; or, First Lessons in French (Introductory to Ollendorff's Larger Grammar). By G. W. Greene, Instructor in Modern Languages in Brown University. Third Edition, enlarged and rewritten. Fcap. 8vo, pp. 248, cloth. 1869. 3s. 6d.

GREENE.—THE HEBREW MIGRATION FROM EGYPT. By J. Baker Greene, LL.B., M.B., Trin. Coll., Dub. Second Edition. Demy 8vo, pp. xii. and 440, cloth. 1882. 10s. 6d.

GREG.—TRUTH VERSUS EDIFICATION. By W. R. Greg. Fcap. 8vo, pp. 32, cloth. 1869. 1s.

GREG.—WHY ARE WOMEN REDUNDANT? By W. R. Greg. Fcap. 8vo, pp. 40, cloth. 1869. 1s.

GREG.—LITERARY AND SOCIAL JUDGMENTS. By W. R. Greg. Fourth Edition, considerably enlarged. 2 vols. crown 8vo, pp. 310 and 288, cloth. 1877. 15s.

GREG.—Mistaken Aims and Attainable Ideals of the Artisan Class. By W. R. Greg. Crown 8vo, pp. vi. and 332, cloth. 1876. 10s. 6d.

GREG.—Enigmas of Life. By W. R. Greg. Fifteenth Edition, with a postscript. Contents: Realisable Ideals. Malthus Notwithstanding. Non-Survival of the Fittest. Limits and Directions of Human Development. The Significance of Life. De Profundis. Elsewhere. Appendix. Post 8vo, pp. xxii. and 314, cloth. 1883. 10s. 6d.

GREG.—Political Problems for our Age and Country. By W. R. Greg. Contents: I. Constitutional and Autocratic Statesmanship. II. England's Future Attitude and Mission. III. Disposal of the Criminal Classes. IV. Recent Change in the Character of English Crime. V. The Intrinsic Vice of Trade-Unions. VI. Industrial and Co-operative Partnerships. VII. The Economic Problem. VIII. Political Consistency. IX. The Parliamentary Career. X. The Price we pay for Self-government. XI. Vestryism. XII. Direct v. Indirect Taxation. XIII. The New Régime, and how to meet it. Demy 8vo, pp. 342, cloth. 1870. 10s. 6d.

GREG.—The Great Duel: Its True Meaning and Issues. By W. R. Greg. Crown 8vo, pp. 96, cloth. 1871. 2s. 6d.

GREG.—The Creed of Christendom. See English and Foreign Philosophical Library, Vols. V. and VI.

GREG.—Rocks Ahead; or, The Warnings of Cassandra. By W. R. Greg. Second Edition, with a Reply to Objectors. Crown 8vo, pp. xliv. and 236, cloth. 1874. 9s.

GREG.—Miscellaneous Essays. By W. R. Greg. First Series. Crown 8vo, pp. iv.-268, cloth. 1881. 7s. 6d.
  Contents:—Rocks Ahead and Harbours of Refuge. Foreign Policy of Great Britain. The Echo of the Antipodes. A Grave Perplexity before us. Obligations of the Soil. The Right Use of a Surplus. The Great Twin Brothers: Louis Napoleon and Benjamin Disraeli. Is the Popular Judgment in Politics more Just than that of the Higher Orders? Harriet Martineau. Verify your Compass. The Prophetic Element in the Gospels. Mr. Frederick Harrison on the Future Life. Can Truths be Apprehended which could not have been Discovered?

GREG.—Miscellaneous Essays. By W. R. Greg. Second Series. Pp. 294. 1884. 7s. 6d.
  Contents:—France since 1848. France in January 1852. England as it is. Sir R. Peel's Character and Policy. Employment of our Asiatic Forces in European Wars.

GRIFFIN.—The Rajas of the Punjab. Being the History of the Principal States in the Punjab, and their Political Relations with the British Government. By Lepel H. Griffin, Bengal Civil Service, Acting Secretary to the Government of the Punjab, Author of "The Punjab Chiefs," &c. Second Edition. Royal 8vo, pp. xvi. and 630, cloth. 1873. £1, 1s.

GRIFFIN.—The World under Glass. By Frederick Griffin, Author of "The Destiny of Man," "The Storm King," and other Poems. Fcap. 8vo, pp. 204, cloth gilt. 1879. 3s. 6d.

GRIFFIN.—The Destiny of Man, The Storm King, and other Poems. By F. Griffin. Second Edition. Fcap. 8vo, pp. vii.-104, cloth. 1883. 2s. 6d.

GRIFFIS.—The Mikado's Empire. Book I. History of Japan, from 660 B.C. to 1872 A.D.—Book II. Personal Experiences, Observations, and Studies in Japan, 1870-1874. By W. E. Griffis, A.M. Second Edition. 8vo, pp. 626, cloth. Illustrated. 1883. 20s.

GRIFFIS.—Japanese Fairy World. Stories from the Wonder-Lore of Japan. By W. E. Griffis. Square 16mo, pp. viii. and 304, with 12 Plates. 1880. 7s. 6d.

Published by Trübner & Co. 29

GRIFFITH.—THE BIRTH OF THE WAR GOD. See Trübner's Oriental Series.

GRIFFITH.—YUSUF AND ZULAIKHA. See Trübner's Oriental Series.

GRIFFITH.—SCENES FROM THE RAMAYANA, MEGHADUTA, &c. Translated by Ralph T. H. Griffith, M.A., Principal of the Benares College. Second Edition. Crown 8vo, pp. xviii. and 244, cloth. 1870. 6s.

CONTENTS.—Preface—Ayodhya—Ravan Doomed—The Birth of Rama—The Heir-Apparent—Manthara's Guile—Dasaratha's Oath—The Step-mother—Mother and Son—The Triumph of Love—Farewell ?—The Hermit's Son—The Trial of Truth—The Forest—The Rape of Sita—Rama's Despair—The Messenger Cloud—Khumbakarna—The Suppliant Dove—True Glory—Feed the Poor—The Wise Scholar.

GRIFFITH.—THE RÁMÁYAN OF VÁLMÍKI. Translated into English Verse. By Ralph T. H. Griffith, M.A., Principal of the Benares College. Vol. I., containing Books I. and II., demy 8vo, pp. xxxii. and 440, cloth. 1870. —Vol. II., containing Book II., with additional Notes and Index of Names. Demy 8vo, pp. 504, cloth. 1871. —Vol. III., demy 8vo, pp. 390, cloth. 1872. —Vol. IV., demy 8vo, pp. viii. and 432, cloth. 1873. —Vol. V., demy 8vo, pp. viii. and 360, cloth. 1875. The complete work, 5 vols. £7, 7s.

GROTE.—REVIEW of the Work of Mr. John Stuart Mill entitled "Examination of Sir William Hamilton's Philosophy." By George Grote, Author of the "History of Ancient Greece," "Plato, and the other Companions of Socrates," &c. 12mo, pp. 112, cloth. 1868. 3s. 6d.

GROUT.—ZULU-LAND; or, Life among the Zulu-Kafirs of Natal and Zulu-Land, South Africa. By the Rev. Lewis Grout. Crown 8vo, pp. 352, cloth. With Map and Illustrations. 7s. 6d.

GROWSE.—MATHURA : A District Memoir. By F. S. Growse, B.C.S., M.A., Oxon, C.I.E., Fellow of the Calcutta University. Second edition, illustrated, revised, and enlarged, 4to, pp. xxiv. and 520, boards. 1880. 42s.

GUBERNATIS.—ZOOLOGICAL MYTHOLOGY; or, The Legends of Animals. By Angelo de Gubernatis, Professor of Sanskrit and Comparative Literature in the Instituto di Studii Superorii e di Perfezionamento at Florence, &c. 2 vols. 8vo, pp. xxvi. and 432, and vii. and 442, cloth. 1872. £1, 8s.

This work is an important contribution to the study of the comparative mythology of the Indo-Germanic nations. The author introduces the denizens of the air, earth, and water in the various characters assigned to them in the myths and legends of all civilised nations, and traces the migration of the mythological ideas from the times of the early Aryans to those of the Greeks, Romans, and Teutons.

GULSHAN I. RAZ : THE MYSTIC ROSE GARDEN OF SA'D UD DIN MAHMUD SHABISTARI. The Persian Text, with an English Translation and Notes, chiefly from the Commentary of Muhammed Bin Yahya Labiji. By E. H. Whinfield, M.A., Barrister-at-Law, late of H.M.B.C.S. 4to, pp. xvi., 94, 60, cloth. 1880. 10s. 6d.

GUMPACH.—TREATY RIGHTS OF THE FOREIGN MERCHANT, and the Transit System in China. By Johannes von Gumpach. 8vo, pp. xviii. and 421, sewed. 10s. 6d.

HAAS.—CATALOGUE OF SANSKRIT AND PALI BOOKS IN THE BRITISH MUSEUM. By Dr. Ernst Haas. Printed by permission of the Trustees of the British Museum. 4to, pp. viii. and 188, paper boards. 1876. 21s.

HAFIZ OF SHIRAZ.—SELECTIONS FROM HIS POEMS. Translated from the Persian by Hermann Bicknell. With Preface by A. S. Bicknell. Demy 4to, pp. xx. and 384, printed on fine stout plate-paper, with appropriate Oriental Bordering in gold and colour, and Illustrations by J. R. Herbert, R.A. 1875. £2, 2s.

HAFIZ.—See Trübner's Oriental Series.

HAGEN.—NORICA ; or, Tales from the Olden Time. Translated from the German of August Hagen. Fcap. 8vo, pp. xiv. and 374. 1850. 5s.

HAGGARD.—CETYWAYO AND HIS WHITE NEIGHBOURS; or, Remarks on Recent Events in Zululand, Natal, and the Transvaal. By H. R. Haggard. Crown 8vo, pp. xvi. and 294, cloth. 1882. 7s. 6d.

HAGGARD.—See "The Vazir of Lankuran."

HAHN.—TSUNI-‖GOAM, the Supreme Being of the Khoi-Khoi. By Theophilus Hahn, Ph.D., Custodian of the Grey Collection, Cape Town, &c., &c. Post 8vo, pp. xiv. and 154. 1882. 7s. 6d.

HALDANE.—See SCHOPENHAUER, or ENGLISH AND FOREIGN PHILOSOPHICAL LIBRARY, vol. xxii.

HALDEMAN.—PENNSYLVANIA DUTCH: A Dialect of South Germany with an Infusion of English. By S. S. Haldeman, A.M., Professor of Comparative Philology in the University of Pennsylvania, Philadelphia. 8vo, pp. viii. and 70, cloth. 1872. 3s. 6d.

HALL.—ON ENGLISH ADJECTIVES IN -ABLE, WITH SPECIAL REFERENCE TO RELIABLE. By FitzEdward Hall, C.E., M.A., Hon. D.C.L. Oxon; formerly Professor of Sanskrit Language and Literature, and of Indian Jurisprudence in King's College, London. Crown 8vo, pp. viii. and 238, cloth. 1877. 7s. 6d.

HALL.—MODERN ENGLISH. By FitzEdward Hall, M.A., Hon. D.C.L. Oxon. Crown 8vo, pp. xvi. and 394, cloth. 1873. 10s. 6d.

HALL.—SUN AND EARTH AS GREAT FORCES IN CHEMISTRY. By T. W. Hall, M.D., L.R.C.S.E. Crown 8vo, pp. xii. and 220, cloth. 1874. 3s.

HALL.—THE PEDIGREE OF THE DEVIL. By F. T. Hall, F.R.A.S. With Seven Autotype Illustrations from Designs by the Author. Demy 8vo, pp. xvi. and 256, cloth. 1883. 7s. 6d.

HALL.—ARCTIC EXPEDITION. See NOURSE.

HALLOCK.—THE SPORTSMAN'S GAZETTEER AND GENERAL GUIDE. The Game Animals, Birds, and Fishes of North America: their Habits and various methods of Capture, &c., &c. With a Directory to the principal Game Resorts of the Country. By Charles Hallock. New Edition. Crown 8vo, cloth. Maps and Portrait. 1883. 15s.

HAM.—THE MAID OF CORINTH. A Drama in Four Acts. By J. Panton Ham. Crown 8vo, pp. 65, sewed. 2s. 6d.

HARDY.—CHRISTIANITY AND BUDDHISM COMPARED. By the late Rev. R. Spence Hardy, Hon. Member Royal Asiatic Society. 8vo, pp. 138, sewed. 1875. 7s. 6d.

HARLEY.—THE SIMPLIFICATION OF ENGLISH SPELLING, specially adapted to the Rising Generation. An Easy Way of Saving Time in Writing, Printing, and Reading. By Dr. George Harley, F.R.S., F.C.S. 8vo. pp. 128, cloth. 1877. 2s. 6d.

HARRISON.—WOMAN'S HANDIWORK IN MODERN HOMES. By Constance Cary Harrison. With numerous Illustrations and Five Coloured Plates, from designs by Samuel Colman, Rosina Emmet, George Gibson, and others. 8vo, pp. xii. and 242, cloth. 1881. 10s.

HARTMANN.—See English and Foreign Philosophical Library, vol. XXV.'

HARTZENBUSCH and LEMMING.—ECO DE MADRID. A Practical Guide to Spanish Conversation. By J. E. Hartzenbusch and H. Lemming. Second Edition. Post 8vo, pp. 250, cloth. 1870. 5s.

HASE.—MIRACLE PLAYS AND SACRED DRAMAS: An Historical Survey. By Dr. Karl Hase. Translated from the German by A. W. Jackson, and Edited by the Rev. W. W. Jackson, Fellow of Exeter College, Oxford. Crown 8vo, pp. 288. 1880. 9s.

HAUG.—GLOSSARY AND INDEX of the Pahlavi Texts of the Book of Arda Viraf, the Tale of Gosht—J. Fryano, the Hadokht Nask, and to some extracts from the Dinkard and Nirangistan; prepared from Destur Hoshangji Jamaspji Asa's Glossary to the Arda Viraf Namak, and from the Original Texts, with Notes on Pahlavi Grammar by E. W. West, Ph.D. Revised by M. Haug, Ph.D., &c. Published by order of the Bombay Government. 8vo, pp. viii. and 352, sewed. 1874. 25s.

HAUG.—THE SACRED LANGUAGE, &c., OF THE PARSIS. See Trübner's Oriental Series.

HAUPT.—THE LONDON ARBITRAGEUR; or, The English Money Market, in connection with Foreign Bourses. A Collection of Notes and Formulæ for the Arbitration of Bills, Stocks, Shares, Bullion, and Coins, with all the Important Foreign Countries. By Ottomar Haupt. Crown 8vo, pp. viii. and 196, cloth. 1870. 7s. 6d.

HAWKEN.—UPA-SASTRĀ: Comments, Linguistic, Doctrinal, on Sacred and Mythic Literature. By J. D. Hawken. Crown 8vo, pp. viii. and 288, cloth. 1877. 7s. 6d.

HAZEN.—THE SCHOOL AND THE ARMY IN GERMANY AND FRANCE, with a Diary of Siege Life at Versailles. By Brevet Major-General W. B. Hazen, U.S.A., Col. 6th Infantry. 8vo, pp. 408, cloth. 1872. 10s. 6d.

HEATH.—EDGAR QUINET. See English and Foreign Philosophical Library, Vol. XIV.

HEATON—AUSTRALIAN DICTIONARY OF DATES AND MEN OF THE TIME. Containing the History of Australasia from 1542 to May 1879. By I. H. Heaton. Royal 8vo, pp. iv. and 554, cloth. 15s.

HEBREW LITERATURE SOCIETY.—Subscription, one guinea per annum. List of publications on application.

HECHLER.—THE JERUSALEM BISHOPRIC DOCUMENTS. With Translations, chiefly derived from "Das Evangelische Bisthum in Jerusalem," Geschichtliche Darlegung mit Urtunden. Berlin, 1842. Published by Command of His Majesty Frederick William IV., King of Prussia. Arranged and Supplemented by the Rev. Prof. William H. Hechler, British Chaplain at Stockholm. 8vo, pp. 212, with Maps, Portrait, and Illustrations, cloth. 1883. 10s. 6d.

HECKER.—THE EPIDEMICS OF THE MIDDLE AGES. Translated by G. B. Babington, M.D., F.R.S. Third Edition, completed by the Author's Treatise on Child-Pilgrimages. By J. F. C. Hecker. 8vo, pp. 384, cloth. 1859. 9s. 6d.
CONTENTS.—The Black Death—The Dancing Mania—The Sweating Sickness—Child Pilgrimages.

HEDLEY.—MASTERPIECES OF GERMAN POETRY. Translated in the Measure of the Originals, by F. H. Hedley. With Illustrations by Louis Wanke. Crown 8vo, pp. viii. and 120, cloth. 1876. 6s.

HEINE.—RELIGION AND PHILOSOPHY IN GERMANY. See English and Foreign Philosophical Library, Vol. XVIII.

HEINE.—WIT, WISDOM, AND PATHOS from the Prose of Heinrich Heine. With a few pieces from the "Book of Songs." Selected and Translated by J. Snodgrass. With Portrait. Crown 8vo, pp. xx. and 340, cloth. 1879. 7s. 6d.

HEINE.—PICTURES OF TRAVEL. Translated from the German of Henry Heine, by Charles G. Leland. 7th Revised Edition. Crown 8vo, pp. 472, with Portrait, cloth. 1873. 7s. 6d.

HEINE.—HEINE'S BOOK OF SONGS. Translated by Charles G. Leland. Fcap. 8vo, pp. xiv. and 240, cloth, gilt edges. 1874. 7s. 6d.

HEITZMANN.—MICROSCOPICAL MORPHOLOGY OF THE ANIMAL BODY IN HEALTH AND DISEASE. By C. HEITZMANN, M.D. Royal 8vo, pp. xx.-850, cloth. 1884. 31s. 6d.

HENDRIK.—MEMOIRS OF HANS HENDRIK, THE ARCTIC TRAVELLER; serving under Kane, Hayes, Hall, and Nares, 1853-76. Written by Himself. Translated from the Eskimo Language, by Dr. Henry Rink. Edited by Prof. Dr. G. Stephens, F.S.A. Crown 8vo, pp. 100, Map, cloth. 1878. 3s. 6d.

HENNELL.—PRESENT RELIGION: As a Faith owning Fellowship with Thought. Vol. I. Part I. By Sara S. Hennell. Crown 8vo, pp. 570, cloth. 1865. 7s. 6d.

HENNELL.—COMPARATIVE ETHICS—I. Sections II. and III. Moral Principle in Regard to Sexhood. Present Religion, Vol. III. By S. Hennell. Crown 8vo, pp. 92, wrapper. 1884. 2s.

HENNELL.—PRESENT RELIGION: As a Faith owning Fellowship with Thought. Part II. First Division. Intellectual Effect: shown as a Principle of Metaphysical Comparativism. By Sara S. Hennell. Crown 8vo, pp. 618, cloth. 1873. 7s. 6d.

HENNELL.—PRESENT RELIGION, Vol. III. Part II. Second Division. The Effect of Present Religion on its Practical Side. By S. S. Hennell. Crown 8vo, pp. 68, paper covers. 1882. 2s.

HENNELL.—COMPARATIVISM shown as Furnishing a Religious Basis to Morality. (Present Religion. Vol. III. Part II. Second Division: Practical Effect.) By Sara S. Hennell. Crown 8vo, pp. 220, stitched in wrapper. 1878. 3s. 6d.

HENNELL.—THOUGHTS IN AID OF FAITH. Gathered chiefly from recent Works in Theology and Philosophy. By Sara S. Hennell. Post 8vo, pp. 428, cloth. 1860. 6s.

HENWOOD.—THE METALLIFEROUS DEPOSITS OF CORNWALL AND DEVON; with Appendices on Subterranean Temperature; the Electricity of Rocks and Veins; the Quantities of Water in the Cornish Mines; and Mining Statistics. (Vol. V. of the Transactions of the Royal Geographical Society of Cornwall.) By William Jory Henwood, F.R.S., F.G.S. 8vo, pp. x. and 515; with 113 Tables, and 12 Plates, half bound. £2, 2s.

HENWOOD.—OBSERVATIONS ON METALLIFEROUS DEPOSITS, AND ON SUBTERRANEAN TEMPERATURE. (Vol. VIII. of the Transactions of the Royal Geological Society of Cornwall.) By William Jory Henwood, F.R.S., F.G.S., President of the Royal Institution of Cornwall. In 2 Parts. 8vo, pp. xxx., vii. and 916; with 38 Tables, 31 Engravings on Wood, and 6 Plates. £1, 16s.

HEPBURN.—A JAPANESE AND ENGLISH DICTIONARY. With an English and Japanese Index. By J. C. Hepburn, M.D., LL.D. Second Edition. Imperial 8vo, pp. xxxii., 632, and 201, cloth. £8, 8s.

HEPBURN.—JAPANESE-ENGLISH AND ENGLISH-JAPANESE DICTIONARY. By J. C. Hepburn, M.D., LL.D. Abridged by the Author. Square fcap., pp. vi. and 536, cloth. 1873. 18s.

HERNISZ.—A GUIDE TO CONVERSATION IN THE ENGLISH AND CHINESE LANGUAGES, for the Use of Americans and Chinese in California and elsewhere. By Stanislas Hernisz. Square 8vo, pp. 274, sewed. 1855. 10s. 6d.

HERSHON.—TALMUDIC MISCELLANY. See Trübner's Oriental Series.

HERZEN.—DU DEVELOPPEMENT DES IDÉES REVOLUTIONNAIRES EN RUSSIE. Par Alexander Herzen. 12mo, pp. xxiii. and 144, sewed. 1853. 2s. 6d.

HERZEN.—A separate list of A. Herzen's works in Russian may be had on application.

HILL.—THE HISTORY OF THE REFORM MOVEMENT in the Dental Profession in Great Britain during the last twenty years. By Alfred Hill, Licentiate in Dental Surgery, &c. Crown 8vo, pp. xvi. and 400, cloth. 1877. 10s. 6d.

HILLEBRAND.—FRANCE AND THE FRENCH IN THE SECOND HALF OF THE NINETEENTH CENTURY. By Karl Hillebrand. Translated from the Third German Edition. Post 8vo, pp. xx. and 262, cloth. 1881. 10s. 6d.

HINDOO MYTHOLOGY POPULARLY TREATED. Being an Epitomised Description of the various Heathen Deities illustrated on the Silver Swami Tea Service presented, as a memento of his visit to India, to H.R.H. the Prince of Wales, K.G., G.C.S.I., by His Highness the Gaekwar of Baroda. Small 4to, pp. 42, limp cloth. 1875. 3s. 6d.

HITTELL.—THE COMMERCE AND INDUSTRIES OF THE PACIFIC COAST OF NORTH AMERICA. By J. S. Hittell, Author of "The Resources of California." 4to, pp. 820. 1882. £1, 10s.

HODGSON.—ACADEMY LECTURES. By J. E. Hodgson, R. A., Librarian and Professor of Painting to the Royal Academy. Cr. 8vo, pp. viiii. and 312, cloth. 1884. 7s. 6d.

HODGSON.—ESSAYS ON THE LANGUAGES, LITERATURE, AND RELIGION OF NÉPAL AND TIBET. Together with further Papers on the Geography, Ethnology, and Commerce of those Countries. By B. H. Hodgson, late British Minister at the Court of Nepál. Royal 8vo, cloth, pp. xii. and 276. 1874. 14s.

HODGSON.— ESSAYS ON INDIAN SUBJECTS. See Trübner's Oriental Series.

HODGSON.—THE EDUCATION OF GIRLS; AND THE EMPLOYMENT OF WOMEN OF THE UPPER CLASSES EDUCATIONALLY CONSIDERED. Two Lectures. By W. B. Hodgson, LL.D. Second Edition. Cr. 8vo, pp. xvi. and 114, cloth. 1869. 3s. 6d.

HODGSON.—TURGOT: His Life, Times, and Opinions. Two Lectures. By W. B. Hodgson, LL.D. Crown 8vo, pp. vi. and 83, sewed. 1870. 2s.

HOERNLE.—A COMPARATIVE GRAMMAR OF THE GAUDIAN LANGUAGES, with Special Reference to the Eastern Hindi. Accompanied by a Language Map, and a Table of Alphabets. By A. F. Rudolf Hoernle. Demy 8vo, pp. 474, cloth. 1880. 18s.

HOLBEIN SOCIETY.—Subscription, one guinea per annum. List of publications on application.

HOLMES-FORBES.—THE SCIENCE OF BEAUTY. An Analytical Inquiry into the Laws of Æsthetics. By Avary W. Holmes-Forbes, of Lincoln's Inn, Barrister-at-Law. Post 8vo, cloth, pp. vi. and 200. 1881. 6s.

HOLST.—THE CONSTITUTIONAL AND POLITICAL HISTORY OF THE UNITED STATES. By Dr. H. von Holst. Translated by J. J. Lalor and A. B. Mason. Royal 8vo. Vol. I. 1750–1833. State Sovereignty and Slavery. Pp. xvi. and 506. 1876. 18s. —Vol. II. 1828–1846. Jackson's Administration—Annexation of Texas. Pp. 720. 1879. £1, 2s.—Vol. III. 1846–1850. Annexation of Texas—Compromise of 1850. Pp. x. and 598. 1881. 18s.

HOLYOAKE.—TRAVELS IN SEARCH OF A SETTLER'S GUIDE-BOOK OF AMERICA AND CANADA. By George Jacob Holyoake, Author of "The History of Co-operation in England." Post 8vo, pp. 148, wrapper. 1884. 2s. 6d.

HOLYOAKE.—THE ROCHDALE PIONEERS. Thirty-three Years of Co-operation in Rochdale. In two parts. Part I. 1844–1857; Part II. 1857–1877. By G. J. Holyoake. Crown 8vo, pp. 174, cloth. 1882. 2s. 6d.

HOLYOAKE.—THE HISTORY OF CO-OPERATION IN ENGLAND: its Literature and its Advocates. By G. J. Holyoake. Vol. I. The Pioneer Period, 1812–44. Crown 8vo, pp. xii. and 420, cloth. 1875. 4s.—Vol. II. The Constructive Period, 1845–78. Crown 8vo, pp. x. and 504, cloth. 1878. 8s.

HOLYOAKE.—THE TRIAL OF THEISM ACCUSED OF OBSTRUCTING SECULAR LIFE. By G. J. Holyoake. Crown 8vo, pp. xvi. and 256, cloth. 1877. 4s.

HOLYOAKE.—REASONING FROM FACTS: A Method of Everyday Logic. By G. J. Holyoake. Fcap., pp. xii. and 94, wrapper. 1877. 1s. 6d.

HOLYOAKE.—SELF-HELP BY THE PEOPLE. Thirty-three Years of Co-operation in Rochdale. In Two Parts. Part I., 1844–1857; Part II., 1857–1877. By G. J. Holyoake. Ninth Edition. Crown 8vo, pp. 174, cloth. 1883. 2s. 6d.

HOPKINS.—ELEMENTARY GRAMMAR OF THE TURKISH LANGUAGE. With a few Easy Exercises. By F. L. Hopkins, M.A., Fellow and Tutor of Trinity Hall, Cambridge. Crown 8vo, pp. 48, cloth. 1877. 3s. 6d.

HORDER.—A SELECTION FROM "THE BOOK OF PRAISE FOR CHILDREN," as Edited by W. Garrett Horder. For the Use of Jewish Children. Fcap. 8vo, pp. 80, cloth. 1883. 1s. 6d.

HOSMER.—THE PEOPLE AND POLITICS; or, The Structure of States and the Significance and Relation of Political Forms. By G. W. Hosmer, M.D. Demy 8vo, pp. viii. and 340, cloth. 1883. 15s.

HOWELLS.—A LITTLE GIRL AMONG THE OLD MASTERS. With Introduction and Comment. By W. D. Howells. Oblong crown 8vo, cloth, pp. 66, with 54 plates. 1884. 10s.

HOWELLS.—DR. BREEN'S PRACTICE: A Novel. By W. D. Howells. English Copyright Edition. Crown 8vo, pp. 272, cloth. 1882. 6s.

HOWSE.—A GRAMMAR OF THE CREE LANGUAGE. With which is combined an Analysis of the Chippeway Dialect. By Joseph Howse, F.R.G.S. 8vo, pp. xx. and 324, cloth. 1865. 7s. 6d.

HULME.—MATHEMATICAL DRAWING INSTRUMENTS, AND HOW TO USE THEM. By F. Edward Hulme, F.L.S.. F.S.A., Art-Master of Marlborough College, Author of "Principles of Ornamental Art," &c. With Illustrations. Second Edition. Imperial 16mo, pp. xvi. and 152, cloth. 1881. 3s. 6d.

HUMBERT.—ON "TENANT RIGHT." By C. F. Humbert. 8vo, pp. 20, sewed. 1875. 1s.

HUMBOLDT.—THE SPHERE AND DUTIES OF GOVERNMENT. Translated from the German of Baron Wilhelm Von Humboldt by Joseph Coulthard, jun. Post 8vo, pp. xv. and 203, cloth. 1854. 5s.

HUMBOLDT.—LETTERS OF WILLIAM VON HUMBOLDT TO A FEMALE FRIEND. A complete Edition. Translated from the Second German Edition by Catherine M. A. Couper, with a Biographical Notice of the Writer. 2 vols. crown 8vo, pp. xxviii. and 592, cloth. 1867. 10s.

HUNT.—THE RELIGION OF THE HEART. A Manual of Faith and Duty. By Leigh Hunt. Fcap. 8vo, pp. xxiv. and 259, cloth. 2s. 6d.

HUNT.—CHEMICAL AND GEOLOGICAL ESSAYS. By Professor T. Sterry Hunt. Second Edition. 8vo, pp. xxii. and 448, cloth. 1879. 12s.

HUNTER.—A COMPARATIVE DICTIONARY OF THE NON-ARYAN LANGUAGES OF INDIA AND HIGH ASIA. With a Dissertation, Political and Linguistic, on the Aboriginal Races. By W. W. Hunter, B.A., M.R.A.S., Hon. Fel. Ethnol. Soc., Author of the "Annals of Rural Bengal," of H.M.'s Civil Service. Being a Lexicon of 144 Languages, illustrating Turanian Speech. Compiled from the Hodgson Lists, Government Archives, and Original MSS., arranged with Prefaces and Indices in English, French, German, Russian, and Latin. Large 4to, toned paper, pp. 230, cloth. 1869. 42s.

HUNTER.—THE INDIAN MUSALMANS. By W. W. Hunter, B.A., LL.D., Director-General of Statistics to the Government of India, &c., Author of the "Annals of Rural Bengal," &c. Third Edition. 8vo, pp. 219, cloth. 1876. 10s. 6d.

HUNTER.—FAMINE ASPECTS OF BENGAL DISTRICTS. A System of Famine Warnings. By W. W. Hunter, B.A., LL.D. Crown 8vo, pp. 216, cloth. 1874. 7s. 6d.

HUNTER.—A STATISTICAL ACCOUNT OF BENGAL. By W. W. Hunter, B.A., LL.D., Director-General of Statistics to the Government of India, &c. In 20 vols. 8vo, half morocco. 1877. £5.

HUNTER.—CATALOGUE OF SANSKRIT MANUSCRIPTS (BUDDHIST). Collected in Nepal by B. H. Hodgson, late Resident at the Court of Nepal. Compiled from Lists in Calcutta, France, and England, by W. W. Hunter, C.I.E., LL.D. 8vo, pp. 28, paper. 1880. 2s.

HUNTER.—THE IMPERIAL GAZETTEER OF INDIA. By W. W. Hunter, C.I.E., LL.D., Director-General of Statistics to the Government of India. In Nine Volumes. 8vo, pp. xxxiii. and 544, 539, 567, xix. and 716, 509, 513, 555, 537, and xii. and 478, half morocco. With Maps. 1881.

HUNTER.—THE INDIAN EMPIRE: Its History, People, and Products. By W. W. Hunter, C.I.E., LL.D. Post 8vo, pp. 568, with Map, cloth. 1882. 16s.

HUNTER.—AN ACCOUNT OF THE BRITISH SETTLEMENT OF ADEN, IN ARABIA. Compiled by Capt. F. M. Hunter, Assistant Political Resident, Aden. 8vo, pp. xii. and 232, half bound. 1877. 7s. 6d.

HUNTER.—A STATISTICAL ACCOUNT OF ASSAM. By W. W. Hunter, B.A., LL.D., C.I.E., Director-General of Statistics to the Government of India, &c. 2 vols. 8vo, pp. 420 and 490, with 2 Maps, half morocco. 1879. 10s.

HUNTER.—A BRIEF HISTORY OF THE INDIAN PEOPLE. By W. W. Hunter, C.I.E., LL.D. Fourth Edition. Crown 8vo, pp. 222, cloth. With Map. 1884. 3s. 6d.

HURST.—HISTORY OF RATIONALISM: embracing a Survey of the Present State of Protestant Theology. By the Rev. John F. Hurst, A.M. With Appendix of Literature. Revised and enlarged from the Third American Edition. Crown 8vo, pp. xvii. and 525, cloth. 1867. 10s. 6d.

HYETT.—PROMPT REMEDIES FOR ACCIDENTS AND POISONS: Adapted to the use of the Inexperienced till Medical aid arrives. By W. H. Hyett, F.R.S. A Broadsheet, to hang up in Country Schools or Vestries, Workshops, Offices of Factories, Mines and Docks, on board Yachts, in Railway Stations, remote Shooting Quarters, Highland Manses, and Private Houses, wherever the Doctor lives at a distance. Sold for the benefit of the Gloncester Eye Institution. In sheets, 21½ by 17½ inches, 2s. 6d.; mounted, 3s. 6d.

HYMANS.—PUPIL *Versus* TEACHER. Letters from a Teacher to a Teacher. Fcap. 8vo, pp. 92, cloth. 1875. 2s.

IHNE.—A LATIN GRAMMAR FOR BEGINNERS. By W. H. Ihne, late Principal of Carlton Terrace School, Liverpool. Crown 8vo, pp. vi. and 184, cloth. 1864. 3s.

IKHWÁNU-S SAFÁ; or, Brothers of Purity. Translated from the Hindustani by Professor John Dowson, M.R.A.S., Staff College, Sandhurst. Crown 8vo, pp. viii. and 156, cloth. 1869. 7s.

INDIA.—ARCHÆOLOGICAL SURVEY OF WESTERN INDIA. See Burgess.

INDIA.—PUBLICATIONS OF THE ARCHÆOLOGICAL SURVEY OF INDIA. A separate list on application.

INDIA.—PUBLICATIONS OF THE GEOGRAPHICAL DEPARTMENT OF THE INDIA OFFICE, LONDON. A separate list, also list of all the Government Maps, on application.

INDIA.—PUBLICATIONS OF THE GEOLOGICAL SURVEY OF INDIA. A separate list on application.

INDIA OFFICE PUBLICATIONS :—

Aden, Statistical Account of. 5s.
Assam, do. do. Vols. I. and II. 5s. each.
Baden Powell, Land Revenues, &c., in India. 12s.
  Do. Jurisprudence for Forest Officers. 12s.
Beal's Buddhist Tripitaka. 4s.
Bengal, Statistical Account of. Vols. I. to XX. 100s. per set.
  Do. do. do. Vols. VI. to XX. 5s. each.
Bombay Code. 21s.
Bombay Gazetteer. Vol. II. 14s. Vol. XIII. (2 parts), 16s.
  Do. do. Vols. III. to VII., and X., XI., XII., XIV., XVI. 8s. each.
Burgess' Archæological Survey of Western India. Vols. I. and III. 42s. each.
  Do. do. do. Vol. II. 63s.
  Do. do. do. Vols. IV. and V. 126s.
Burma (British) Gazetteer. 2 vols. 50s.
Catalogue of Manuscripts and Maps of Surveys. 12s.
Chambers' Meteorology (Bombay) and Atlas. 30s.
Cole's Agra and Muttra. 70s.
Cook's Gums and Resins. 5s.
Corpus Inscriptionem Indicarum. Vol. I. 32s.
Cunningham's Archæological Survey. Vols. I. to XV. 10s. and 12s. each.
  Do. Stupa of Bharut. 63s.
Egerton's Catalogue of Indian Arms. 2s. 6d.
Ferguson and Burgess, Cave Temples of India. 42s.
  Do. Tree and Serpent Worship. 105s.
Finance and Revenue Accounts of the Government of India for 1882-3. 2s. 6d.

INDIA OFFICE PUBLICATIONS—*continued.*
Gamble, Manual of Indian Timbers. 10s.
Hunter's Imperial Gazetteer. 9 vols.
Jaschke's Tibetan-English Dictionary. 30s.
King. Chinchona-Planting. 1s.
Kurz. Forest Flora of British Burma. Vols. I. and II. 15s. each.
Liotard's Materials for Paper. 2s. 6d.
Liotard's Silk in India. Part I. 2s.
Markham's Tibet. 21s.
    Do.   Memoir of Indian Surveys. 10s. 6d.
    Do.   Abstract of Reports of Surveys. 1s. 6d.
Mitra (Rajendralala), Buddha Gaya. 60s.
Moir, Torrent Regions of the Alps. 1s.
Mueller. Select Plants for Extra-Tropical Countries. 8s.
Mysore and Coorg Gazetteer. Vols. I. and II. 10s. each.
    Do.   do.   Vol. III. 5s.
N. W. P. Gazetteer. Vols. I. and II. 10s. each.
    Do.   do.   Vols. III. to VI. and IX., X. and XIII. 12s. each.
    Do.   do.   Vol. VII. 8s.
Oudh   do.   Vols. I. to III. 10s. each.
Pharmacopœia of India, The. 6s.
People of India, The. Vols. I. to VIII. 45s. each.
Raverty's Notes on Afghanistan and Baluchistan. Sections I. and II. 2s. Section III. 5s. Section IV. 3s.
Rajputana Gazetteer. 3 vols. 15s.
Saunders' Mountains and River Basins of India. 3s.
Sewell's Amaravati Tope. 3s.
Smith's (Brough) Gold Mining in Wynaad. 1s.
Taylor. Indian Marine Surveys. 2s. 6d.
Trigonometrical Survey, Synopsis of Great. Vols. I. to VI. 10s. 6d. each.
Trumpp's Adi Granth. 52s. 6d.
Watson's Cotton for Trials. Boards, 10s. 6d. Paper, 10s.'
    Do.   Rhea Fibre. 2s. 6d.
    Do.   Tobacco. 5s.
Wilson. Madras Army. Vols. I. and II.

INDIAN GAZETTEERS.—See GAZETTEER, and INDIA OFFICE PUBLICATIONS.

INGLEBY.—See SHAKESPEARE.

INMAN.—NAUTICAL TABLES. Designed for the use of British Seamen. By the Rev. James Inman, D.D., late Professor at the Royal Naval College, Portsmouth. Demy 8vo, pp. xvi. and 410, cloth. 1877. 15s.

INMAN.—HISTORY OF THE ENGLISH ALPHABET : A Paper read before the Liverpool Literary and Philosophical Society. By T. Inman, M.D. 8vo, pp. 36, sewed. 1872. 1s.

IN SEARCH OF TRUTH. Conversations on the Bible and Popular Theology, for Young People. By A. M. Y. Crown 8vo, pp. x. and 138, cloth. 1875. 2s. 6d.

INTERNATIONAL NUMISMATA ORIENTALIA (THE).—Royal 4to, in paper wrapper. Part I. Ancient Indian Weights. By E. Thomas, F.R.S. Pp. 84, with a Plate and Map of the India of Manu. 9s. 6d.—Part II. Coins of the Urtukí Turkumáns. By Stanley Lane Poole, Corpus Christi College, Oxford. Pp. 44, with 6 Plates. 9s.—Part III. The Coinage of Lydia and Persia, from the Earliest Times to the Fall of the Dynasty of the Achæmenidæ. By Barclay V. Head, Assistant-Keeper of Coins, British Museum. Pp. viii.-56, with 3 Autotype Plates. 10s. 6d.—Part IV. The Coins of the Tuluni Dynasty. By Edward Thomas Rogers. Pp. iv.-22, and 1 Plate. 5s.—Part V. The Parthian Coinage. By Percy Gardner, M.A. Pp. iv.-66, and 8 Autotype Plates. 18s.—Part VI. The Ancient Coins and Measures of Ceylon. By T. W. Rhys Davids. Pp. iv. and 60, and 1 Plate. 10s.—Vol. I., containing the first six parts, as specified above. Royal 4to, half bound. £3, 13s. 6d.

INTERNATIONAL NUMISMATA—*continued.*
Vol. II. COINS OF THE JEWS. Being a History of the Jewish Coinage and Money in the Old and New Testaments. By Frederick W. Madden, M.R.A.S., Member of the Numismatic Society of London, Secretary of the Brighton College, &c., &c. With 279 woodcuts and a plate of alphabets. Royal 4to, pp. xii. and 330, sewed. 1881. £2.

THE COINS OF ARAKAN, OF PEGU, AND OF BURMA. By Lieut.-General Sir Arthur Phayre, C.B., K.C.S.I., G.C.M.G., late Commissioner of British Burma. Royal 4to, pp. viii. and 48, with Five Autotype Illustrations, wrapper. 1882. 8s. 6d.

JACKSON.—ETHNOLOGY AND PHRENOLOGY AS AN AID TO THE HISTORIAN. By the late J. W. Jackson. Second Edition. With a Memoir of the Author, by his Wife. Crown 8vo, pp. xx. and 324, cloth. 1875. 4s. 6d.

JACKSON.—THE SHROPSHIRE WORD-BOOK. A Glossary of Archaic and Provincial Words, &c., used in the County. By Georgina F. Jackson. Crown 8vo, pp. civ. and 524, cloth. 1881. 31s. 6d.

JACOB.—HINDU PANTHEISM. See Trübner's Oriental Series.

JAGIELSKI.—ON MARIENBAD SPA, and the Diseases Curable by its Waters and Baths. By A. V. Jagielski, M.D., Berlin. Second Edition. Crown 8vo, pp. viii. and 186. With Map. Cloth. 1874. 5s.

JAMISON.—THE LIFE AND TIMES OF BERTRAND DU GUESCLIN. A History of the Fourteenth Century. By D. F. Jamison, of South Carolina. Portrait. 2 vols. 8vo, pp. xvi., 287, and viii., 314, cloth. 1864. £1, 1s.

JAPAN.—MAP OF NIPPON (Japan): Compiled from Native Maps, and the Notes of most recent Travellers. By R. Henry Brunton, M.I.C.E., F.R.G.S., 1880. Size, 5 feet by 4 feet, 20 miles to the inch. In 4 Sheets, £1, 1s.; Roller, varnished, £1, 11s. 6d.; Folded, in Case, £1, 5s. 6d.

JASCHKE.—A TIBETAN-ENGLISH DICTIONARY. With special reference to the Prevailing Dialects. To which is added an English-Tibetan Vocabulary. By H. A. Jäschke, late Moravian Missionary at Kyèlang, British Lahoul. Imperial 8vo, pp. xxiv.-672, cloth. 1881. £1, 10s.

JASCHKE.—TIBETAN GRAMMAR. By H. A. Jäschke. Crown 8vo, pp. viii.-104, cloth. 1883. 5s.

JATAKA (THE), together with its COMMENTARY : being tales of the Anterior Births of Gotama Buddha. Now first published in Pali, by V. Fausboll. Text. 8vo. Vol. I., pp. viii. and 512, cloth. 1877. 28s.—Vol. II., pp. 452, cloth. 1879. 28s.—Vol. III., pp. viii. and 544, cloth. 1883. 28s. (For Translation see Trübner's Oriental Series, "Buddhist Birth Stories.")

JENKINS.—A PALADIN OF FINANCE : Contemporary Manners. By E. Jenkins, Author of "Ginx's Baby." Crown 8vo, pp. iv. and 392, cloth. 1882. 7s. 6d.

JENKINS.—VEST-POCKET LEXICON. An English Dictionary of all except familiar Words, including the principal Scientific and Technical Terms, and Foreign Moneys, Weights and Measures; omitting what everybody knows, and containing what everybody wants to know and cannot readily find. By Jabez Jenkins. 64mo, pp. 564, cloth. 1879. 1s. 6d.

JOHNSON.—ORIENTAL RELIGIONS. See English and Foreign Philosophical Library, Extra Series, Vols. IV. and V.

JOLLY.—See NARADÍYA.

JOMINI.—THE ART OF WAR. By Baron de Jomini, General and Aide-de-Camp to the Emperor of Russia. A New Edition, with Appendices and Maps. Translated from the French. By Captain G. H. Mendell, and Captain W. O. Craighill. Crown 8vo, pp. 410, cloth. 1879. 9s.

JOSEPH.—RELIGION, NATURAL AND REVEALED. A Series of Progressive Lessons for Jewish Youth. By N. S. Joseph. Crown 8vo, pp. xii.-296, cloth. 1879. 3s.

JUVENALIS SATIRÆ. With a Literal English Prose Translation and Notes. By J. D. Lewis, M.A., Trin. Coll. Camb. Second Edition. Two vols. 8vo, pp. xii. and 230 and 400, cloth. 1882. 12s.

KARCHER.—QUESTIONNAIRE FRANÇAIS. Questions on French Grammar, Idiomatic Difficulties, and Military Expressions. By Theodore Karcher, LL.B. Fourth Edition, greatly enlarged. Crown 8vo, pp. 224, cloth. 1879. 4s. 6d. Interleaved with writing paper, 5s. 6d.

KARDEC.—THE SPIRIT'S BOOK. Containing the Principles of Spiritist Doctrine on the Immortality of the Soul, &c., &c., according to the Teachings of Spirits of High Degree, transmitted through various mediums, collected and set in order by Allen Kardec. Translated from the 120th thousand by Anna Blackwell. Crown 8vo, pp. 512, cloth. 1875. 7s. 6d.

KARDEC.—THE MEDIUM'S BOOK; or, Guide for Mediums and for Evocations. Containing the Theoretic Teachings of Spirits concerning all kinds of Manifestations, the Means of Communication with the Invisible World, the Development of Medianimity, &c., &c. By Allen Kardec. Translated by Anna Blackwell. Crown 8vo, pp. 456, cloth. 1876. 7s. 6d.

KARDEC.—HEAVEN AND HELL; or, the Divine Justice Vindicated in the Plurality of Existences. By Allen Kardec. Translated by Anna Blackwell. Crown 8vo, pp. viii. and 448, cloth. 1878. 7s. 6d.

KEMP. See SCHOPENHAUER.

KENDRICK.—GREEK OLLENDORFF. A Progressive Exhibition of the Principles of the Greek Grammar. By Asahel C. Kendrick. 8vo, pp. 371, cloth. 1870. 9s.

KERMODE.—NATAL: Its Early History, Rise, Progress, and Future Prospects as a Field for Emigration. By W. Kermode, of Natal. Crown 8vo, pp. xii. and 228, with Map, cloth. 1883. 3s. 6d.

KEYS OF THE CREEDS (THE). Third Revised Edition. Crown 8vo, pp. 210, cloth. 1876. 5s.

KINAHAN.—VALLEYS AND THEIR RELATION TO FISSURES, FRACTURES, AND FAULTS. By G. H. Kinahan, M.R.I.A., F.R.G.S.I., &c. Dedicated by permission to his Grace the Duke of Argyll. Crown 8vo, pp. 256, cloth, illustrated. 7s. 6d.

KING'S STRATAGEM (The); OR, THE PEARL OF POLAND; A Tragedy in Five Acts. By Stella. Second Edition. Crown 8vo, pp. 94, cloth. 1874. 2s. 6d.

KINGSTON.—THE UNITY OF CREATION. A Contribution to the Solution of the Religious Question. By F. H. Kingston. Crown 8vo, pp. viii. and 152, cloth. 1874. 5s.

KISTNER.—BUDDHA AND HIS DOCTRINES. A Bibliographical Essay. By Otto Kistner. 4to, pp. iv. and 32, sewed. 1869. 2s. 6d.

KNOX.—ON A MEXICAN MUSTANG. See under SWEET.

KLEMM.—MUSCLE BEATING; or, Active and Passive Home Gymnastics, for Healthy and Unhealthy People. By C. Klemm. With Illustrations. 8vo, pp. 60, wrapper. 1878. 1s.

KOHL.—TRAVELS IN CANADA AND THROUGH THE STATES OF NEW YORK AND PENNSYLVANIA. By J. G. Kohl. Translated by Mrs. Percy Sinnett. Revised by the Author. Two vols. post 8vo, pp. xiv. and 794, cloth. 1861. £1, 1s.

KRAPF.—DICTIONARY OF THE SUAHILI LANGUAGE. Compiled by the Rev. Dr. L. Krapf, missionary of the Church Missionary Society in East Africa. With an Appendix, containing an outline of a Suahili Grammar. Medium 8vo, pp. xl. and 434, cloth. 1882. 30s.

KRAUS.—CARLSBAD AND ITS NATURAL HEALING AGENTS, from the Physiological and Therapeutical Point of View. By J. Kraus, M.D. With Notes Introductory by the Rev. J. T. Walters, M.A. Second Edition. Revised and enlarged. Crown 8vo, pp. 104, cloth. 1880. 5s.

KROEGER.—THE MINNESINGER OF GERMANY. By A. E. Kroeger. Fcap. 8vo, pp. 290, cloth. 1873. 7s.

KURZ.—FOREST FLORA OF BRITISH BURMA. By S. Kurz, Curator of the Herbarium, Royal Botanical Gardens, Calcutta. 2 vols. crown 8vo, pp. xxx., 550, and 614, cloth. 1877. 30s.

LACERDA'S JOURNEY TO CAZEMBE in 1798. Translated and Annotated by Captain R. F. Burton, F.R.G.S. Also Journey of the Pombeiros, &c. Demy 8vo, pp. viii. and 272. With Map, cloth. 1873. 7s. 6d.

LANARI.—COLLECTION OF ITALIAN AND ENGLISH DIALOGUES. By A. Lanari. Fcap. 8vo, pp. viii. and 200, cloth. 1874. 3s. 6d.

LAND.—THE PRINCIPLES OF HEBREW GRAMMAR. By J. P. N. Land, Professor of Logic and Metaphysics in the University of Leyden. Translated from the Dutch, by Reginald Lane Poole, Balliol College, Oxford. Part I. Sounds. Part II. Words. With Large Additions by the Author, and a new Preface. Crown 8vo, pp. xx. and 220, cloth. 1876. 7s. 6d.

LANE.—THE KORAN. See Trübner's Oriental Series.

LANGE.—A HISTORY OF MATERIALISM. See English and Foreign Philosophical Library, Vols. I. to III.

LANGE.—GERMANIA. A German Reading-book Arranged Progressively. By F. K. W. Lange, Ph.D. Part I. Anthology of German Prose and Poetry, with Vocabulary and Biographical Notes. 8vo, pp. xvi. and 216, cloth, 1881, 3s. 6d. Part II. Essays on German History and Institutions, with Notes. 8vo, pp. 124, cloth. Parts I. and II. together. 5s. 6d.

LANGE.—GERMAN PROSE WRITING. Comprising English Passages for Translation into German. Selected from Examination Papers of the University of London, the College of Preceptors, London, and the Royal Military Academy, Woolwich, arranged progressively, with Notes and Theoretical as well as Practical Treatises on themes for the writing of Essays. By F. K. W. Lange, Ph.D., Assistant German Master, Royal Academy, Woolwich; Examiner, Royal College of Preceptors London. Crown 8vo, pp. viii. and 176, cloth. 1881. 4s.

LANGE.—GERMAN GRAMMAR PRACTICE. By F. K. W. Lange, Ph.D. Crown 8vo, pp. viii. and 64, cloth. 1882. 1s. 6d.

LANGE.—COLLOQUIAL GERMAN GRAMMAR. With Special Reference to the Anglo-Saxon Element in the English Language. By F. K. W. Lange, Ph.D., &c. Crown 8vo, pp. xxxii. and 380, cloth. 1882. 4s. 6d.

LANMAN.—A SANSKRIT READER. With Vocabulary and Notes. By Charles Rockwell Lanman, Professor of Sanskrit in Harvard College. Imperial 8vo, pp. xx. and 294, cloth. 1884. 10s. 6d.

LARSEN.—DANISH-ENGLISH DICTIONARY. By A. Larsen. Crown 8vo, pp. viii. and 646, cloth. 1884. 7s. 6d.

LASCARIDES.—A COMPREHENSIVE PHRASEOLOGICAL ENGLISH-ANCIENT AND MODERN GREEK LEXICON. Founded upon a manuscript of G. P. Lascarides, and Compiled by L. Myrianthcus, Ph.D. 2 vols. 18mo, pp. xi. and 1338, cloth. 1882. £1, 10s.

LATHE (THE) AND ITS USES; or, Instruction in the Art of Turning Wood and Metal, including a description of the most modern appliances for the Ornamentation of Plain and Curved Surfaces, &c. Sixth Edition. With additional Chapters and Index. Illustrated. 8vo, pp. iv. and 316, cloth. 1883. 10s. 6d.

LE-BRUN.—MATERIALS FOR TRANSLATING FROM ENGLISH INTO FRENCH; being a short Essay on Translation, followed by a Graduated Selection in Prose and Verse. By L. Le-Brun. Seventh Edition. Revised and corrected by Henri Van Laun. Post 8vo, pp. xii. and 204, cloth. 1882. 4s. 6d.

LEE.—ILLUSTRATIONS OF THE PHYSIOLOGY OF RELIGION. In Sections adapted for the use of Schools. Part I. By Henry Lee, F.R.C.S., formerly Professor of Surgery, Royal College of Surgeons, &c. Crown 8vo, pp. viii. and 108, cloth. 1880. 3s. 6d.

LEES.—A PRACTICAL GUIDE TO HEALTH, AND TO THE HOME TREATMENT OF THE COMMON AILMENTS OF LIFE : With a Section on Cases of Emergency, and Hints to Mothers on Nursing, &c. By F. Arnold Lees, F.L.S. Crown 8vo, 1 p. 334, stiff covers. 1874. 3s.

LEGGE.—THE CHINESE CLASSICS. With a Translation, Critical and Exegetical, Notes, Prolegomena, and copious Indexes. By James Legge, D.D., of the London Missionary Society. In 7 vols. Royal 8vo. Vols. I.-V. in Eight Parts, published, cloth. £2, 2s. each Part.

LEGGE.—THE CHINESE CLASSICS, translated into English. With Preliminary Essays and Explanatory Notes. Popular Edition. Reproduced for General Readers from the Author's work, containing the Original Text. By James Legge, D.D. Crown 8vo. Vol. I. The Life and Teachings of Confucius. Third Edition. Pp. vi. and 338, cloth. 1872. 10s. 6d.—Vol. II. The Works of Mencius. Pp. x. and 402, cloth, 12s.—Vol. III. The She-King; or, The Book of Poetry. Pp. vi. and 432, cloth. 1876. 12s.

LEGGE.—CONFUCIANISM IN RELATION TO CHRISTIANITY. A Paper read before the Missionary Conference in Shanghai, on May 11th, 1877. By Rev. James Legge, D.D., LL.D., &c. 8vo, pp. 12, sewed. 1877. 1s. 6d.

LEGGE.—A LETTER TO PROFESSOR MAX MÜLLER, chiefly on the Translation into English of the Chinese Terms Ti and $Shang\ Ti$. By James Legge, Professor of the Chinese Language and Literature in the University of Oxford. Crown 8vo, pp. 30, sewed. 1880. 1s.

LEIGH.—THE RELIGION OF THE WORLD. By H. Stone Leigh. 12mo, pp. xii. and 66, cloth. 1869. 2s. 6d.

LEIGH.—THE STORY OF PHILOSOPHY. By Aston Leigh. Post 8vo, pp. xii. and 210, cloth. 1881. 6s.

LEÏLA-HANOUM.—A TRAGEDY IN THE IMPERIAL HAREM AT CONSTANTINOPLE. By Leïla-Hanoum. Translated from the French, with Notes by General R. E. Colston. 16mo, pp. viii. and 300, cloth. 1883. 4s. Paper, 2s. 6d.

LELAND.—THE BREITMANN BALLADS. The only authorised Edition. Complete in 1 vol., including Nineteen Ballads, illustrating his Travels in Europe (never before printed), with Comments by Fritz Schwackenhammer. By Charles G. Leland. Crown 8vo, pp. xxviii. and 292, cloth. 1872. 6s.

LELAND.—THE MUSIC LESSON OF CONFUCIUS, and other Poems. By Charles G. Leland. Fcap. 8vo, pp. viii. and 168, cloth. 1871. 3s. 6d.

LELAND.—GAUDEAMUS. Humorous Poems translated from the German of Joseph Victor Scheffel and others. By Charles G. Leland. 16mo, pp. 176, cloth 1872. 3s. 6d.

LELAND.—THE EGYPTIAN SKETCH-BOOK. By C. G. Leland. Crown 8vo, pp. viii. and 316, cloth. 1873. 7s. 6d.

LELAND.—THE ENGLISH GIPSIES AND THEIR LANGUAGE. By Charles G. Leland. Second Edition. Crown 8vo, pp. xvi. and 260, cloth. 1874. 7s. 6d.

LELAND.—FU-SANG; OR, THE DISCOVERY OF AMERICA by Chinese Buddhist Priests in the Fifth Century. By Charles G. Leland. Crown 8vo, pp. 232, cloth. 1875. 7s. 6d.

LELAND.—PIDGIN-ENGLISH SING-SONG; or, Songs and Stories in the China-English Dialect. With a Vocabulary. By Charles G. Leland. Crown 8vo, pp. viii. and 140, cloth. 1876. 5s.

LELAND.—THE GYPSIES. By C. G. Leland. Crown 8vo, pp. 372, cloth. 1882. 10s. 6d.

LEOPARDI.—See English and Foreign Philosophical Library, Vol. XVII.

LEO.—FOUR CHAPTERS OF NORTH'S PLUTARCH, Containing the Lives of Caius Marcius, Coriolanus, Julius Cæsar, Marcus Antonius, and Marcus Brutus, as Sources to Shakespeare's Tragedies; Coriolanus, Julius Cæsar, and Antony and Cleopatra; and partly to Hamlet and Timon of Athens. Photolithographed in the size of the Edition of 1595. With Preface, Notes comparing the Text of the Editions of 1579, 1595, 1603, and 1612; and Reference Notes to the Text of the Tragedies of Shakespeare. Edited by Professor F. A. Leo, Ph.D., Vice-President of the New Shakespeare Society; Member of the Directory of the German Shakespeare Society; and Lecturer at the Academy of Modern Philology at Berlin. Folio, pp. 22, 130 of facsimiles, half-morocco. Library Edition (limited to 250 copies), £1, 11s. 6d.; Amateur Edition (50 copies on a superior large hand-made paper), £3, 3s.

LERMONTOFF.—THE DEMON. By Michael Lermontoff. Translated from the Russian by A. Condie Stephen. Crown 8vo, pp. 88, cloth. 1881. 2s. 6d.

LESLEY.—MAN'S ORIGIN AND DESTINY. Sketched from the Platform of the Physical Sciences. By. J. P. Lesley, Member of the National Academy of the United States, Professor of Geology, University of Pennsylvania. Second (Revised and considerably Enlarged) Edition, crown 8vo, pp. viii. and 142, cloth. 1881. 7s. 6d.

LESSING.—LETTERS ON BIBLIOLATRY. By Gotthold Ephraim Lessing. Translated from the German by the late H. H. Bernard, Ph.D. 8vo, pp. 184, cloth. 1862. 5s.

LESSING.—See English and Foreign Philosophical Library, Extra Series, Vols. I. and II.

LETTERS ON THE WAR BETWEEN GERMANY AND FRANCE. By Mommsen, Strauss, Max Müller, and Carlyle. Second Edition. Crown 8vo, pp. 120, cloth. 1871. 2s. 6d.

LEWES.—PROBLEMS OF LIFE AND MIND. By George Henry Lewes. First Series: The Foundations of a Creed. Vol. I., demy 8vo. Fourth edition, pp. 488, cloth. 1884. 12s.—Vol. II., demy 8vo, pp. 552, cloth. 1875. 16s.

LEWES.—PROBLEMS OF LIFE AND MIND. By George Henry Lewes. Second Series. THE PHYSICAL BASIS OF MIND. 8vo, with Illustrations, pp. 508, cloth. 1877. 16s. Contents.—The Nature of Life; The Nervous Mechanism; Animal Automatism; The Reflex Theory.

LEWES.—PROBLEMS OF LIFE AND MIND. By George Henry Lewes. Third Series. Problem the First—The Study of Psychology: Its Object, Scope, and Method. Demy 8vo, pp. 200, cloth. 1879. 7s. 6d.

LEWES.—PROBLEMS OF LIFE AND MIND. By George Henry Lewes. Third Series. Problem the Second—Mind as a Function of the Organism. Problem the Third—The Sphere of Sense and Logic of Feeling. Problem the Fourth—The Sphere of Intellect and Logic of Signs. Demy 8vo, pp. x. and 500, cloth. 1879. 15s.

LEWIS.—See JUVENAL and PLINY.

LIBRARIANS, TRANSACTIONS AND PROCEEDINGS OF THE CONFERENCE OF, held in London, October 1877. Edited by Edward B. Nicholson and Henry R. Tedder. Imperial 8vo, pp. 276, cloth. 1878. £1, 8s.

LIBRARY ASSOCIATION OF THE UNITED KINGDOM, Transactions and Proceedings of the Annual Meetings of the. Imperial 8vo, cloth. FIRST, held at Oxford, October 1, 2, 3, 1878. Edited by the Secretaries, Henry R. Tedder, Librarian of the Athenæum Club, and Ernest C. Thomas, late Librarian of the Oxford Union Society. Pp. viii. and 192. 1879. £1, 8s.—SECOND, held at Manchester, September 23, 24, and 25, 1879. Edited by H. R. Tedder and E. C. Thomas. Pp. x. and 184. 1880. £1, 1s.—THIRD, held at Edinburgh, October 5, 6, and 7, 1880. Edited by E. C. Thomas and C. Welsh. Pp. x. and 202. 1881. £1, 1s.

LIEBER.—THE LIFE AND LETTERS OF FRANCIS LIEBER. Edited by T. S. Perry. 8vo, pp. iv. and 440, cloth, with Portrait. 1882. 14s.

LITTLE FRENCH READER (THE). Extracted from "The Modern French Reader." Third Edition. Crown 8vo, pp. 112, cloth. 1884. 2s.

LLOYD AND NEWTON.—PRUSSIA'S REPRESENTATIVE MAN. By F. Lloyd of the Universities of Halle and Athens, and W. Newton, F.R.G.S. Crown 8vo, pp. 648, cloth. 1875. 10s. 6d.

LOBSCHEID.—CHINESE AND ENGLISH DICTIONARY, arranged according to the Radicals. By W. Lobscheid. 1 vol. imperial 8vo, pp. 600, cloth. £2, 8s.

LOBSCHEID.—ENGLISH AND CHINESE DICTIONARY, with the Punti and Mandarin Pronunciation. By W. Lobscheid. Four Parts. Folio, pp. viii. and 2016, boards. £8, 8s.

LONG.—EASTERN PROVERBS. See Trübner's Oriental Series.

LOVETT.—THE LIFE AND STRUGGLES OF WILLIAM LOVETT in his pursuit of Bread, Knowledge, and Freedom; with some short account of the different Associations he belonged to, and of the Opinions he entertained. 8vo, pp. vi. and 474, cloth. 1876. 5s.

LOVELY.—WHERE TO GO FOR HELP: Being a Companion for Quick and Easy Reference of Police Stations, Fire-Engine Stations, Fire-Escape Stations, &c., &c., of London and the Suburbs. Compiled by W. Lovely, R.N. Third Edition. 18mo, pp. 16, sewed. 1882. 3d.

LOWELL.—THE BIGLOW PAPERS. By James Russell Lowell. Edited by Thomas Hughes, Q.C. A Reprint of the Authorised Edition of 1859, together with the Second Series of 1862. First and Second Series in 1 vol. Fcap., pp. lxviii.-140 and lxiv.-190, cloth. 1880. 2s. 6d.

LUCAS.—THE CHILDREN'S PENTATEUCH: With the Haphtarahs or Portions from the Prophets. Arranged for Jewish Children. By Mrs. Henry Lucas. Crown 8vo, pp. viii. and 570, cloth. 1878. 5s.

LUDEWIG.—THE LITERATURE OF AMERICAN ABORIGINAL LANGUAGES. By Hermann E. Ludewig. With Additions and Corrections by Professor Wm. W. Turner. Edited by Nicolas Trübner. 8vo, pp. xxiv. and 258, cloth. 1858. 10s. 6d.

LUKIN.—THE BOY ENGINEERS: What they did, and how they did it. By the Rev. L. J. Lukin, Author of "The Young Mechanic," &c. A Book for Boys; 30 Engravings. Imperial 16mo, pp. viii. and 344, cloth. 1877. 7s. 6d.

LUX E TENEBRIS; OR, THE TESTIMONY OF CONSCIOUSNESS. A Theoretic Essay. Crown 8vo, pp. 376, with Diagram, cloth. 1874. 10s. 6d.

MACCORMAC.—THE CONVERSATION OF A SOUL WITH GOD : A Theodicy. By Henry MacCormac, M.D. 16mo, pp. xvi. and 144, cloth. 1877. 3s. 6d.

MACHIAVELLI.—THE HISTORICAL, POLITICAL, AND DIPLOMATIC WRITINGS OF NICCOLO MACHIAVELLI. Translated from the Italian by C. E. Detmold. With Portraits. 4 vols. 8vo, cloth, pp. xli., 420, 464, 488, and 472. 1882. £3, 3s.

MADDEN.—COINS OF THE JEWS. Being a History of the Jewish Coinage and Money in the Old and New Testaments. By Frederick W. Madden, M.R.A.S. Member of the Numismatic Society of London, Secretary of the Brighton College, &c., &c. With 279 Woodcuts and a Plate of Alphabets. Royal 4to, pp. xii. and 330, cloth. 1881. £2, 2s.

MADELUNG.—THE CAUSES AND OPERATIVE TREATMENT OF DUPUYTREN'S FINGER CONTRACTION. By Dr. Otto W. Madelung, Lecturer of Surgery at the University, and Assistant Surgeon at the University Hospital, Bonn. 8vo, pp. 24, sewed. 1876. 1s.

MAHAPARINIBBANASUTTA.—See CHILDERS.

MAHA-VIRA-CHARITA; or, The Adventures of the Great Hero Rama. An Indian Drama in Seven Acts. Translated into English Prose from the Sanskrit of Bhavabhūti. By John Pickford, M.A. Crown 8vo, cloth. 5s.

MALLESON.—ESSAYS AND LECTURES ON INDIAN HISTORICAL SUBJECTS. By Colonel G. B. Malleson, C.S.I. Second Issue. Crown 8vo, pp. 348, cloth. 1876. 5s.

MANDLEY.—WOMAN OUTSIDE CHRISTENDOM. An Exposition of the Influence exerted by Christianity on the Social Position and Happiness of Women. By J. G. Mandley. Crown 8vo, pp. viii. and 160, cloth. 1880. 5s.

MANIPULUS VOCABULORUM. A Rhyming Dictionary of the English Language. By Peter Levins (1570). Edited, with an Alphabetical Index, by Henry B. Wheatley. 8vo, pp. xvi. and 370, cloth. 1867. 14s.

MANŒUVRES.—A RETROSPECT OF THE AUTUMN MANŒUVRES, 1871. With 5 Plans. By a Recluse. 8vo, pp. xii. and 133, cloth. 1872. 5s.

MARIETTE-BEY.—THE MONUMENTS OF UPPER EGYPT : a translation of the "Itinéraire de la Haute Egypte" of Auguste Mariette-Bey. Translated by Alphonse Mariette. Crown 8vo, pp. xvi. and 262, cloth. 1877. 7s. 6d.

MARKHAM.—QUICHUA GRAMMAR AND DICTIONARY. Contributions towards a Grammar and Dictionary of Quichua, the Language of the Yncas of Peru. Collected by Clements R. Markham, F.S.A. Crown 8vo, pp. 223, cloth. £1, 11s. 6d.

MARKHAM.—OLLANTA : A Drama in the Quichua Language. Text, Translation, and Introduction. By Clements R. Markham, C.B. Crown 8vo, pp. 128, cloth. 1871. 7s. 6d.

MARKHAM.—A MEMOIR OF THE LADY ANA DE OSORIO, Countess of Chinchon, and Vice-Queen of Peru, A.D. 1629-39. With a Plea for the correct spelling of the Chinchona Genus. By Clements R. Markham, C.B., Member of the Imperial Academy Naturæ Curiosorum, with the Cognomen of Chinchon. Small 4to, pp. xii. and 100. With 2 Coloured Plates, Map, and Illustrations. Handsomely bound. 1874. 28s.

MARKHAM.—A MEMOIR ON THE INDIAN SURVEYS. By Clements R. Markham, C.B., F.R.S., &c., &c. Published by Order of H. M. Secretary of State for India in Council. Illustrated with Maps. Second Edition. Imperial 8vo, pp. xxx. and 481, boards. 1878. 10s. 6d.

MARKHAM.—NARRATIVES OF THE MISSION OF GEORGE BOGLE TO TIBET, and of the Journey of Thomas Manning to Lhasa. Edited with Notes, an Introduction, and Lives of Mr. Bogle and Mr. Manning. By Clements R. Markham, C.B., F.R.S. Second Edition. 8vo, pp. clxv. and 362, cloth. With Maps and Illustrations. 1879. 21s.

MARMONTEL.—BELISAIRE. Par Marmontel. Nouvelle Edition. 12mo, pp. xii. and 123, cloth. 1867. 2s. 6d.

MARSDEN.—NUMISMATA ORIENTALIA ILLUSTRATA. THE PLATES OF THE ORIENTAL COINS, ANCIENT AND MODERN, of the Collection of the late William Marsden, F.R.S., &c. &c. Engraved from Drawings made under his Directions. 4to, 57 Plates, cloth. 31s. 6d.

MARTIN AND TRÜBNER.—THE CURRENT GOLD AND SILVER COINS OF ALL COUNTRIES, their Weight and Fineness, and their Intrinsic Value in English Money, with Facsimiles of the Coins. By Leopold C. Martin, of Her Majesty's Stationery Office, and Charles Trübner. In 1 vol. medium 8vo, 141 Plates, printed in Gold and Silver, and representing about 1000 Coins, with 160 pages of Text, handsomely bound in embossed cloth, richly gilt, with Emblematical Designs on the Cover, and gilt edges. 1863. £2. 2s.

MARTIN.—THE CHINESE: THEIR EDUCATION, PHILOSOPHY, AND LETTERS. By W. A. P. Martin, D.D., LL.D., President of the Tungwen College, Pekin. 8vo, pp. 320, cloth. 1881. 7s. 6d.

MARTINEAU.—ESSAYS, PHILOSOPHICAL AND THEOLOGICAL. By James Martineau. 2 vols. crown 8vo, pp. iv. and 414—x. and 430, cloth. 1875. £1, 4s.

MARTINEAU.—LETTERS FROM IRELAND. By Harriet Martineau. Reprinted from the *Daily News.* Post 8vo, pp. viii. and 220, cloth. 1852. 6s. 6d.

MASON.—BURMA: ITS PEOPLE AND PRODUCTIONS; or, Notes on the Fauna, Flora, and Minerals of Tenasserim, Pegu and Burma. By the Rev. F. Mason, D.D., M.R.A.S., Corresponding Member of the American Oriental Society, of the Boston Society of Natural History, and of the Lyceum of Natural History, New York. Vol. I. GEOLOGY, MINERALOGY AND ZOOLOGY. Vol. II. BOTANY. Rewritten and Enlarged by W. Theobald, late Deputy-Superintendent Geological Survey of India. Two Vols., royal 8vo, pp. xxvi. and 560; xvi. and 788 and xxxvi., cloth. 1884. £3.

MATHEWS.—ABRAHAM IBN EZRA'S COMMENTARY ON THE CANTICLES AFTER THE FIRST RECENSION. Edited from the MSS., with a translation, by H. J. Mathews, B.A., Exeter College, Oxford. Crown 8vo, pp. x., 34, and 24, limp cloth. 1874. 2s. 6d.

MAXWELL.—A MANUAL OF THE MALAY LANGUAGE. By W. E. MAXWELL, of the Inner Temple, Barrister-at-Law; Assistant Resident, Perak, Malay Peninsula. With an Introductory Sketch of the Sanskrit Element in Malay. Crown 8vo, pp. viii. and 182, cloth. 1882. 7s. 6d.

MAY.—A BIBLIOGRAPHY OF ELECTRICITY AND MAGNETISM. 1860 to 1883. With Special Reference to Electro-Technics. Compiled by G. May. With an Index by O. Salle, Ph.D. Crown 8vo, pp. viii.-204, cloth. 1884. 5s.

MAYER.—ON THE ART OF POTTERY: with a History of its Rise and Progress in Liverpool. By Joseph Mayer, F.S.A., F.R.S.N.A., &c. 8vo, pp. 100, boards. 1873. 5s.

MAYERS.—TREATIES BETWEEN THE EMPIRE OF CHINA AND FOREIGN POWERS, together with Regulations for the conduct of Foreign Trade, &c. Edited by W. F. Mayers, Chinese Secretary to H.B.M.'s Legation at Peking. 8vo, pp. 246, cloth. 1877. 25s.

MAYERS.—THE CHINESE GOVERNMENT: a Manual of Chinese Titles, categorically arranged and explained, with an Appendix. By Wm. Fred. Mayers, Chinese Secretary to H.B.M.'s Legation at Peking, &c., &c. Royal 8vo, pp. viii. and 160, cloth. 1878. 30s.

M'CRINDLE.—ANCIENT INDIA, AS DESCRIBED BY MEGASTHENES AND ARRIAN; being a translation of the fragments of the Indika of Megasthenes collected by Dr. Schwanbeck, and of the first part of the Indika of Arrian. By J. W. M'Crindle, M.A., Principal of the Government College, Patna, &c. With Introduction, Notes, and Map of Ancient India. Post 8vo, pp. xi. and 224, cloth. 1877. 7s. 6d.

M'CRINDLE.—THE COMMERCE AND NAVIGATION OF THE ERYTHRÆAN SEA. Being a Translation of the Periplus Maris Erythræi, by an Anonymous Writer, and of Arrian's Account of the Voyage of Nearkhos, from the Mouth of the Indus to the Head of the Persian Gulf. With Introduction, Commentary, Notes, and Index. By J. W. M'Crindle, M.A., Edinburgh, &c. Post 8vo, pp. iv. and 238, cloth. 1879. 7s. 6d.

M'CRINDLE.—Ancient India as Described by Ktesias the Knidian; being a Translation of the Abridgment of his "Indika" by Photius, and of the Fragments of that Work preserved in other Writers. With Introduction, Notes, and Index. By J. W. M'Crindle, M.A., M.R.S.A. 8vo, pp. viii. and 104, cloth. 1882. 6s.

MECHANIC (THE YOUNG). A Book for Boys, containing Directions for the use of all kinds of Tools, and for the construction of Steam Engines and Mechanical Models, including the Art of Turning in Wood and Metal. Fifth Edition. Imperial 16mo, pp. iv. and 346, and 70 Engravings, cloth. 1878. 6s.

MECHANIC'S WORKSHOP (AMATEUR). A Treatise containing Plain and Concise Directions for the Manipulation of Wood and Metals, including Casting, Forging, Brazing, Soldering, and Carpentry. By the Author of "The Lathe and its Uses." Sixth Edition. Demy 8vo, pp. iv. and 148. Illustrated, cloth. 1880. 6s.

MEDITATIONS ON DEATH AND ETERNITY. Translated from the German by Frederica Rowan. Published by Her Majesty's gracious permission. 8vo, pp. 386, cloth. 1862. 10s. 6d.

DITTO. Smaller Edition, crown 8vo, printed on toned paper, pp. 352, cloth. 1884. 6s.

MEDITATIONS ON LIFE AND ITS RELIGIOUS DUTIES. Translated from the German by Frederica Rowan. Dedicated to H.R.H. Princess Louis of Hesse. Published by Her Majesty's gracious permission. Being the Companion Volume to "Meditations on Death and Eternity." 8vo, pp. vi. and 370, cloth. 1863. 10s. 6d.

DITTO. Smaller Edition, crown 8vo, printed on toned paper, pp. 338. 1863. 6s.

MEDLICOTT.—A MANUAL OF THE GEOLOGY OF INDIA, chiefly compiled from the observations of the Geological Survey. By H. B. Medlicott, M.A., Superintendent, Geological Survey of India, and W. T. Blanford, A.R.S.M., F.R.S., Deputy Superintendent. Published by order of the Government of India. 2 vols. 8vo, pp. xviii.-lxxx.-818. with 21 Plates and large coloured Map mounted in case, uniform, cloth. 1879. 16s. (For Part III. see BALL.)

MEGHA-DUTA (THE). (Cloud-Messenger.) By Kālidāsa. Translated from the Sanskrit into English Verse by the late H. H. Wilson, M.A., F.R.S. The Vocabulary by Francis Johnson. New Edition. 4to, pp. xi. and 180, cloth. 10s. 6d.

MENKE.—Orbis Antiqui Descriptio : An Atlas illustrating Ancient History and Geography, for the Use of Schools ; containing 18 Maps engraved on Steel and Coloured, with Descriptive Letterpress. By D. T. Menke. Fourth Edition. Folio, half bound morocco. 1866. 5s.

MEREDYTH.—Arca, a Repertoire of Original Poems, Sacred and Secular. By F. Meredyth, M.A., Canon of Limerick Cathedral. Crown 8vo, pp. 124, cloth. 1875. 5s.

METCALFE.—The Englishman and the Scandinavian. By Frederick Metcalfe, M.A., Fellow of Lincoln College, Oxford; Translator of "Gallus" and "Charicles;" and Author of "The Oxonian in Iceland." Post 8vo, pp. 512, cloth. 1880. 18s.

MICHEL.—Les Écossais en France, Les Français en Écosse. Par Francisque Michel, Correspondant de l'Institut de France, &c. In 2 vols. 8vo, pp. vii., 547, and 551, rich blue cloth, with emblematical designs. With upwards of 100 Coats of Arms, and other Illustrations. Price, £1, 12s.—Also a Large-Paper Edition (limited to 100 Copies), printed on Thick Paper. 2 vols. 4to, half morocco, with 3 additional Steel Engravings. 1862. £3, 3s.

MICKIEWICZ.—Konrad Wallenrod. An Historical Poem. By A. Mickiewicz. Translated from the Polish into English Verse by Miss M. Biggs. 18mo, pp. xvi. and 100, cloth. 1882. 2s. 6d.

MILL.—Auguste Comte and Positivism. By the late John Stuart Mill, M.P. Third Edition. 8vo, pp. 200, cloth. 1882. 3s. 6d.

MILLHOUSE.—Manual of Italian Conversation. For the Use of Schools. By John Millhouse. 18mo, pp. 126, cloth. 1866. 2s.

MILLHOUSE.—New English and Italian Pronouncing and Explanatory Dictionary. By John Millhouse. Vol. I. English-Italian. Vol. II. Italian-English. Fourth Edition. 2 vols. square 8vo, pp. 654 and 740, cloth. 1867. 12s.

MILNE.—Notes on Crystallography and Crystallo-physics. Being the Substance of Lectures delivered at Yedo during the years 1876-1877. By John Milne, F.G.S. 8vo, pp. viii. and 70, cloth. 1879. 3s.

MINOCHCHERJI.—Pahlavi, Gujârati, and English Dictionary. By Jamashji Dastur Minochcherji. Vol. I., with Photograph of Author. 8vo, pp. clxxii. and 168, cloth. 1877. 14s.

MITRA.—Buddha Gaya : The Hermitage of Sákya Muni. By Rajendralala Mitra, LL.D., C.I.E., &c. 4to, pp. xvi. and 258, with 51 Plates, cloth. 1879. £3.

MOCATTA.—Moral Biblical Gleanings and Practical Teachings, Illustrated by Biographical Sketches Drawn from the Sacred Volume. By J. L. Mocatta. 8vo, pp. viii. and 446, cloth. 1872. 7s.

MODERN FRENCH READER (The). Prose. Junior Course. Tenth Edition. Edited by Ch. Cassal, LL.D., and Théodore Karcher, LL.B. Crown 8vo, pp. xiv. and 224, cloth. 1884. 2s. 6d.

Senior Course. Third Edition. Crown 8vo, pp. xiv. and 418, cloth. 1880. 4s.

MODERN FRENCH READER.—A Glossary of Idioms, Gallicisms, and other Difficulties contained in the Senior Course of the Modern French Reader ; with Short Notices of the most important French Writers and Historical or Literary Characters, and hints as to the works to be read or studied. By Charles Cassal, LL.D., &c. Crown 8vo, pp. viii. and 104, cloth. 1881. 2s. 6d.

MODERN FRENCH READER.—SENIOR COURSE AND GLOSSARY combined. 6s.

MORELET.—TRAVELS IN CENTRAL AMERICA, including Accounts of some Regions unexplored since the Conquest. From the French of A. Morelet, by Mrs. M. F. Squier. Edited by E. G. Squier. 8vo, pp. 430, cloth. 1871. 8s. 6d.

MORFILL.—SIMPLIFIED POLISH GRAMMAR. See Trübner's Collection.

MORFIT.—A PRACTICAL TREATISE ON THE MANUFACTURE OF SOAPS. By Campbell Morfit, M.D., F.C.S., formerly Professor of Applied Chemistry in the University of Maryland. With Illustrations. Demy 8vo, pp. xii. and 270, cloth. 1871. £2, 12s. 6d.

MORFIT.—A PRACTICAL TREATISE ON PURE FERTILIZERS, and the Chemical Conversion of Rock Guanos, Marlstones, Coprolites, and the Crude Phosphates of Lime and Alumina generally into various valuable Products. By Campbell Morfit, M.D., F.C.S., formerly Professor of Applied Chemistry in the University of Maryland. With 28 Plates. 8vo, pp. xvi. and 547, cloth. 1873. £4, 4s.

MORRIS.—A DESCRIPTIVE AND HISTORICAL ACCOUNT OF THE GODAVERY DISTRICT, IN THE PRESIDENCY OF MADRAS. By Henry Morris, formerly of the Madras Civil Service, author of "A History of India, for use in Schools," and other works. With a Map. 8vo, pp. xii. and 390, cloth. 1878. 12s.

MOSENTHAL.—OSTRICHES AND OSTRICH FARMING. By J. de Mosenthal, late Member of the Legistive Council of the Cape of Good Hope, &c., and James E. Harting, F.L.S., F.Z.S., Member of the British Ornithologist's Union, &c. Second Edition. With 8 full-page illustrations and 20 woodcuts. Royal 8vo, pp. xxiv. and 246, cloth. 1879. 10s. 6d.

MOTLEY.—JOHN LOTHROP MOTLEY: a Memoir. By Oliver Wendell Holmes. English Copyright Edition. Crown 8vo, pp. xii. and 275, cloth. 1878. 6s.

MUELLER.—THE ORGANIC CONSTITUENTS OF PLANTS AND VEGETABLE SUBSTANCES, and their Chemical Analysis. By Dr. G. C. Wittstein. Authorised Translation from the German Original, enlarged with numerous Additions, by Baron Ferd. von Mueller, K.C.M.G., M. & Ph. D., F.R.S. Crown 8vo, pp. xviii. and 332, wrapper. 1880. 14s.

MUELLER.—SELECT EXTRA-TROPICAL PLANTS READILY ELIGIBLE FOR INDUSTRIAL CULTURE OR NATURALISATION. With Indications of their Native Countries and some of their Uses. By F. Von Mueller, K.C.M.G., M.D., Ph.D., F.R.S. 8vo, pp. x., 394, cloth. 1880. 8s.

MUHAMMED.—THE LIFE OF MUHAMMED. Based on Muhammed Ibn Ishak. By Abd El Malik Ibn Hisham. Edited by Dr. Ferdinand Wüstenfeld. One volume containing the Arabic Text. 8vo, pp. 1026, sewed. £1, 1s. Another volume, containing Introduction, Notes, and Index in German. 8vo, pp. lxxii. and 266, sewed. 7s. 6d. Each part sold separately.

MUIR.—EXTRACTS FROM THE CORAN. In the Original, with English rendering. Compiled by Sir William Muir, K.C.S.I., LL.D., Author of "The Life of Mahomet." Crown 8vo, pp. viii. and 64, cloth. 1880. 3s. 6d.

MUIR.—ORIGINAL SANSKRIT TEXTS, on the Origin and History of the People of India, their Religion and Institutions. Collected, Translated, and Illustrated by John Muir, D.C.L., LL.D., Ph.D., &c. &c.

Vol. I. Mythical and Legendary Accounts of the Origin of Caste, with an Inquiry into its existence in the Vedic Age. Second Edition, rewritten and greatly enlarged. 8vo, pp. xx. and 532, cloth. 1868. £1, 1s.

MUIR.—ORIGINAL SANSKRIT TEXTS—*continued.*
Vol. II. The Trans-Himalayan Origin of the Hindus, and their Affinity with the Western Branches of the Aryan Race. Second Edition, revised, with Additions. 8vo, pp. xxxii. and 512, cloth. 1871. £1, 1s.
Vol. III. The Vedas: Opinions of their Authors, and of later Indian Writers, on their Origin, Inspiration, and Authority. Second Edition, revised and enlarged. 8vo, pp. xxxii. and 312, cloth. 1868. 16s.
Vol. IV. Comparison of the Vedic with the later representation of the principal Indian Deities. Second Edition, revised. 8vo, pp. xvi. and 524, cloth. 1873. £1, 1s.
Vol. V. Contributions to a Knowledge of the Cosmogony, Mythology, Religious Ideas, Life and Manners of the Indians in the Vedic Age. Third Edition. 8vo, pp. xvi. and 492, cloth. 1884. £1, 1s.

MUIR.—TRANSLATIONS FROM THE SANSKRIT. See Trübner's Oriental Series.

MÜLLER.—OUTLINE DICTIONARY, for the Use of Missionaries, Explorers, and Students of Language. With an Introduction on the proper Use of the Ordinary English Alphabet in transcribing Foreign Languages. By F. Max Müller, M.A. The Vocabulary compiled by John Bellows. 12mo, pp. 368, morocco. 1867. 7s. 6d.

MÜLLER.—LECTURE ON BUDDHIST NIHILISM. By F. Max Müller, M.A. Fcap. 8vo, sewed. 1869. 1s.

MÜLLER.—THE SACRED HYMNS OF THE BRAHMINS, as preserved to us in the oldest collection of religious poetry, the Rig-Veda-Sanhita. Translated and explained, by F. Max Müller, M.A., Fellow of All Souls' College, Professor of Comparative Philology at Oxford, Foreign Member of the Institute of France, &c., &c. Vol. I. Hymns to the Maruts or the Storm-Gods. 8vo, pp. clii. and 264, cloth. 1869. 12s. 6d.

MÜLLER.—THE HYMNS OF THE RIG-VEDA, in the Samhita and Pada Texts. Reprinted from the Editio Princeps. By F. Max Müller, M.A., &c. Second Edition, with the two Texts on Parallel Pages. In two vols. 8vo, pp. 1704, sewed. £1, 12s.

MÜLLER.—A SHORT HISTORY OF THE BOURBONS. From the Earliest Period down to the Present Time. By R. M. Müller, Ph.D., Modern Master at Forest School, Walthamstow, and Author of " Parallèle entre ' Jules César,' par Shakespeare, et ' Le Mort de César,' par Voltaire," &c. Fcap. 8vo, pp. 30, wrapper. 1882. 1s.

MÜLLER.—ANCIENT INSCRIPTIONS IN CEYLON. By Dr. Edward Müller. 2 Vols. Text, crown 8vo, pp. 220, cloth, and Plates, oblong folio, cloth. 1883. 21s.

MULLEY.—GERMAN GEMS IN AN ENGLISH SETTING. Translated by Jane Mulley. Fcap., pp. xii. and 180, cloth. 1877. 3s. 6d.

NÁGÁNANDA; OR, THE JOY OF THE SNAKE WORLD. A Buddhist Drama in Five Acts. Translated into English Prose, with Explanatory Notes, from the Sanskrit of Sri-Harsha-Deva, by Palmer Boyd, B.A. With an Introduction by Professor Cowell. Crown 8vo, pp. xvi. and 100, cloth. 1872. 4s. 6d.

NAPIER.—FOLK LORE; or, Superstitious Beliefs in the West of Scotland within this Century. With an Appendix, showing the probable relation of the modern Festivals of Christmas, May Day, St. John's Day, and Hallowe'en, to ancient Sun and Fire Worship. By James Napier, F.R.S.E., &c. Crown 8vo, pp. vii. and 190, cloth. 1878. 4s.

NARADÍYA DHARMA-SASTRA; OR, THE INSTITUTES OF NARADA. Translated, for the first time, from the unpublished Sanskrit original. By Dr. Julius Jolly, University, Wurzburg. With a Preface, Notes, chiefly critical, an Index of Quotations from Narada in the principal Indian Digests, and a general Index. Crown 8vo, pp. xxxv. and 144, cloth. 1876. 10s. 6d.

NEVILL.—HAND LIST OF MOLLUSCA IN THE INDIAN MUSEUM, CALCUTTA. By Geoffrey Nevill, C.M.Z.S., &c., First Assistant to the Superintendent of the Indian Museum. Part I. Gastropoda, Pulmonata, and Prosobranchia-Neurobranchia. 8vo, pp. xvi. and 338, cloth. 1878. 15s.

NEWMAN.—THE ODES OF HORACE. Translated into Unrhymed Metres, with Introduction and Notes. By F. W. Newman. Second Edition. Post 8vo, pp. xxi. and 247, cloth. 1876. 4s.

NEWMAN.—THEISM, DOCTRINAL AND PRACTICAL; or, Didactic Religious Utterances. By F. W. Newman. 4to, pp. 184, cloth. 1858. 4s. 6d.

NEWMAN.—HOMERIC TRANSLATION IN THEORY AND PRACTICE. A Reply to Matthew Arnold. By F. W. Newman. Crown 8vo, pp. 104, stiff covers. 1861. 2s. 6d.

NEWMAN.—HIAWATHA: Rendered into Latin. With Abridgment. By F. W. Newman. 12mo, pp. vii. and 110, sewed. 1862. 2s. 6d.

NEWMAN.—A HISTORY OF THE HEBREW MONARCHY from the Administration of Samuel to the Babylonish Captivity. By F. W. Newman. Third Edition. Crown 8vo, pp. x. and 354, cloth. 1865. 8s. 6d.

NEWMAN.—PHASES OF FAITH; or, Passages from the History of my Creed. New Edition; with Reply to Professor Henry Rogers, Author of the "Eclipse of Faith." Crown 8vo, pp. viii. and 212, cloth. 1881. 3s. 6d.

NEWMAN.—A HANDBOOK OF MODERN ARABIC, consisting of a Practical Grammar, with numerous Examples, Dialogues, and Newspaper Extracts, in European Type. By F. W. Newman. Post 8vo, pp. xx. and 192, cloth. 1866. 6s.

NEWMAN.—TRANSLATIONS OF ENGLISH POETRY INTO LATIN VERSE. Designed as Part of a New Method of Instructing in Latin. By F. W. Newman. Crown 8vo, pp. xiv. and 202, cloth. 1868. 6s.

NEWMAN.—THE SOUL: Her Sorrows and her Aspirations. An Essay towards the Natural History of the Soul, as the True Basis of Theology. By F. W. Newman. Tenth Edition. Post 8vo, pp. xii. and 162, cloth. 1882. 3s. 6d.

NEWMAN.—MISCELLANIES; chiefly Addresses, Academical and Historical. By F. W. Newman. 8vo, pp. iv. and 356, cloth. 1869. 7s. 6d.

NEWMAN.—THE ILIAD OF HOMER, faithfully translated into Unrhymed English Metre, by F. W. Newman. Royal 8vo, pp. xvi. and 384, cloth. 1871. 10s. 6d.

NEWMAN.—A DICTIONARY OF MODERN ARABIC. 1. Anglo-Arabic Dictionary. 2. Anglo-Arabic Vocabulary. 3. Arabo-English Dictionary. By F. W. Newman. In 2 vols. crown 8vo, pp. xvi. and 376–464, cloth. 1871. £1, 1s.

NEWMAN.—HEBREW THEISM. By F. W. Newman. Royal 8vo, pp. viii. and 172. Stiff wrappers. 1874. 4s. 6d.

NEWMAN.—THE MORAL INFLUENCE OF LAW. A Lecture by F. W. Newman, May 20, 1860. Crown 8vo, pp. 16, sewed. 3d.

NEWMAN.—RELIGION NOT HISTORY. By F. W. Newman. Foolscap, pp. 58, paper wrapper. 1877. 1s.

NEWMAN.—MORNING PRAYERS IN THE HOUSEHOLD OF A BELIEVER IN GOD. By F. W. Newman. Second Edition. Crown 8vo, pp. 80, limp cloth. 1882. 1s. 6d.

NEWMAN.—REORGANIZATION OF ENGLISH INSTITUTIONS. A Lecture by Emeritus Professor F. W. Newman. Delivered in the Manchester Athenæum, October 15, 1875. Crown 8vo, pp. 28, sewed. 1880. 6d.

NEWMAN.—WHAT IS CHRISTIANITY WITHOUT CHRIST? By F. W. Newman, Emeritus Professor of University College, London. 8vo, pp. 28, stitched in wrapper. 1881. 1s.

D

NEWMAN.—LIBYAN VOCABULARY. An Essay towards Reproducing the Ancient Numidian Language out of Four Modern Languages. By F. W. Newman. Crown 8vo, pp. vi. and 204, cloth. 1882. 10s. 6d.

NEWMAN.—A CHRISTIAN COMMONWEALTH. By F. W. Newman. Crown 8vo, pp. 60, cloth. 1883. 1s.

NEW SOUTH WALES, PUBLICATIONS OF THE GOVERNMENT OF. List on application.

NEW SOUTH WALES.—JOURNAL AND PROCEEDINGS OF THE ROYAL SOCIETY OF. Published annually. Price 10s. 6d. List of Contents on application.

NEWTON.—PATENT LAW AND PRACTICE: showing the mode of obtaining and opposing Grants, Disclaimers, Confirmations, and Extensions of Patents. With a Chapter on Patent Agents. By A. V. Newton. Enlarged Edition. Crown 8vo, pp. xii. and 104, cloth. 1879. 2s. 6d.

NEW ZEALAND INSTITUTE PUBLICATIONS:—

I. TRANSACTIONS AND PROCEEDINGS of the New Zealand Institute. Demy 8vo, stitched. Vols. I. to XVI., 1868 to 1883. £1, 1s. each.

II. AN INDEX TO THE TRANSACTIONS AND PROCEEDINGS of the New Zealand Institute. Vols. I. to VIII. Edited and Published under the Authority of the Board of Governors of the Institute. By James Hector, C.M.G., M.D., F.R.S. Demy, 8vo, 44 pp., stitched. 1877. 2s. 6d.

NEW ZEALAND.—GEOLOGICAL SURVEY. List of Publications on application.

NOIRIT.—A FRENCH COURSE IN TEN LESSONS. By Jules Noirit, B.A. Lessons I.-IV. Crown 8vo, pp. xiv. and 80, sewed. 1870. 1s. 6d.

NOIRIT.—FRENCH GRAMMATICAL QUESTIONS for the use of Gentlemen preparing for the Army, Civil Service, Oxford Examinations, &c., &c. By Jules Noirit. Crown 8vo, pp. 62, cloth. 1870. 1s. Interleaved, 1s. 6d.

NOURSE.—NARRATIVE OF THE SECOND ARCTIC EXPEDITION MADE BY CHARLES F. HALL. His Voyage to Repulse Bay; Sledge Journeys to the Straits of Fury and Hecla, and to King William's Land, and Residence among the Eskimos during the years 1864-69. Edited under the orders of the Hon. Secretary of the Navy, by Prof. J. E. Nourse, U.S.N. 4to, pp. l. and 644, cloth. With maps, heliotypes, steel and wood engravings. 1880. £1, 8s.

NUGENT'S IMPROVED FRENCH AND ENGLISH AND ENGLISH AND FRENCH POCKET DICTIONARY. Par Smith. 24mo, pp. 489 and 320, cloth. 1873. 3s.

NUTT.—TWO TREATISES ON VERBS CONTAINING FEEBLE AND DOUBLE LETTERS. By R. Jehuda Hayug of Fez. Translated into Hebrew from the original Arabic by R. Moses Gikatilia of Cordova, with the Treatise on Punctuation by the same author, translated by Aben Ezra. Edited from Bodleian MSS., with an English translation, by J. W. Nutt, M.A. Demy 8vo, pp. 312, sewed. 1870. 5s.

NUMISMATA ORIENTALIA ILLUSTRATA. See MARSDEN.

NUTT.—A SKETCH OF SAMARITAN HISTORY, DOGMA, AND LITERATURE. An Introduction to "Fragments of a Samaritan Targum." By J. W. Nutt, M.A., &c., &c. Demy 8vo, pp. 180, cloth. 1874. 5s.

OEHLENSCHLÄGER.—AXEL AND VALBORG: a Tragedy, in Five Acts, and other Poems. Translated from the Danish of Adam Oehlenschläger by Pierce Butler, M.A., late Rector of Ulcombe, Kent. Edited by Professor Palmer, M.A., of St. John's Coll., Camb. With a Memoir of the Translator. Fcap. 8vo, pp. xii. and 164, cloth. 1874. 5s.

OERA LINDA BOOK (THE).—From a Manuscript of the 13th Century, with the permission of the proprietor, C. Over de Linden of the Helder. The Original Frisian Text as verified by Dr. J. O. Ottema, accompanied by an English Version of Dr. Ottema's Dutch Translation. By W. R. Sandbach. 8vo, pp. xxv. and 254, cloth. 1876. 5s.

OGAREFF.—ESSAI SUR LA SITUATION RUSSE. Lettres à un Anglais. Par N. Ogareff. 12mo, pp. 150, sewed. 1862. 3s.

OLCOTT.—A BUDDHIST CATECHISM, according to the Canon of the Southern Church. By Colonel H. S. Olcott, President of the Theosophical Society. 24mo, pp. 32. 1s.

OLCOTT.—THE YOGA PHILOSOPHY: Being the Text of Patanjali, with Bhojarajah's Commentary. A Reprint of the English Translation of the above, by the late Dr. Ballantyne and Govind Shastri Deva ; to which are added Extracts from Various Authors. With an Introduction by Colonel H. S. Olcott, President of the Theosophical Society. The whole Edited by Tukaram Tatia, F.T.S. Crown 8vo, pp. xvi.-294, wrapper. 1882. 7s. 6d.

OLLENDORFF.—METODO PARA APRENDER A LEER, escribir y hablar el Inglés segun el sistema de Ollendorff. Por Ramon Palenzuela y Juan de la Carreño. 8vo, pp. xlvi. and 460, cloth. 1873. 7s. 6d.
KEY to Ditto. Crown 8vo, pp. 112, cloth. 1873. 4s.

OLLENDORFF.—METODO PARA APRENDER A LEER, escribir y hablar el Francés, segun el verdadero sistema de Ollendorff ; ordenado en lecciones progresivas, consistiendo de ejercicios orales y escritos ; enriquecido de la pronunciacion figurada como se estila en la conversacion ; y de un Apéndice abrazando las reglas de la sintáxis, la formacion de los verbos regulares, y la conjugacion de los irregulares. Por Teodoro Simonné, Professor de Lenguas. Crown 8vo, pp. 342, cloth. 1873. 6s.
KEY to Ditto. Crown 8vo, pp. 80, cloth. 1873. 3s. 6d.

OPPERT.—ON THE CLASSIFICATION OF LANGUAGES : A Contribution to Comparative Philology. By Dr. Gustav Oppert, Ph.D., Professor of Sanskrit, Presidency College, Madras. 8vo, paper, pp. viii. and 146. 1883. 7s. 6d.

OPPERT.—LISTS OF SANSKRIT MANUSCRIPTS in Private Libraries of Southern India, Compiled, Arranged, and Indexed by Gustav Oppert, Ph.D., Professor of Sanskrit, Presidency College, Madras. Vol. I. 8vo, pp. vii. and 620, cloth. 1883. £1, 1s.

OPPERT.—ON THE WEAPONS, ARMY ORGANISATION, AND POLITICAL MAXIMS OF THE ANCIENT HINDUS ; with special reference to Gunpowder and Firearms. By Dr. Gustav Oppert, Ph.D., Professor of Sanskrit, Presidency College, Madras. 8vo, paper, pp. vi. and 162. 1883. 7s. 6d.

ORIENTAL SERIES.—See TRÜBNER'S ORIENTAL SERIES.

ORIENTAL TEXT SOCIETY'S PUBLICATIONS. A list may be had on application.

ORIENTAL CONGRESS.—REPORT OF THE PROCEEDINGS OF THE SECOND INTERNATIONAL CONGRESS OF ORIENTALISTS HELD IN LONDON, 1874. Royal 8vo, pp. viii. and 68, sewed. 1874. 5s.

ORIENTALISTS.—TRANSACTIONS OF THE SECOND SESSION OF THE INTERNATIONAL CONGRESS OF ORIENTALISTS. Held in London in September 1874. Edited by Robert K. Douglas, Hon. Sec. 8vo, pp. viii. and 456, cloth. 1876. 21s.

OTTÉ.—HOW TO LEARN DANISH (Dano-Norwegian) : a Manual for Students of Danish based on the Ollendorffian system of teaching languages, and adapted for self-instruction. By E. C. Otté. Second Edition. Crown 8vo, pp. xx. and 333, cloth. 1884. 7s. 6d.
Key to above. Crown 8vo, pp. 84, cloth. 3s.

OTTÉ.—SIMPLIFIED DANISH AND SWEDISH GRAMMARS. See TRÜBNER'S COLLECTION.

OVERBECK.—CATHOLIC ORTHODOXY AND ANGLO-CATHOLICISM. A Word about the Intercommunion between the English and Orthodox Churches. By J. J. Overbeck, D.D. 8vo, pp. viii. and 200, cloth. 1866. 5s.

OVERBECK.—BONN CONFERENCE. By J. J. Overbeck, D.D. Crown 8vo, pp. 48, sewed. 1876. 1s.

OVERBECK.—A PLAIN VIEW OF THE CLAIMS OF THE ORTHODOX CATHOLIC CHURCH AS OPPOSED TO ALL OTHER CHRISTIAN DENOMINATIONS. By J. J. Overbeck, D.D. Crown 8vo, pp. iv. and 133, wrapper. 1881. 2s. 6d.

OWEN.—FOOTFALLS ON THE BOUNDARY OF ANOTHER WORLD. With Narrative Illustrations. By R. D. Owen. An enlarged English Copyright Edition. Post 8vo, pp. xx. and 392, cloth. 1875. 7s. 6d.

OWEN.—THE DEBATABLE LAND BETWEEN THIS WORLD AND THE NEXT. With Illustrative Narrations. By Robert Dale Owen. Second Edition. Crown 8vo, pp. 456, cloth. 1874. 7s. 6d.

OWEN.—THREADING MY WAY: Twenty-Seven Years of Autobiography. By R. D. Owen. Crown 8vo, pp. 344, cloth. 1874. 7s. 6d.

OYSTER (THE): WHERE, HOW, AND WHEN TO FIND, BREED, COOK, AND EAT IT. Second Edition, with a New Chapter, "The Oyster-Seeker in London." 12mo, pp. viii. and 106, boards. 1863. 1s.

PALESTINE.—MEMOIRS OF THE SURVEY OF WESTERN PALESTINE. Edited by W. Besant, M.A., and E. H. Palmer, M.A., under the Direction of the Committee of the Palestine Exploration Fund. Complete in seven volumes. Demy 4to, cloth, with a Portfolio of Plans, and large scale Map. Second Issue. Price Twenty Guineas.

PALMER.—A CONCISE ENGLISH-PERSIAN DICTIONARY; together with a simplified Grammar of the Persian Language. By the late E. H. Palmer, M.A., Lord Almoner's Reader, and Professor of Arabic, Cambridge, &c. Completed and Edited, from the MS. left imperfect at his death, by G. Le Strange. Royal 16mo, pp. 606, cloth. 1883. 10s. 6d.

PALMER.—A CONCISE PERSIAN-ENGLISH DICTIONARY. By E. H. Palmer, M.A., of the Middle Temple, Barrister-at-Law, Lord Almoner's Reader, and Professor of Arabic, and Fellow of St. John's College in the University of Cambridge. Royal 16mo, pp. 726, cloth. 1884. 10s. 6d.

PALMER.—THE SONG OF THE REED, AND OTHER PIECES. By E. H. Palmer, M.A., Cambridge. Crown 8vo, pp. 203, cloth. 1876. 5s.

PALMER.—HINDUSTANI, ARABIC, AND PERSIAN GRAMMAR. See Trübner's Collection.

PALMER.—THE PATRIARCH AND THE TSAR. Translated from the Russ by William Palmer, M.A. Demy 8vo, cloth. Vol. I. THE REPLIES OF THE HUMBLE NICON. Pp. xl. and 674. 1871. 12s.—Vol. II. TESTIMONIES CONCERNING THE PATRIARCH NICON, THE TSAR, AND THE BOYARS. Pp. lxxviii. and 554. 1873. 12s.—Vol. III. HISTORY OF THE CONDEMNATION OF THE PATRIARCH NICON. Pp. lxvi. and 558. 1873. 12s.—Vols. IV., V., and VI. SERVICES OF THE PATRIARCH NICON TO THE CHURCH AND STATE OF HIS COUNTRY, &c. Pp. lxxviii. and 1 to 660; xiv.-661-102?, and 1 to 254; xxvi.-1029-1656, and 1-72. 1876. 36s.

PARKER.—THEODORE PARKER'S CELEBRATED DISCOURSE ON MATTERS PERTAINING TO RELIGION. People's Edition. Cr. 8vo, pp. 351. 1872. Stitched, 1s. 6d.; cl., 2s.

PARKER.—THEODORE PARKER. A Biography. By O. B. Frothingham. Crown 8vo, pp. viii. and 588, cloth, with Portrait. 1876. 12s.

PARKER.—THE COLLECTED WORKS OF THEODORE PARKER, Minister of the Twenty-eighth Congregational Society at Boston, U.S. Containing his Theological, Polemical, and Critical Writings; Sermons, Speeches, and Addresses; and Literary Miscellanies. In 14 vols. 8vo, cloth. 6s. each.
    Vol. I. Discourse on Matters Pertaining to Religion. Preface by the Editor, and Portrait of Parker from a medallion by Saulini. Pp. 380.
    Vol. II. Ten Sermons and Prayers. Pp. 360.
    Vol. III. Discourses of Theology. Pp. 318.
    Vol. IV. Discourses on Politics. Pp. 312.
    Vol. V. Discourses of Slavery. I. Pp. 336.
    Vol. VI. Discourses of Slavery. II. Pp. 323.
    Vol. VII. Discourses of Social Science. Pp. 296.
    Vol. VIII. Miscellaneous Discourses. Pp. 230.
    Vol. IX. Critical Writings. I. Pp. 292.
    Vol. X. Critical Writings. II. Pp. 308.

PARKER.—COLLECTED WORKS—*continued.*
Vol. XI. Sermons of Theism, Atheism, and Popular Theology. Pp. 257.
Vol. XII. Autobiographical and Miscellaneous Pieces. Pp. 356.
Vol. XIII. Historic Americans. Pp. 236.
Vol. XIV. Lessons from the World of Matter and the World of Man. Pp. 352.

PARKER.—MALAGASY GRAMMAR. See Trübner's Collection.

PATERSON.—NOTES ON MILITARY SURVEYING AND RECONNAISSANCE. By Lieut.-Colonel William Paterson. Sixth Edition. With 16 Plates. Demy 8vo, pp. xii. and 146, cloth. 1882. 7s. 6d.

PATERSON.—TOPOGRAPHICAL EXAMINATION PAPERS. By Lieut.-Col. W. Paterson. 8vo, pp. 32, with 4 Plates. Boards. 1882. 2s.

PATERSON.—TREATISE ON MILITARY DRAWING. With a Course of Progressive Plates. By Captain W. Paterson, Professor of Military Drawing at the Royal Military College, Sandhurst. Oblong 4to, pp. xii. and 31, cloth. 1862. £1, 1s.

PATERSON.—THE OROMETER FOR HILL MEASURING, combining Scales of Distances, Protractor, Clinometer, Scale of Horizontal Equivalents, Scale of Shade, and Table of Gradients. By Captain William Paterson. On cardboard. 1s.

PATERSON.—CENTRAL AMERICA. By W. Paterson, the Merchant Statesman. From a MS. in the British Museum, 1701. With a Map. Edited by S. Bannister, M.A. 8vo, pp. 70, sewed. 1857. 2s. 6d.

PATON.—A HISTORY OF THE EGYPTIAN REVOLUTION, from the Period of the Mamelukes to the Death of Mohammed Ali; from Arab and European Memoirs, Oral Tradition, and Local Research. By A. A. Paton. Second Edition. 2 vols. demy 8vo, pp. xii. and 395, viii. and 446, cloth. 1870. 7s. 6d.

PATON.—HENRY BEYLE (otherwise DE STENDAHL). A Critical and Biographical Study, aided by Original Documents and Unpublished Letters from the Private Papers of the Family of Beyle. By A. A. Paton. Crown 8vo, pp. 340, cloth. 1874. 7s. 6d.

PATTON.—THE DEATH OF DEATH; or, A Study of God's Holiness in Connection with the Existence of Evil, in so far as Intelligent and Responsible Beings are Concerned. By an Orthodox Layman (John M. Patton). Revised Edition, crown 8vo, pp. xvi. and 252, cloth. 1881. 6s.

PAULI.—SIMON DE MONTFORT, EARL OF LEICESTER, the Creator of the House of Commons. By Reinhold Pauli. Translated by Una M. Goodwin. With Introduction by Harriet Martineau. Crown 8vo, pp. xvi. and 340, cloth. 1876. 6s.

PETTENKOFER.—THE RELATION OF THE AIR TO THE CLOTHES WE WEAR, THE HOUSE WE LIVE IN, AND THE SOIL WE DWELL ON. Three Popular Lectures delivered before the Albert Society at Dresden. By Dr. Max Von Pettenkofer, Professor of Hygiene at the University of Munich, &c. Abridged and Translated by Augustus Hess, M.D., M.R.C.P., London, &c. Cr. 8vo, pp. viii. and 96, limp cl. 1873. 2s. 6d.

PETRUCCELLI.—PRELIMINAIRES DE LA QUESTION ROMAINE DE M. ED. ABOUT. Par F. Petruccelli de la Gattina. 8vo, pp. xv. and 364, cloth. 1860. 7s. 6d.

PEZZI.—ARYAN PHILOLOGY, according to the most recent researches (Glottologia Aria Recentissima). Remarks Historical and Critical. By Domenico Pezzi. Translated by E. S. Roberts, M.A. Crown 8vo, pp. xvi. and 200, cloth. 1879. 6s.

PHAYRE.—A HISTORY OF BURMA. See Trübner's Oriental Series.

PHAYRE.—THE COINS OF ARAKAN, OF PEGU, AND OF BURMA. By Sir Arthur Phayre, C.B., K.C.S.I., G.C.M.G., late Commissioner of British Burma. Royal 4to, pp. viii.-48, with Autotype Illustrative Plates. Wrapper. 1882. 8s. 6d.

PHILLIPS.—THE DOCTRINE OF ADDAI, THE APOSTLE, now first edited in a complete form in the Original Syriac, with English Translation and Notes. By George Phillips, D.D., President of Queen's College, Cambridge. 8vo, pp. xv. and 52 and 53, cloth. 1876. 7s. 6d.

PHILOLOGICAL SOCIETY, TRANSACTIONS OF, published irregularly. List of publications on application.

PHILOSOPHY (THE) OF INSPIRATION AND REVELATION. By a Layman. With a preliminary notice of an Essay by the present Lord Bishop of Winchester, contained in a volume entitled "Aids to Faith." 8vo, pp. 20, sewed. 1875. 6d.

PICCIOTTO.—SKETCHES OF ANGLO-JEWISH HISTORY. By James Picciotto. Demy 8vo, pp. xi. and 420, cloth. 1875. 12s.

PIESSE.—CHEMISTRY IN THE BREWING-ROOM: being the substance of a Course of Lessons to Practical Brewers. With Tables of Alcohol, Extract, and Original Gravity. By Charles H. Piesse, F.C.S., Public Analyst. Fcap., pp. viii. and 62, cloth. 1877. 5s.

PIRY.—LE SAINT EDIT, ÉTUDE DE LITTERATURE CHINOISE. Préparée par A. Théophile Piry, du Service des Douanes Maritimes de Chine. 4to, pp. xx. and 320, cloth. 1879. 21s.

PLAYFAIR.—THE CITIES AND TOWNS OF CHINA. A Geographical Dictionary. By G. M. H. Playfair, of Her Majesty's Consular Service in China. 8vo, pp. 506, cloth. 1879. £1, 5s.

PLINY.—THE LETTERS OF PLINY THE YOUNGER. Translated by J. D. Lewis, M.A., Trinity College, Cambridge. Post 8vo, pp. vii. and 390, cloth. 1879. 5s.

PLUMPTRE.—KING'S COLLEGE LECTURES ON ELOCUTION; on the Physiology and Culture of Voice and Speech and the Expression of the Emotions by Language, Countenance, and Gesture. To which is added a Special Lecture on the Causes and Cure of the Impediments of Speech. Being the substance of the Introductory Course of Lectures annually delivered by Charles John Plumptre, Lecturer on Public Reading and Speaking at King's College, London, in the Evening Classes Department. Dedicated by permission to H.R.H. the Prince of Wales. Fourth, greatly Enlarged Illustrated, Edition. Post 8vo, pp. xviii. and 494, cloth. 1883. 15s.

PLUMPTRE.—GENERAL SKETCH OF THE HISTORY OF PANTHEISM. By C. E. Plumptre. Vol. I., from the Earliest Times to the Age of Spinoza; Vol. II., from the Age of Spinoza to the Commencement of the 19th Century. 2 vols. demy 8vo, pp. viii. and 395; iv. and 348, cloth. 1881. 18s.

POLE.—THE PHILOSOPHY OF MUSIC. See English and Foreign Philosophical Library. Vol. XI.

PONSARD.—CHARLOTTE CORDAY. A Tragedy. By F. Ponsard. Edited, with English Notes and Notice on Ponsard, by Professor C. Cassal, LL.D. 12mo, pp. xi. and 133, cloth. 1867. 2s. 6d.

PONSARD.—L'HONNEUR ET L'ARGENT. A Comedy. By François Ponsard. Edited, with English Notes and Memoir of Ponsard, by Professor C. Cassal, LL.D. Fcap. 8vo, pp. xvi. and 172, cloth. 1869. 3s. 6d.

POOLE.—AN INDEX TO PERIODICAL LITERATURE. By W. F. Poole, LL.D., Librarian of the Chicago Public Library. Third Edition, brought down to January 1882. 1 vol. royal 8vo, pp. xxviii. and 1442, cloth. 1883. £3, 13s. 6d. Wrappers, £3, 10s.

PRACTICAL GUIDES :—
FRANCE, BELGIUM, HOLLAND, AND THE RHINE. 1s.—ITALIAN LAKES. 1s.—WINTERING PLACES OF THE SOUTH. 2s.—SWITZERLAND, SAVOY, AND NORTH ITALY. 2s. 6d.—GENERAL CONTINENTAL GUIDE. 5s.—GENEVA. 1s.—PARIS. 1s.—BERNESE OBERLAND. 1s.—ITALY. 4s.

PRATT.—A GRAMMAR AND DICTIONARY OF THE SAMOAN LANGUAGE. By Rev. George Pratt, Forty Years a Missionary of the London Missionary Society in Samoa. Second Edition. Edited by Rev. S. J. Whitmee, F.R.G.S. Crown 8vo, pp. viii. and 380, cloth. 1878. 18s.

PSYCHICAL RESEARCH, SOCIETY FOR, PROCEEDINGS. Published irregularly. Vol. I. Post 8vo, pp. 338, cloth. 1884. 10s.

QUINET.—EDGAR QUINET. See English and Foreign Philosophical Library, Vol. XIV.

RAM RAZ.—ESSAY ON THE ARCHITECTURE OF THE HINDUS. By Ram Raz, Native Judge and Magistrate of Bangalore, Corr. Mem. R.A.S. With 48 Plates. 4to, pp. xiv. and 64, sewed. 1834. £2, 2s.

RAMSAY.—TABULAR LIST OF ALL THE AUSTRALIAN BIRDS AT PRESENT KNOWN TO THE AUTHOR, showing the distribution of the species. By E. P. Ramsay, F.L.S., &c., Curator of the Australian Museum, Sydney. 8vo, pp. 36, and Map ; boards. 1878. 5s.

RASK.—GRAMMAR OF THE ANGLO-SAXON TONGUE, from the Danish of Erasmus Rask. By Benjamin Thorpe. Third Edition, corrected and improved, with Plate. Post 8vo, pp. vi. and 192, cloth. 1879. 5s. 6d.

RASK.—A SHORT TRACTATE on the Longevity ascribed to the Patriarchs in the Book of Genesis, and its relation to the Hebrew Chronology; the Flood, the Exodus of the Israelites, the Site of Eden, &c. From the Danish of the late Professor Rask, with his manuscript corrections, and large additions from his autograph, now for the first time printed. With a Map of Paradise and the circumjacent Lands. Crown 8vo, pp. 134, cloth. 1863. 2s. 6d.

RATTON.—A HANDBOOK OF COMMON SALT. By J. J. L. Ratton, M.D., M.C., Surgeon, Madras Army. 8vo, pp. xviii. and 282, cloth. 1879. 7s. 6d.

RAVENSTEIN.—THE RUSSIANS ON THE AMUR ; its Discovery, Conquest, and Colonization, with a Description of the Country, its Inhabitants, Productions, and Commercial Capabilities, and Personal Accounts of Russian Travellers. By E. G. Ravenstein, F.R.G.S. With 4 tinted Lithographs and 3 Maps. 8vo, pp. 500, cloth. 1861. 15s.

RAVENSTEIN AND HULLEY.—THE GYMNASIUM AND ITS FITTINGS. By E. G. Ravenstein and John Hulley. With 14 Plates of Illustrations. 8vo, pp. 32, sewed. 1867. 2s. 6d.

RAVERTY.—NOTES ON AFGHANISTAN AND PART OF BALUCHISTAN, Geographical, Ethnographical, and Historical, extracted from the Writings of little known Afghan, and Tajyik Historians, &c., &c., and from Personal Observation. By Major H. G. Raverty, Bombay Native Infantry (Retired). Foolscap folio. Sections I. and II., pp. 98, wrapper. 1880. 2s. Section III., pp. vi. and 218. 1881. 5s. Section IV. 1884. 3s.

READE.—THE MARTYRDOM OF MAN. By Winwood Reade. Eighth Edition. Crown 8vo, pp. viii. and 544, cloth. 1884. 7s. 6d.

RECORD OFFICE.—A SEPARATE CATALOGUE OF THE OFFICIAL PUBLICATIONS OF THE PUBLIC RECORD OFFICE, on sale by Trübner & Co., may be had on application.

RECORDS OF THE HEART. By Stella, Author of "Sappho," "The King's Stratagem," &c. Second English Edition. Crown 8vo, pp. xvi. and 188, with six steel-plate engravings, cloth. 1881. 3s. 6d.

REDHOUSE.—THE TURKISH VADE-MECUM OF OTTOMAN COLLOQUIAL LANGUAGE: Containing a Concise Ottoman Grammar ; a Carefully Selected Vocabulary Alphabetically Arranged, in two Parts, English and Turkish, and Turkish and English ; Also a few Familiar Dialogues and Naval and Military Terms. The whole in English Characters, the Pronunciation being fully indicated. By J. W. Redhouse, M.R.A.S. Third Edition. 32mo, pp. viii. and 372, cloth. 1882. 6s.

REDHOUSE.—On the History, System, and Varieties of Turkish Poetry. Illustrated by Selections in the Original and in English Paraphrase, with a Notice of the Islamic Doctrine of the Immortality of Woman's Soul in the Future State. By J. W. Redhouse, Esq., M.R.A.S. 8vo, pp. 62, cloth, 2s. 6d.; wrapper, 1s. 6d. 1879.

REDHOUSE.—The Mesnevi. See Trübner's Oriental Series.

REDHOUSE.—Simplified Ottoman-Turkish Grammar. See Trübner's Collection.

REEMELIN.—A Critical Review of American Politics. By C. Reemelin, of Cincinnati, Ohio. Demy 8vo, pp. xxiv. and 630, cloth. 1881. 14s.

RELIGION in Europe Historically Considered: An Essay in Verse. By the Author of "The Thames." Fcap. 8vo, pp. iv. and 152, cloth. 1883. 2s.

RENAN.—Philosophical Dialogues and Fragments. From the French of Ernest Renan. Translated, with the sanction of the Author, by Ras Bihari Mukharji. Post 8vo, pp. xxxii. and 182, cloth. 1883. 7s. 6d.

RENAN.—An Essay on the Age and Antiquity of the Book of Nabathæan Agriculture. To which is added an Inaugural Lecture on the Position of the Shemitic Nations in the History of Civilisation. By Ernest Renan. Crown 8vo, pp. xvi. and 148, cloth. 1862. 3s. 6d.

RENAN.—The Life of Jesus. By Ernest Renan. Authorised English Translation. Crown 8vo, pp. xii. and 312, cloth. 2s. 6d.; sewed, 1s. 6d.

RENAN.—The Apostles. By Ernest Renan. Translated from the original French. 8vo, pp. viii. and 288, cloth. 1869. 7s. 6d.

REPORT of a General Conference of Liberal Thinkers, for the discussion of matters pertaining to the religious needs of our time, and the methods of meeting them. Held June 13th and 14th, 1878, at South Place Chapel, Finsbury, London. 8vo, pp. 77, sewed. 1878. 1s.

RHODES.—Universal Curve Tables for Facilitating the Laying out of Circular Arcs on the Ground for Railways, Canals, &c. Together with Table of Tangential Angles and Multiples. By Alexander Rhodes, C.E. Oblong 18mo, band, pp. ix. and 104, roan. 1881. 5s.

RHYS.—Lectures on Welsh Philology. By John Rhys, M.A., Professor of Celtic at Oxford, Honorary Fellow of Jesus College, &c., &c. Second Edition, Revised and Enlarged. Crown 8vo, pp. xiv. and 467, cloth. 1879. 15s.

RICE.—Mysore and Coorg. A Gazetteer compiled for the Government of India. By Lewis Rice, Director of Public Instruction, Mysore and Coorg. Vol. I. Mysore in General. With 2 Coloured Maps. Vol. II. Mysore, by Districts. With 10 Coloured Maps. Vol. III. Coorg. With a Map. 3 vols. royal 8vo, pp. xii. 670 and xvi.; 544 and xxii.; and 427 and xxvii., cloth. 1878. 25s.

RICE.—Mysore Inscriptions. Translated for the Government by Lewis Rice. 8vo, pp. xcii. and 336-xxx., with a Frontispiece and Map, boards. 1879. 30s.

RIDLEY.—Kámilarói, and other Australian Languages. By the Rev. William Ridley, B.A. Second Edition, revised and enlarged by the author; with comparative Tables of Words from twenty Australian Languages, and Songs, Traditions, Laws, and Customs of the Australian Race. Small 4to, pp. vi. and 172, cloth. 1877. 10s. 6d.

RIG-VEDA-SANHITA. A Collection of Ancient Hindu Hymns. Constituting the 1st to the 8th Ashtakas, or Books of the Rig-Veda; the oldest authority for the Religious and Social Institutions of the Hindus. Translated from the Original Sanskrit. By the late H. H. Wilson, M.A., F.R.S., &c., &c.
    Vol. I. 8vo, pp. lii. and 348, cloth. 21s.
    Vol. II. 8vo, pp. xxx. and 346, cloth. 1854. 21s.
    Vol. III. 8vo, pp. xxiv. and 525, cloth. 1857. 21s.
    Vol. IV. Edited by E. B. Cowell, M.A. 8vo, pp. 214, cloth. 1866. 14s.
    Vols. V. and VI. in the Press.

RILEY.—MEDIÆVAL CHRONICLES OF THE CITY OF LONDON. Chronicles of the Mayors and Sheriffs of London, and the Events which happened in their Days, from the Year A.D. 1188 to A.D. 1274. Translated from the original Latin of the "Liber de Antiquis Legibus" (published by the Camden Society), in the possession of the Corporation of the City of London; attributed to Arnold Fitz-Thedmar, Alderman of London in the Reign of Henry III.—Chronicles of London, and of the Marvels therein, between the Years 44 Henry III., A.D. 1260, and 17 Edward III., A.D. 1343. Translated from the original Anglo-Norman of the "Croniques de London," preserved in the Cottonian Collection (Cleopatra A. iv.) in the British Museum. Translated, with copious Notes and Appendices, by Henry Thomas Riley, M.A., Clare Hall, Cambridge, Barrister-at-Law. 4to, pp. xii. and 319, cloth. 1863. 12s.

RIOLA.—How to Learn Russian: a Manual for Students of Russian, based upon the Ollendorffian System of Teaching Languages, and adapted for Self-Instruction. By Henry Riola, Teacher of the Russian Language. With a Preface by W.R.S. Ralston, M.A. Second Edition. Crown 8vo, pp. 576, cloth. 1883. 12s. Key to the above. Crown 8vo, pp. 126, cloth. 1878. 5s.

RIOLA.—A Graduated Russian Reader, with a Vocabulary of all the Russian Words contained in it. By Henry Riola, Author of "How to Learn Russian." Crown 8vo, pp. viii. and 314, cloth. 1879. 10s. 6d.

RIPLEY.—Sacred Rhetoric; or, Composition and Delivery of Sermons. By Henry I. Ripley. 12mo, pp. 234, cloth. 1858. 2s. 6d.

ROCHE.—A French Grammar, for the use of English Students, adopted for the Public Schools by the Imperial Council of Public Instruction. By A. Roche. Crown 8vo, pp. xii. and 176, cloth. 1869. 3s.

ROCHE.—Prose and Poetry. Select Pieces from the best English Authors, for Reading, Composition, and Translation. By A. Roche. Second Edition. Fcap. 8vo, pp. viii. and 226, cloth. 1872. 2s. 6d.

ROCKHILL.—Udanavarga. See Trübner's Oriental Series.

RODD.—The Birds of Cornwall and the Scilly Islands. By the late Edward Hearle Rodd. Edited, with an Introduction, Appendix, and Memoir, by J. E. Harting. 8vo, pp. lvi. and 320, with Portrait and Map, cloth. 1880. 14s.

ROGERS.—The Waverley Dictionary: An Alphabetical Arrangement of all the Characters in Sir Walter Scott's Waverley Novels, with a Descriptive Analysis of each Character, and Illustrative Selections from the Text. By May Rogers. 12mo, pp. 358, cloth. 1879. 10s.

ROSING.—English-Danish Dictionary. By S. Rosing. Crown 8vo, pp. x. and 722, cloth. 8s. 6d.

ROSS.—Alphabetical Manual of Blowpipe Analysis; showing all known Methods, Old and New. By Lieut.-Colonel W. A. Ross, late R.A., Member of the German Chemical Society (Author of "Pyrology, or Fire Chemistry"). Crown 8vo, pp. xii. and 148, cloth. 1880. 5s.

ROSS.—Pyrology, or Fire Chemistry; a Science interesting to the General Philosopher, and an Art of infinite importance to the Chemist, Metallurgist, Engineer, &c., &c. By W. A. Ross, lately a Major in the Royal Artillery. Small 4to, pp. xxviii. and 346, cloth. 1875. 36s.

ROSS.—Celebrities of the Yorkshire Wolds. By Frederick Ross, Fellow of the Royal Historical Society. 12mo, pp. 202, cloth. 1878. 4s.

ROSS.—The Early History of Land Holding among the Germans. By Denman W. Ross, Ph.D. 8vo, pp. viii. and 274, cloth. 1883. 12s.

ROSS.—Corean Primer: being Lessons in Corean on all Ordinary Subjects. Transliterated on the principles of the "Mandarin Primer," by the same author. By Rev. John Ross, Newchwang. 8vo, pp. 90, wrapper. 1877. 10s.

ROSS.—HONOUR OR SHAME? By R. S. Ross. 8vo, pp. 183. 1878. Cloth. 3s. 6d.; paper, 2s. 6d.

ROSS.—REMOVAL OF THE INDIAN TROOPS TO MALTA. By R. S. Ross. 8vo, pp. 77, paper. 1878. 1s. 6d.

ROSS.—THE MONK OF ST. GALL. A Dramatic Adaptation of Scheffel's "Ekkehard." By R. S. Ross. Crown 8vo, pp. xii. and 218. 1879. 5s.

ROSS.—ARIADNE IN NAXOS. By R. S. Ross. Square 16mo, pp. 200, cloth. 1882. 5s.

ROTH.—NOTES ON CONTINENTAL IRRIGATION. By H. L. Roth. Demy 8vo, pp. 40, with 8 Plates, cloth. 1882. 5s.

ROUGH NOTES OF JOURNEYS made in the years 1868-1873 in Syria, down the Tigris, India, Kashmir, Ceylon, Japan, Mongolia, Siberia, the United States, the Sandwich Islands, and Australasia. Demy 8vo, pp. 624, cloth. 1875. 14s.

ROUSTAING.—THE FOUR GOSPELS EXPLAINED BY THEIR WRITERS. With an Appendix on the Ten Commandments. Edited by J. B. Roustaing. Translated by W. E. Kirby. 3 vols. crown 8vo, pp. 440-456-304, cloth. 1881. 15s.

ROUTLEDGE.—ENGLISH RULE AND NATIVE OPINION IN INDIA. From Notes taken in 1870-74. By James Routledge. 8vo, pp. x. and 338, cloth. 1878. 10s. 6d.

ROWE.—AN ENGLISHMAN'S VIEWS ON QUESTIONS OF THE DAY IN VICTORIA. By C. J. Rowe, M.A. Crown 8vo, pp. 122, cloth. 1882. 4s.

ROWLEY.—ORNITHOLOGICAL MISCELLANY. By George Dawson Rowley, M.A., F.Z.S.
Vol. I. Part 1, 15s.—Part 2, 20s.—Part 3, 15s.—Part 4, 20s.
Vol. II. Part 5, 20s.—Part 6, 20s.—Part 7, 10s. 6d.—Part 8, 10s. 6d.—Part 9, 10s. 6d.—Part 10, 10s. 6d.
Vol. III. Part 11, 10s. 6d.—Part 12, 10s. 6d.—Part 13, 10s. 6d.—Part 14, 20s.

ROYAL SOCIETY OF LONDON (THE).—CATALOGUE OF SCIENTIFIC PAPERS (1800-1863), Compiled and Published by the Royal Society of London. Demy 4to, cloth, per vol. £1; in half-morocco, £1, 8s. Vol. I. (1867), A to Cluzel. pp. lxxix. and 960; Vol. II. (1868), Coaklay—Graydon. pp. iv. and 1012; Vol. III. (1869), Greatheed—Leze. pp. v. and 1002; Vol. IV. (1870), L'Héritier de Brutille—Pozzetti. pp. iv. and 1006; Vol. V. (1871), Prang—Tizzani. pp. iv. and 1000; Vol. VI. (1872), Tkalec—Zylius, Anonymous and Additions. pp. xi. and 763. Continuation of above (1864-1873); Vol. VII. (1877), A to Hyrtl. pp. xxxi. and 1047; Vol. VIII. (1879), Ibañez—Zwicky. pp. 1310. A List of the Publications of the Royal Society (Separate Papers from the Philosophical Transactions), on application.

RUNDALL.—A SHORT AND EASY WAY TO WRITE ENGLISH AS SPOKEN. Méthode Rapide et Facile d'Ecrire le Français comme on le Parle. Kurze und Leichte Weise Deutsch zu Schreiben wie man es Spricht. By J. B. Rundall, Certificated Member of the London Shorthand Writers' Association. 6d. each.

RUTHERFORD.—THE AUTOBIOGRAPHY OF MARK RUTHERFORD, Dissenting Minister. Edited by his friend, Reuben Shapcott. Crown 8vo, pp. xii. and 180, boards. 1881. 5s.

RUTTER.—See BUNYAN.

SÂMAVIDHÂNABRÂHMANA (THE) (being the Third Brâhmana) of the Sâma Veda. Edited, together with the Commentary of Sâyana, an English Translation, Introduction, and Index of Words, by A. C. Burnell. Vol. I. Text and Commentary, with Introduction. Demy 8vo, pp. xxxviii. and 104, cloth. 1873. 12s. 6d.

SAMUELSON.—HISTORY OF DRINK. A Review, Social, Scientific, and Political. By James Samuelson, of the Middle Temple, Barrister-at-Law. Second Edition. 8vo, pp. xxviii. and 288, cloth. 1880. 6s.

SAND.—MOLIÈRE. A Drama in Prose. By George Sand. Edited, with Notes, by Th. Karcher, LL.B. 12mo, pp. xx. and 170, cloth. 1868. 3s. 6d.

SARTORIUS.—MEXICO. Landscapes and Popular Sketches. By C. Sartorius. Edited by Dr. Gaspey. With Engravings, from Sketches by M. Rugendas. 4to, pp. vi. and 202, cloth gilt. 1859. 18s.

SATOW.—AN ENGLISH JAPANESE DICTIONARY OF THE SPOKEN LANGUAGE. By Ernest Mason Satow, Japanese Secretary to H.M. Legation at Yedo, and Ishibashi Masakata of the Imperial Japanese Foreign Office. Second Edition. Imperial 32mo, pp. xv. and 416, cloth. 1879. 12s. 6d.

SAVAGE.—THE MORALS OF EVOLUTION. By M. J. Savage, Author of "The Religion of Evolution," &c. Crown 8vo, pp. 192, cloth. 1880. 5s.

SAVAGE.—BELIEF IN GOD; an Examination of some Fundamental Theistic Problems. By M. J. Savage. To which is added an Address on the Intellectual Basis of Faith. By W. H. Savage. 8vo, pp. 176, cloth. 1881. 5s.

SAVAGE.—BELIEFS ABOUT MAN. By M. J. Savage. Crown 8vo, pp. 130, cloth. 1882. 5s.

SAYCE.—AN ASSYRIAN GRAMMAR for Comparative Purposes. By A. H. Sayce, M.A., Fellow and Tutor of Queen's College, Oxford. Crown 8vo, pp. xvi. and 188, cloth. 1872. 7s. 6d.

SAYCE.—THE PRINCIPLES OF COMPARATIVE PHILOLOGY. By A. H. Sayce, M.A. Crown 8vo, pp. 384, cloth. 1874. 10s. 6d.

SCHAIBLE.—AN ESSAY ON THE SYSTEMATIC TRAINING OF THE BODY. By C. H. Schaible, M.D., &c., &c. A Memorial Essay, Published on the occasion of the first Centenary Festival of Frederick L. Jahn, with an Etching by H. Herkomer. Crown 8vo, pp. xviii. and 124, cloth. 1878. 5s.

SCHEFFEL.—MOUNTAIN PSALMS. By J. V. von Scheffel. Translated by Mrs. F. Brunnow. Fcap., pp. 62, with 6 Plates after designs by A. Von Werner. Parchment. 1882. 3s. 6d.

SCHILLER.—THE BRIDE OF MESSINA. Translated from the German of Schiller in English Verse. By Emily Allfrey. Crown 8vo, pp. viii. and 110, cloth. 1876. 2s.

SCHLAGINTWEIT.—BUDDHISM IN TIBET: Illustrated by Literary Documents and Objects of Religious Worship. By Emil Schlagintweit, LL.D. With a folio Atlas of 20 Plates, and 20 Tables of Native Print in the Text. Roy. 8vo, pp. xxiv. and 404. 1863. £2, 2s.

SCHLAU, SCHLAUER, AM SCHLÄUESTEN.—Facsimile of a Manuscript supposed to have been found in an Egyptian Tomb by the English Soldiers. Royal 8vo, in ragged canvas covers, with string binding, and dilapidated edges (? just as discovered). 1884. 6s.

SCHLEICHER.—A COMPENDIUM OF THE COMPARATIVE GRAMMAR OF THE INDO-EUROPEAN, SANSKRIT, GREEK, AND LATIN LANGUAGES. By August Schleicher. Translated from the Third German Edition, by Herbert Bendall, B.A., Chr. Coll., Camb. 8vo. Part I., Phonology. Pp. 184, cloth. 1874. 7s. 6d. Part II., Morphology. Pp. viii. and 104, cloth. 1877. 6s.

SCHOPENHAUER.—THE WORLD AS WILL AND IDEA. By Arthur Schopenhauer. Translated from the German by R. B. HALDANE, M.A., and J. KEMP, M.A. Vol. I., containing Four Books. Post 8vo, pp. xxxii.-532, cloth. 1883. 18s.

SCHULTZ.—UNIVERSAL DOLLAR TABLES (Complete United States). Covering all Exchanges between the United States and Great Britain, France, Belgium, Switzerland, Italy, Spain, and Germany. By C. W. H. Schultz. 8vo, cloth. 1874. 15s.

SCHULTZ.—UNIVERSAL INTEREST AND GENERAL PERCENTAGE TABLES: On the Decimal System. With a Treatise on the Currency of the World, and numerous examples for Self-Instruction. By C. W. H. Schultz. 8vo, cloth. 1874. 10s. 6d.

SCHULTZ.—ENGLISH GERMAN EXCHANGE TABLES. By C. W. H. Schultz. With a Treatise on the Currency of the World. 8vo, boards. 1874. 5s.

SCHWENDLER.—INSTRUCTIONS FOR TESTING TELEGRAPH LINES, and the Technical Arrangements in Offices. Written on behalf of the Government of India, under the Orders of the Director-General of Telegraphs in India. By Louis Schwendler. Vol. I., demy 8vo, pp. 248, cloth. 1878. 12s. Vol. II., demy 8vo, pp. xi. and 268, cloth. 1880. 9s.

SCOONES.—FAUST. A Tragedy. By Goethe. Translated into English Verse, by William Dalton Scoones. Fcap., pp. vi. and 230, cloth. 1879. 5s.

SCOTT.—THE ENGLISH LIFE OF JESUS. By Thomas Scott. Crown 8vo, pp. xxviii. and 350, cloth. 1879. 2s. 6d.

SCOTUS.—A NOTE ON MR. GLADSTONE'S "The Peace to Come." By Scotus. 8vo, pp. 106. 1878. Cloth, 2s. 6d.; paper wrapper, 1s. 6d.

SELL.—THE FAITH OF ISLAM. By the Rev. E. Sell, Fellow of the University of Madras. Demy 8vo, pp. xiv. and 270, cloth. 1881. 6s. 6d.

SELL.—IHN-I-TAJWID; OR, ART OF READING THE QURAN. By the Rev. E. Sell, B.D. 8vo, pp. 48, wrappers. 1882. 2s. 6d.

SELSS.—GOETHE'S MINOR POEMS. Selected, Annotated, and Rearranged. By Albert M. Selss, Ph.D. Crown 8vo, pp. xxxi. and 152, cloth. 1875. 3s. 6d.

SERMONS NEVER PREACHED. By Philip Phosphor. Crown 8vo, pp. vi. and 124, cloth. 1878. 2s. 6d.

SEWELL.—REPORT ON THE AMARAVATI TOPE, and Excavations on its Site in 1877. By Robert Sewell, of the Madras C.S., &c. With four plates. Royal 4to, pp. 70, boards. 1880. 3s.

SHADWELL.—POLITICAL ECONOMY FOR THE PEOPLE. By J. L. Shadwell, Author of "A System of Political Economy." Fcap., pp. vi. and 154, limp cloth. 1880. 1s. 6d.

SHAKESPEARE.—A NEW STUDY OF SHAKESPEARE: An Inquiry into the connection of the Plays and Poems, with the origins of the Classical Drama, and with the Platonic Philosophy, through the Mysteries. Demy 8vo, pp. xii. and 372, with Photograph of the Stratford Bust, cloth. 1884. 10s. 6d.

SHAKESPEARE'S CENTURIE OF PRAYSE; being Materials for a History of Opinion on Shakespeare and his Works, culled from Writers of the First Century after his Rise. By C. M. Ingleby. Medium 8vo, pp. xx. and 384. Stiff cover. 1874. £1, 1s. Large paper, fcap. 4to, boards. £2, 2s.

SHAKESPEARE.—HERMENEUTICS; OR, THE STILL LION. Being an Essay towards the Restoration of Shakespeare's Text. By C. M. Ingleby, M.A., LL.D., of Trinity College, Cambridge. Small 4to, pp. 168, boards. 1875. 6s.

SHAKESPEARE.—THE MAN AND THE BOOK. By C. M. Ingleby, M.A., LL.D. Small 4to. Part I., pp. 172, boards. 1877. 6s.

SHAKESPEARE.—OCCASIONAL PAPERS ON SHAKESPEARE; being the Second Part of "Shakespeare: the Man and the Book." By C. M. Ingleby, M.A., LL.D., V.P.R.S.L. Small 4to, pp. x. and 194, paper boards. 1881. 6s.

SHAKESPEARE'S BONES.—The Proposal to Disinter them, considered in relation to their possible bearing on his Portraiture: Illustrated by instances of Visits of the Living to the Dead. By C. M. Ingleby, LL.D., V.P.R.S.L. Fcap. 4to, pp. viii. and 48, boards. 1883. 1s. 6d.

SHAKESPEARE.—A NEW VARIORUM EDITION OF SHAKESPEARE. Edited by Horace Howard Furness. Royal 8vo. Vol. I. Romeo and Juliet. Pp. xxiii. and 480, cloth. 1871. 18s.—Vol. II. Macbeth. Pp. xix. and 492. 1873. 18s.—Vols. III. and IV. Hamlet. 2 vols. pp. xx. and 474 and 430. 1877. 36s.—Vol. V. King Lear. Pp. vi. and 504. 1880. 18s.

SHAKESPEARE.—CONCORDANCE TO SHAKESPEARE'S POEMS. By Mrs. H. H. Furness. Royal 8vo, cloth. 18s.

SHAKSPERE SOCIETY (THE NEW).—Subscription, One Guinea per annum. List of Publications on application.

SHERRING.—THE SACRED CITY OF THE HINDUS. An Account of Benares in Ancient and Modern Times. By the Rev. M. A. Sherring, M.A., LL.D.; and Prefaced with an Introduction by FitzEdward Hall, D.C.L. With Illustrations. 8vo, pp. xxxvi. and 388, cloth. 21s.

SHERRING.—HINDU TRIBES AND CASTES; together with an Account of the Mohamedan Tribes of the North-West Frontier and of the Aboriginal Tribes of the Central Provinces. By the Rev. M. A. Sherring, M.A., LL.B., Lond., &c. 4to. Vol. II. Pp. lxviii. and 376, cloth. 1879. £2, 8s.—Vol. III., with Index of 3 vols. Pp. xii. and 336, cloth. 1881. 32s.

SHERRING.—THE HINDOO PILGRIMS. By Rev. M. A. Sherring, M.A., LL.D. Crown 8vo, pp. 126, cloth. 1878. 5s.

SHIELDS.—THE FINAL PHILOSOPHY; or, System of Perfectible Knowledge issuing from the Harmony of Science and Religion. By Charles W. Shields, D.D., Professor in Princeton College. Royal 8vo, pp. viii. and 610, cloth. 1878. 18s.

SIBREE.—THE GREAT AFRICAN ISLAND. Chapters on Madagascar. A Popular Account of Recent Researches in the Physical Geography, Geology, and Exploration of the Country, and its Natural History and Botany; and in the Origin and Divisions, Customs and Language, Superstitions, Folk-lore, and Religious Beliefs and Practices of the Different Tribes. Together with Illustrations of Scripture and Early Church History from Native Habits and Missionary Experience. By the Rev. James Sibree, jun., F.R.G.S., Author of "Madagascar and its People," &c. 8vo, pp. xii. and 272, with Physical and Ethnological Maps and Four Illustrations, cloth. 1879. 12s.

SIBREE.—POEMS; including "Fancy," "A Resting Place," &c. By John Sibree, M.A., London. Crown 8vo, pp. iv. and 134, cloth. 1884. 4s.

SIMCOX.—EPISODES IN THE LIVES OF MEN, WOMEN, AND LOVERS. By Edith Simcox. Crown 8vo, pp. 312, cloth. 1882. 7s. 6d.

SIMCOX.—NATURAL LAW. See English and Foreign Philosophical Library, Vol. IV.

SIME.—LESSING. See English and Foreign Philosophical Library, Extra Series, Vols. I. and II.

SIMPSON-BAIKIE.—THE DRAMATIC UNITIES IN THE PRESENT DAY. By E. Simpson-Baikie. Third Edition. Fcap. 8vo, pp. iv. and 108, cloth. 1878. 2s. 6d.

SIMPSON-BAIKIE.—THE INTERNATIONAL DICTIONARY for Naturalists and Sportsmen in English, French, and German. By Edwin Simpson-Baikie. 8vo, pp. iv. and 284, cloth. 1880. 15s.

SINCLAIR.—THE MESSENGER: A Poem. By Thomas Sinclair, M.A. Foolscap 8vo, pp. 174, cloth. 1875. 5s.

SINCLAIR.—LOVE'S TRILOGY: A Poem. By Thomas Sinclair, M.A. Crown 8vo, pp. 150, cloth. 1876. 5s.

SINCLAIR.—THE MOUNT: Speech from its English Heights. By Thomas Sinclair, M.A. Crown 8vo, pp. viii. and 302, cloth. 1877. 10s.

SINCLAIR.—GODDESS FORTUNE: A Novel. By Thomas Sinclair, Author of "The Messenger," &c. Three vols., post 8vo, pp. viii.-302, 302, 274, cloth. 1884. 31s. 6d.

SINGER.—HUNGARIAN GRAMMAR. See Trübner's Collection.

SINNETT.—THE OCCULT WORLD. By A. P. Sinnett. Fourth Edition. 8vo, pp. xx. and 206, cloth. 1884. 3s. 6d.

SINNETT.—ESOTERIC BUDDHISM. By A. P. Sinnett, Author of "The Occult World," President of the Simla Eclectic Philosophical Society. Third Edition. Crown 8vo, pp. xx.-216, cloth. 1884. 7s. 6d.

SMITH.—THE DIVINE GOVERNMENT. By S. Smith, M.D. Fifth Edition. Crown 8vo, pp. xii. and 276, cloth. 1866. 6s.

SMITH.—THE RECENT DEPRESSION OF TRADE. Its Nature, its Causes, and the Remedies which have been suggested for it. By Walter E. Smith, B.A., New College. Being the Oxford Cobden Prize Essay for 1879. Crown 8vo, pp. vi. and 108, cloth. 1880. 3s.

SMYTH.—THE ABORIGINES OF VICTORIA. With Notes relating to the Habits of the Natives of other Parts of Australia and Tasmania. Compiled from various sources for the Government of Victoria. By R. Brough Smyth, F.L.S., F.G.S., &c., &c. 2 vols. royal 8vo, pp. lxxii.-484 and vi.-456, Maps, Plates, and Woodcuts, cloth. 1878. £3, 3s.

SNOW—A THEOLOGICO-POLITICAL TREATISE. By G. D. Snow. Crown 8vo, pp. 180, cloth. 1874. 4s. 6d.

SOLLING.—DIUTISKA: An Historical and Critical Survey of the Literature of Germany, from the Earliest Period to the Death of Goethe. By Gustav Solling. 8vo, pp. xviii. and 368. 1863. 10s. 6d.

SOLLING.—SELECT PASSAGES FROM THE WORKS OF SHAKESPEARE. Translated and Collected. German and English. By G. Solling. 12mo, pp. 155, cloth. 1866. 3s. 6d.

SOLLING.—MACBETH. Rendered into Metrical German (with English Text adjoined). By Gustav Solling. Crown 8vo, pp. 160, wrapper. 1878. 3s. 6d.

SONGS OF THE SEMITIC IN ENGLISH VERSE. By G. E. W. Crown 8vo, pp. iv. and 134, cloth. 1877. 5s.

SOUTHALL.—THE EPOCH OF THE MAMMOTH AND THE APPARITION OF MAN UPON EARTH. By James C. Southall, A.M., LL.D. Crown 8vo, pp. xii. and 430, cloth. Illustrated. 1878. 10s. 6d.

SPANISH REFORMERS OF TWO CENTURIES FROM 1520; Their Lives and Writing, according to the late Benjamin B. Wiffen's Plan, and with the Use of His Materials. Described by E. Boehmer, D.D., Ph.D. Vol. I. With B. B. Wiffen's Narrative of the Incidents attendant upon the Republication of Reformistas Antiguos Españoles, and with a Memoir of B. B. Wiffen. By Isaline Wiffen. Royal 8vo, pp. xvi. and 216, cloth. 1874. 12s. 6d. Roxburghe, 15s.—Vol. II. Royal 8vo, pp. xii.-374, cloth. 1883. 18s.

SPEDDING.—THE LIFE AND TIMES OF FRANCIS BACON. Extracted from the Edition of his Occasional Writings, by James Spedding. 2 vols. post 8vo, pp. xx.-710 and xiv.-708, cloth. 1878. 21s.

SPIERS.—THE SCHOOL SYSTEM OF THE TALMUD. By the Rev. B. Spiers. 8vo, pp. 48, cloth. 1882. 2s. 6d.

SPINOZA.—BENEDICT DE SPINOZA: his Life, Correspondence, and Ethics. By R. Willis, M.D. 8vo, pp. xliv. and 648, cloth. 1870. 21s.

SPINOZA.—ETHIC DEMONSTRATED IN GEOMETRICAL ORDER AND DIVIDED INTO FIVE PARTS, which treat—I. Of God; II. Of the Nature and Origin of the Mind; III. Of the Origin and Nature of the Affects; IV. Of Human Bondage, or of the Strength of the Affects; V. Of the Power of the Intellect, or of Human Liberty. By Benedict de Spinoza. Translated from the Latin by W. Hale White. Post 8vo, pp. 328, cloth. 1883. 10s. 6d.

SPIRITUAL EVOLUTION, AN ESSAY ON, considered in its bearing upon Modern Spiritualism, Science, and Religion. By J. P. B. Crown 8vo, pp. 156, cloth. 1879. 3s.

SPRUNER.—DR. KARL VON SPRUNER'S HISTORICO-GEOGRAPHICAL HAND-ATLAS, containing 26 Coloured Maps. Obl. cloth. 1861. 15s.

SQUIER.—HONDURAS; Descriptive, Historical, and Statistical. By E. G. Squier, M.A., F.S.A. Cr. 8vo, pp. viii. and 278, cloth. 1870. 3s. 6d.

STATIONERY OFFICE.—PUBLICATIONS OF HER MAJESTY'S STATIONERY OFFICE. List on application.

STEDMAN.—OXFORD: Its Social and Intellectual Life. With Remarks and Hints on Expenses, the Examinations, &c. By Algernon M. M. Stedman, B.A., Wadham College, Oxford. Crown 8vo, pp. xvi. and 309, cloth. 1878. 7s. 6d.

STEELE.—AN EASTERN LOVE STORY. Kusa Játakaya: A Buddhistic Legendary Poem, with other Stories. By Th. Steele. Cr. 8vo, pp. xii. and 260, cl. 1871. 6s.

STENT.—THE JADE CHAPLET. In Twenty-four Beads. A Collection of Songs, Ballads, &c. (from the Chinese). By G. C. Stent, M.N.C.B.R.A.S. Post 8vo, pp. viii. and 168, cloth. 1874. 5s.

STENZLER.—See AUCTORES SANSKRITI, Vol. II.

STOCK.—ATTEMPTS AT TRUTH. By St. George Stock. Crown 8vo, pp. vi. and 248, cloth. 1882. 5s.

STOKES.—GOIDELICA—Old and Early-Middle Irish Glosses: Prose and Verse. Edited by Whitley Stokes. 2d Edition. Med. 8vo, pp. 192, cloth. 1872. 18s.

STOKES.—BEUNANS MERIASEK. The Life of Saint Meriasek, Bishop and Confessor. A Cornish Drama. Edited, with a Translation and Notes, by Whitley Stokes. Med. 8vo, pp. xvi. and 280, and Facsimile, cloth. 1872. 15s.

STOKES.—TOGAIL TROY, THE DESTRUCTION OF TROY. Transcribed from the Facsimile of the Book of Leinster, and Translated, with a Glossarial Index of the Rarer Words, by Whitley Stokes. Crown 8vo, pp. xvi. and 188, paper boards. 1882. 18s.

STOKES.—THREE MIDDLE-IRISH HOMILIES ON THE LIVES OF SAINTS—PATRICK, BRIGIT, AND COLUMBA. Edited by Whitley Stokes. Crown 8vo, pp. xii. and 140, paper boards. 1882. 10s. 6d.

STRANGE.—THE BIBLE; is it "The Word of God"? By Thomas Lumisden Strange. Demy 8vo, pp. xii. and 384, cloth. 1871. 7s.

STRANGE.—THE SPEAKER'S COMMENTARY. Reviewed by T. L. Strange. Cr. 8vo, pp. viii. and 159, cloth. 1871. 2s. 6d.

STRANGE.—THE DEVELOPMENT OF CREATION ON THE EARTH. By T. L. Strange. Demy 8vo, pp. xii. and 110, cloth. 1874. 2s. 6d.

STRANGE.—THE LEGENDS OF THE OLD TESTAMENT. By T. L. Strange. Demy 8vo, pp. xii. and 244, cloth. 1874. 5s.

STRANGE.—THE SOURCES AND DEVELOPMENT OF CHRISTIANITY. By Thomas Lumisden Strange. Demy 8vo, pp. xx. and 256, cloth. 1875. 5s.

STRANGE.—WHAT IS CHRISTIANITY? An Historical Sketch. Illustrated with a Chart. By T. L. Strange. Foolscap 8vo, pp. 72, cloth. 1880. 2s. 6d.

STRANGE.—CONTRIBUTIONS TO A SERIES OF CONTROVERSIAL WRITINGS, issued by the late Mr. Thomas Scott, of Upper Norwood. By Thomas Lumisden Strange. Fcap. 8vo, pp. viii. and 312, cloth. 1881. 2s. 6d.

STRANGFORD.—ORIGINAL LETTERS AND PAPERS OF THE LATE VISCOUNT STRANGFORD UPON PHILOLOGICAL AND KINDRED SUBJECTS. Edited by Viscountess Strangford. Post 8vo, pp. xxii. and 284, cloth. 1878. 12s. 6d.

STRATMANN.—THE TRAGICALL HISTORIE OF HAMLET, PRINCE OF DENMARKE. By William Shakespeare. Edited according to the first printed Copies, with the various Readings and Critical Notes. By F. H. Stratmann. 8vo, pp. vi. and 120, sewed. 3s. 6d.

STRATMANN.—A DICTIONARY OF THE OLD ENGLISH LANGUAGE. Compiled from Writings of the Twelfth, Thirteenth, Fourteenth, and Fifteenth Centuries. By F. H. Stratmann. Third Edition. 4to, pp. x. and 662, sewed. 1878. 30s.

STUDIES OF MAN. By a Japanese. Crown 8vo, pp. 124, cloth. 1874. 2s. 6d.

SUMNER.—WHAT SOCIAL CLASSES OWE TO EACH OTHER. By W. G. Sumner, Professor of Political and Social Science in Yale College. 18mo, pp. 170, cloth. 1884. 3s. 6d.

SUYEMATZ.—GENJI MONOGATARI. The Most Celebrated of the Classical Japanese Romances. Translated by K. Suyematz. Crown 8vo, pp. xvi. and 254, cloth. 1882. 7s. 6d.

SWEET.—SPELLING REFORM AND ENGLISH LITERATURE. By Henry Sweet, M.A. 8vo, pp. 8, wrapper. 1884. 2d.

SWEET.—HISTORY OF ENGLISH SOUNDS, from the Earliest Period, including an Investigation of the General Laws of Sound Change, and full Word Lists. By Henry Sweet. Demy 8vo, pp. iv.-164, cloth. 1874. 4s. 6d.

SWEET.—ON A MEXICAN MUSTANG THROUGH TEXAS FROM THE GULF TO THE RIO GRANDE. By Alex. E. Sweet and J. Armoy Knox, Editors of "Texas Siftings." English Copyright Edition. Demy 8vo, pp. 672. Illustrated, cloth. 1883. 10s.

SYED AHMAD.—A SERIES OF ESSAYS ON THE LIFE OF MOHAMMED, and Subjects subsidiary thereto. By Syed Ahmad Khan Bahadur, C.S.I. 8vo, pp. 532, with 4 Tables, 2 Maps, and Plate, cloth. 1870. 30s.

TALBOT.—ANALYSIS OF THE ORGANISATION OF THE PRUSSIAN ARMY. By Lieutenant Gerald F. Talbot, 2d Prussian Dragoon Guards. Royal 8vo, pp. 78, cloth. 1871. 3s.

TAYLER.—A RETROSPECT OF THE RELIGIOUS LIFE OF ENGLAND; or, Church, Puritanism, and Free Inquiry. By J. J. Tayler, B.A. Second Edition. Reissued, with an Introductory Chapter on Recent Development, by James Martineau, LL.D., D.D. Post 8vo, pp. 380, cloth. 1876. 7s. 6d.

TAYLOR.—PRINCE DEUKALION: A Lyrical Drama. By Bayard Taylor. Small 4to, pp. 172. Handsomely bound in white vellum. 1878. 12s.

TECHNOLOGICAL DICTIONARY of the Terms employed in the Arts and Sciences; Architecture; Civil Engineering; Mechanics; Machine-Making; Shipbuilding and Navigation; Metallurgy; Artillery; Mathematics; Physics; Chemistry; Mineralogy, &c. With a Preface by Dr. K. Karmarsch. Second Edition. 3 vols.
    Vol. I. German-English-French. 8vo, pp. 646. 12s.
    Vol. II. English-German-French. 8vo, pp. 666. 12s.
    Vol. III. French-German-English. 8vo, pp. 618. 12s.

TECHNOLOGICAL DICTIONARY.—A POCKET DICTIONARY OF TECHNICAL TERMS USED IN ARTS AND MANUFACTURES. English-German-French, Deutsch-Englisch-Französisch, Français-Allemand-Anglais. Abridged from the above Technological Dictionary by Rumpf, Mothes, and Unverzagt. With the addition of Commercial Terms. 3 vols. sq. 12mo, cloth, 12s.

THEÁTRE FRANÇAIS MODERNE.—A Selection of Modern French Plays. Edited by the Rev. P. H. E. Brette, B.D., C. Cassal, LL.D., and Th. Karcher, LL.B.
    First Series, in 1 vol. crown 8vo, cloth, 6s., containing—
CHARLOTTE CORDAY. A Tragedy. By F. Ponsard. Edited, with English Notes and Notice on Ponsard, by Professor C. Cassal, LL.D. Pp. xii. and 134. Separately, 2s. 6d.
DIANE. A Drama in Verse. By Emile Augier. Edited, with English Notes and Notice on Augier, by Th. Karcher, LL.B. Pp. xiv. and 145. Separately, 2s. 6d.
LE VOYAGE À DIEPPE, A Comedy in Prose. By Wafflard and Fulgence. Edited, with English Notes, by the Rev. P. H. E. Brette, B.D. Pp. 104. Separately, 2s. 6d.
    Second Series, crown 8vo, cloth, 6s., containing—
MOLIÈRE. A Drama in Prose. By George Sand. Edited, with English Notes and Notice of George Sand, by Th. Karcher, LL.B. Fcap. 8vo, pp. xx. and 170, cloth. Separately, 3s. 6d.
LES ARISTOCRATIES. A Comedy in Verse. By Etienne Arago. Edited, with English Notes and Notice of Etienne Arago, by the Rev. P. H. E. Brette, B.D. 2d Edition. Fcap. 8vo, pp. xiv. and 236, cloth. Separately, 4s

THEÁTRE FRANÇAIS MODERNE—*continued*.
Third Series, crown 8vo, cloth, 6s., containing—
LES FAUX BONSHOMMES. A Comedy. By Théodore Barrière and Ernest Capendu. Edited, with English Notes and Notice on Barrière, by Professor C. Cassal, LL.D. Fcap. 8vo, pp. xvi. and 304. 1868. Separately, 4s.

L'HONNEUR ET L'ARGENT. A Comedy. By François Ponsard. Edited, with English Notes and Memoir of Ponsard, by Professor C. Cassal, LL.D. 2d Edition. Fcap. 8vo, pp. xvi. and 171, cloth. 1869. Separately, 3s. 6d.

THEISM.—A CANDID EXAMINATION OF THEISM. By Physicus. Post 8vo, pp. xviii. and 198, cloth. 1878. 7s. 6d.

THEOSOPHY AND THE HIGHER LIFE; or, Spiritual Dynamics and the Divine and Miraculous Man. By G. W., M.D., Edinburgh. President of the British Theosophical Society. 12mo, pp. iv. and 138, cloth. 1880. 3s.

THOM.—ST. PAUL'S EPISTLES TO THE CORINTHIANS. An Attempt to convey their Spirit and Significance. By the Rev. J. H. Thom. 8vo, pp. xii. and 408, cloth. 1851. 5s.

THOMAS.—EARLY SASSANIAN INSCRIPTIONS, SEALS, AND COINS, illustrating the Early History of the Sassanian Dynasty, containing Proclamations of Ardeshir Babek, Sapor I., and his Successors. With a Critical Examination and Explanation of the celebrated Inscription in the Hájíábad Cave, demonstrating that Sapor, the Conqueror of Valerian, was a professing Christian. By Edward Thomas. Illustrated. 8vo, pp. 148, cloth. 7s. 6d.

THOMAS.—THE CHRONICLES OF THE PATHAN KINGS OF DEHLI. Illustrated by Coins, Inscriptions, and other Antiquarian Remains. By E. Thomas, F.R.A.S. With Plates and Cuts. Demy 8vo, pp. xxiv. and 467, cloth. 1871. 28s.

THOMAS.—THE REVENUE RESOURCES OF THE MUGHAL EMPIRE IN INDIA, from A.D. 1593 to A.D. 1707. A Supplement to "The Chronicles of the Pathán Kings of Delhi." By E. Thomas, F.R.S. 8vo, pp. 60, cloth. 3s. 6d.

THOMAS.—SASSANIAN COINS. Communicated to the Numismatic Society of London. By E. Thomas, F.R.S. Two Parts, 12mo, pp. 43, 3 Plates and a Cut, sewed. 5s.

THOMAS.—JAINISM; OR, THE EARLY FAITH OF ASOKA. With Illustrations of the Ancient Religions of the East, from the Pantheon of the Indo-Scythians. To which is added a Notice on Bactrian Coins and Indian Dates. By Edward Thomas, F.R.S. 8vo, pp. viii.-24 and 82. With two Autotype Plates and Woodcuts. 1877. 7s. 6d.

THOMAS.—THE THEORY AND PRACTICE OF CREOLE GRAMMAR. By J. J. Thomas. 8vo, pp. viii. and 135, boards. 12s.

THOMAS.—RECORDS OF THE GUPTA DYNASTY. Illustrated by Inscriptions, Written History, Local Tradition, and Coins. To which is added a Chapter on the Arabs in Sind. By Edward Thomas, F.R.S. Folio, with a Plate, pp. iv. and 64, cloth. 14s.

THOMAS.—BOYHOOD LAYS. By William Henry Thomas. 18mo, pp. iv. and 74, cloth. 1877. 2s. 6d.

THOMPSON.—DIALOGUES, RUSSIAN AND ENGLISH. Compiled by A. R. Thompson, sometime Lecturer of the English Language in the University of St. Vladimir Kieff. Crown 8vo, pp. iv. and 132, cloth. 1882. 5s.

THOMSON.—EVOLUTION AND INVOLUTION. By George Thomson, Author of "The World of Being," &c. Crown 8vo, pp. viii. and 206, cloth. 1880. 5s.

E

THORBURN.—BANNÚ; OR, OUR AFGHAN FRONTIER. By S. S. Thorburn, F.C.S., Settlement Officer of the Bannú District. 8vo, pp. x. and 480, cloth. 1876. 18s.

THORPE.—DIPLOMATARIUM ANGLICUM ÆVI SAXONICI. A Collection of English Charters, from the reign of King Æthelberht of Kent, A.D. DCV., to that of William the Conqueror. Containing: I. Miscellaneous Charters. II. Wills. III. Guilds. IV. Manumissions and Acquittances. With a Translation of the Anglo-Saxon. By the late Benjamin Thorpe, Member of the Royal Academy of Sciences at Munich, and of the Society of Netherlandish Literature at Leyden. 8vo, pp. xlii. and 682, cloth. 1865. £1, 1s.

THOUGHTS ON LOGIC; or, the S.N.I.X. Propositional Theory. Crown 8vo, pp. iv. and 76, cloth. 1877. 2s. 6d.

THOUGHTS ON THEISM, with Suggestions towards a Public Religious Service in Harmony with Modern Science and Philosophy. Ninth Thousand. Revised and Enlarged. 8vo, pp. 74, sewed. 1882. 1s.

THURSTON.—FRICTION AND LUBRICATION. Determinations of the Laws and Coefficients of Friction by new Methods and with new Apparatus. By Robert H. Thurston, A.M., C.E., &c. Crown 8vo, pp. xvi. and 212, cloth. 1879. 6s. 6d.

TIELE.—See English and Foreign Philosophical Library, Vol. VII. and Trübner's Oriental Series.

TOLHAUSEN.—A SYNOPSIS OF THE PATENT LAWS OF VARIOUS COUNTRIES. By A. Tolhausen, Ph.D. Third Edition. 12mo, pp. 62, sewed. 1870. 1s. 6d.

TONSBERG.—NORWAY. Illustrated Handbook for Travellers. Edited by Charles Tönsberg. With 134 Engravings on Wood, 17 Maps, and Supplement. Crown 8vo, pp. lxx., 482, and 32, cloth. 1875. 18s.

TOPOGRAPHICAL WORKS.—A LIST OF THE VARIOUS WORKS PREPARED AT THE TOPOGRAPHICAL AND STATISTICAL DEPARTMENT OF THE WAR OFFICE may be had on application.

TORCEANU.—ROUMANIAN GRAMMAR. See Trübner's Collection.

TORRENS.—EMPIRE IN ASIA: How we came by it. A Book of Confessions. By W. M. Torrens, M.P. Med. 8vo, pp. 426, cloth. 1872. 14s.

TOSCANI.—ITALIAN CONVERSATIONAL COURSE. A New Method of Teaching the Italian Language, both Theoretically and Practically. By Giovanni Toscani, Professor of the Italian Language and Literature in Queen's Coll., London, &c. Fourth Edition. 12mo, pp. xiv. and 300, cloth. 1872. 5s.

TOSCANI.—ITALIAN READING COURSE. By G. Toscani. Fcap. 8vo, pp. xii. and 160. With table. Cloth. 1875. 4s. 6d.

TOULON.—ITS ADVANTAGES AS A WINTER RESIDENCE FOR INVALIDS AND OTHERS. By an English Resident. The proceeds of this pamphlet to be devoted to the English Church at Toulon. Crown 8vo, pp. 8, sewed. 1873. 6d.

TRADLEG.—A SON OF BELIAL. Autobiographical Sketches. By Nitram Tradleg, University of Bosphorus. Crown 8vo, pp. viii.-260, cloth. 1882. 5s.

TRIMEN.—SOUTH-AFRICAN BUTTERFLIES; a Monograph of the Extra-Tropical Species. By Roland Trimen, F.L.S., F.Z.S., M.E.S., Curator of the South African Museum, Cape Town. Royal 8vo. [In preparation.

TRÜBNER'S AMERICAN, EUROPEAN, AND ORIENTAL LITERARY RECORD. A Register of the most Important Works published in America, India, China, and the British Colonies. With Occasional Notes on German, Dutch, Danish, French, Italian, Spanish, Portuguese, and Russian Literature. The object of the Publishers in issuing this publication is to give a full and particular account of every publication of importance issued in America and the East. Small 4to, 6d. per number. Subscription, 5s. per volume.

TRÜBNER.—TRÜBNER'S BIBLIOGRAPHICAL GUIDE TO AMERICAN LITERATURE: A Classed List of Books published in the United States of America, from 1817 to 1857. With Bibliographical Introduction, Notes, and Alphabetical Index. Compiled and Edited by Nicolas Trübner. In 1 vol. 8vo, half bound, pp. 750. 1859. 18s.

TRÜBNER'S CATALOGUE OF DICTIONARIES AND GRAMMARS OF THE PRINCIPAL LANGUAGES AND DIALECTS OF THE WORLD. Considerably Enlarged and Revised, with an Alphabetical Index. A Guide for Students and Booksellers. Second Edition, 8vo, pp. viii. and 170, cloth. 1882. 5s.

TRÜBNER'S COLLECTION OF SIMPLIFIED GRAMMARS OF THE PRINCIPAL ASIATIC AND EUROPEAN LANGUAGES. Edited by Reinhold Rost, LL.D., Ph.D. Crown 8vo, cloth, uniformly bound.
   I.—HINDUSTANI, PERSIAN, AND ARABIC. By E. H. Palmer, M.A. Pp. 112. 1882. 5s.
   II.—HUNGARIAN. By I. Singer. Pp. vi. and 88. 1882. 4s. 6d.
   III.—BASQUE. By W. Van Eys. Pp. xii. and 52. 1883. 3s. 6d.
   IV.—MALAGASY. By G. W. Parker. Pp. 66, with Plate. 1883. 5s.
   V.—MODERN GREEK. By E. M. Geldart, M.A. Pp. 68. 1883. 2s. 6d.
   VI.—ROUMANIAN. By R. Torceanu. Pp. viii. and 72. 1883. 5s.
   VII.—TIBETAN GRAMMAR. By H. A. JASCHKE. Pp. viii.-104. 1883. 5s.
   VIII.—DANISH. By E. C. Otté. Pp. viii. and 66. 1884. 2s. 6d.
   IX.—TURKISH. By J. W. Redhouse, M.R.A.S. Pp. xii. and 204. 1884. 10s.6d.
   X.—SWEDISH. By E. C. Otté. Pp. xii.-70. 1884. 2s. 6d.
   XI.—POLISH. By W. R. Morfill, M.A. Pp. viii. and 64. 1884. 3s. 6d.

TRÜBNER'S ORIENTAL SERIES :—
   Post 8vo, cloth, uniformly bound.
ESSAYS ON THE SACRED LANGUAGE, WRITINGS, AND RELIGION OF THE PARSIS. By Martin Haug, Ph.D., late Professor of Sanskrit and Comparative Philology at the University of Munich. Third Edition. Edited and Enlarged by E. W. West, Ph.D. To which is also added, A Biographical Memoir of the late Dr. Haug. By Professor E. P. Evans. Pp. xlviii. and 428. 1884. 16s.

TEXTS FROM THE BUDDHIST CANON, commonly known as Dhammapada. With Accompanying Narratives. Translated from the Chinese by S. Beal, B.A., Trinity College, Cambridge, Professor of Chinese, University College, London. Pp. viii. and 176. 1878. 7s. 6d.

THE HISTORY OF INDIAN LITERATURE. By Albrecht Weber. Translated from the German by J. Mann, M.A., and Dr. T. Zachariae, with the Author's sanction and assistance. 2d Edition. Pp. 368. 1882. 10s. 6d.

A SKETCH OF THE MODERN LANGUAGES OF THE EAST INDIES. Accompanied by Two Language Maps, Classified List of Languages and Dialects, and a List of Authorities for each Language. By Robert Cust, late of H.M.I.C.S., and Hon. Librarian of R.A.S. Pp. xii. and 198. 1878. 12s.

THE BIRTH OF THE WAR-GOD: A Poem. By Kálidasá. Translated from the Sanskrit into English Verse, by Ralph T. H. Griffiths, M.A., Principal of Benares College. Second Edition. Pp. xii. and 116. 1879. 5s.

A CLASSICAL DICTIONARY OF HINDU MYTHOLOGY AND HISTORY, GEOGRAPHY AND LITERATURE. By John Dowson, M.R.A.S., late Professor in the Staff College. Pp. 432. 1879. 16s.

METRICAL TRANSLATIONS FROM SANSKRIT WRITERS; with an Introduction, many Prose Versions, and Parallel Passages from Classical Authors. By J. Muir, C.I.E., D.C.L., &c. Pp. xliv.-376. 1879. 14s.

MODERN INDIA AND THE INDIANS: being a Series of Impressions, Notes, and Essays. By Monier Williams, D.C.L., Hon. LL.D. of the University of Calcutta, Boden Professor of Sanskrit in the University of Oxford. Third Edition, revised and augmented by considerable additions. With Illustrations and Map, pp. vii. and 368. 1879. 14s.

A Catalogue of Important Works,

TRÜBNER'S ORIENTAL SERIES—*continued.*

THE LIFE OR LEGEND OF GAUDAMA, the Buddha of the Burmese. With Annotations, the Ways to Neibban, and Notice on the Phongyies, or Burmese Monks. By the Right Rev. P. Bigandet, Bishop of Ramatha, Vicar Apostolic of Ava and Pegu. Third Edition. 2 vols. Pp. xx.-368 and viii.-326. 1880. 21s.

MISCELLANEOUS ESSAYS, relating to Indian Subjects. By B. H. Hodgson, late British Minister at Nepal. 2 vols., pp. viii.-408, and viii.-348. 1880. 28s.

SELECTIONS FROM THE KORAN. By Edward William Lane, Author of an "Arabic-English Lexicon," &c. A New Edition, Revised, with an Introduction. By Stanley Lane Poole. Pp. cxii. and 174. 1879. 9s.

CHINESE BUDDHISM. A Volume of Sketches, Historical and Critical. By J. Edkins, D.D., Author of "China's Place in Philology," "Religion in China," &c., &c. Pp. lvi. and 454. 1880. 18s.

THE GULISTAN; OR, ROSE GARDEN OF SHEKH MUSHLIU'D-DIN SADI OF SHIRAZ. Translated for the first time into Prose and Verse, with Preface and a Life of the Author, from the Atish Kudah, by E. B. Eastwick, F.R.S., M.R.A.S. 2d Edition. Pp. xxvi. and 244. 1880. 10s. 6d.

A TALMUDIC MISCELLANY; or, One Thousand and One Extracts from the Talmud, the Midrashim, and the Kabbalah. Compiled and Translated by P. J. Hershon. With a Preface by Rev. F. W. Farrar, D.D., F.R.S., Chaplain in Ordinary to Her Majesty, and Canon of Westminster. With Notes and Copious Indexes. Pp. xxviii. and 362. 1880. 14s.

THE HISTORY OF ESARHADDON (Son of Sennacherib), King of Assyria, B.C. 681-668. Translated from the Cuneiform Inscriptions upon Cylinders and Tablets in the British Museum Collection. Together with Original Texts, a Grammatical Analysis of each word, Explanations of the Ideographs by Extracts from the Bi-Lingual Syllabaries, and List of Eponyms, &c. By E. A. Budge, B.A., M.R.A.S., Assyrian Exhibitioner, Christ's College, Cambridge. Post 8vo, pp. xii. and 164, cloth. 1880. 10s. 6d.

BUDDHIST BIRTH STORIES; or, Jātaka Tales. The oldest Collection of Folk-Lore extant: being the Jātakatthavannanā, for the first time edited in the original Pali, by V. Fausböll, and translated by T. W. Rhys Davids. Translation. Vol. I. Pp. cxvi. and 348. 1880. 18s.

THE CLASSICAL POETRY OF THE JAPANESE. By Basil Chamberlain, Author of "Yeigio Henkaku, Ichiran." Pp. xii. and 228. 1880. 7s. 6d.

LINGUISTIC AND ORIENTAL ESSAYS. Written from the year 1846-1878. By R. Cust, Author of "The Modern Languages of the East Indies." Pp. xii. and 484. 1880. 18s.

INDIAN POETRY. Containing a New Edition of "The Indian Song of Songs," from the Sanskrit of the Gita Govinda of Jayadeva; Two Books from "The Iliad of India" (Mahábhárata); "Proverbial Wisdom" from the Shlokas of the Hitopadésa, and other Oriental Poems. By Edwin Arnold, C.S.I., &c. Third Edition. Pp. viii. and 270. 1884. 7s. 6d.

THE RELIGIONS OF INDIA. By A. Barth. Authorised Translation by Rev. J. Wood. Pp. xx. and 310. 1881. 16s.

HINDU PHILOSOPHY. The Sânkhya Kârikâ of Iswara Krishna. An Exposition of the System of Kapila. With an Appendix on the Nyaya and Vaiseshika Systems. By John Davies, M.A., M.R.A.S. Pp. vi. and 151. 1881. 6s.

TRÜBNER'S ORIENTAL SERIES—continued.

A MANUAL OF HINDU PANTHEISM. The Vedantasara. Translated with Copious Annotations. By Major G. A. Jacob, Bombay Staff Corps, Inspector of Army Schools. With a Preface by E. B. Cowell, M.A., Professor of Sanskrit in the University of Cambridge. Pp. x. and 130 1881. 6s.

THE MESNEVĪ (usually known as the Mesnevīyi Sherīf, or Holy Mesnevī) of Mevlānā (Our Lord) Jelālu-'d-Din Muhammed, Er-Rūmī. Book the First. Together with some Account of the Life and Acts of the Author, of his Ancestors, and of his Descendants. Illustrated by a selection of Characteristic Anecdotes as collected by their Historian Mevlānā Shemsu-'d-Dīn Ahmed, El Eflākī El Arifī. Translated, and the Poetry Versified by James W. Redhouse, M.R.A.S., &c. Pp. xvi. and 136, vi. and 290. 1881. £1, 1s.

EASTERN PROVERBS AND EMBLEMS ILLUSTRATING OLD TRUTHS. By the Rev. J. Long, Member of the Bengal Asiatic Society, F.R.G.S. Pp. xv. and 280. 1881. 6s.

THE QUATRAINS OF OMAR KHAYYÁM. A New Translation. By E. H. Whinfield, late of H.M. Bengal Civil Service. Pp. 96. 1881. 5s.

THE QUATRAINS OF OMAR KHAYYÁM. The Persian Text, with an English Verse Translation. By E. H. Whinfield. Pp. xxxii.-335. 1883. 10s. 6d.

THE MIND OF MENCIUS; or, Political Economy Founded upon Moral Philosophy. A Systematic Digest of the Doctrines of the Chinese Philosopher Mencius. The Original Text Classified and Translated, with Comments, by the Rev. E. Faber, Rhenish Mission Society. Translated from the German, with Additional Notes, by the Rev. A. B. Hutchinson, Church Mission, Hong Kong. Author in Chinese of "Primer Old Testament History," &c., &c. Pp. xvi. and 294. 1882. 10s. 6d.

YÚSUF AND ZULAIKHA. A Poem by Jami. Translated from the Persian into English Verse. By R. T. H. Griffith. Pp. xiv. and 304. 1882. 8s. 6d.

TSUNI-ǁGOAM: The Supreme Being of the Khoi-Khoi. By Theophilus Hahn, Ph.D., Custodian of the Grey Collection, Cape Town, Corresponding Member of the Geographical Society, Dresden; Corresponding Member of the Anthropological Society, Vienna, &c., &c. Pp. xii. and 154. 1882. 7s. 6d.

A COMPREHENSIVE COMMENTARY TO THE QURAN. To which is prefixed Sale's Preliminary Discourse, with Additional Notes and Emendations. Together with a Complete Index to the Text, Preliminary Discourse, and Notes. By Rev. E. M. Wherry, M.A., Lodiana. Vol. I. Pp. xii. and 392. 1882. 12s. 6d. Vol. II. Pp. xi. and 408. 1884. 12s. 6d.

HINDU PHILOSOPHY. THE BHAGAVAD GITÂ; or, The Sacred Lay. A Sanskrit Philosophical Lay. Translated, with Notes, by John Davies, M.A. Pp. vi. and 208. 1882. 8s. 6d.

THE SARVA-DARSANA-SAMGRAHA; or, Review of the Different Systems of Hindu Philosophy. By Madhava Acharya. Translated by E. B. Cowell, M.A., Cambridge, and A. E. Gough, M.A., Calcutta. Pp. xii. and 282. 1882. 10s. 6d.

TIBETAN TALES. Derived from Indian Sources. Translated from the Tibetan of the Kay-Gyur. By F. Anton von Schiefner. Done into English from the German, with an Introduction. By W. R. S. Ralston, M.A. Pp. lxvi. and 368. 1882. 14s.

LINGUISTIC ESSAYS. By Carl Abel, Ph.D. Pp. viii. and 265. 1882. 9s.

THE INDIAN EMPIRE: Its History, People, and Products. By W. W. Hunter, C.I.E., LL.D. Pp. 568. 1882. 16s.

TRÜBNER'S ORIENTAL SERIES—*continued.*

HISTORY OF THE EGYPTIAN RELIGION. By Dr. C. P. Tiele, Leiden. Translated by J. Ballingal. Pp. xxiv. and 230. 1882. 7s. 6d.

THE PHILOSOPHY OF THE UPANISHADS. By A. E. Gough, M.A., Calcutta. Pp. xxiv.-268. 1882. 9s.

UDANAVARGA. A Collection of Verses from the Buddhist Canon. Compiled by Dharmatrâta. Being the Northern Buddhist Version of Dhammapada. Translated from the Tibetan of Bkah-hgyur, with Notes, and Extracts from the Commentary of Pradjnavarman, by W. Woodville Rockhill. Pp. 240. 1883. 9s.

A HISTORY OF BURMA, including Burma Proper, Pegu, Taungu, Tenasserim, and Arakan. From the Earliest Time to the End of the First War with British India. By Lieut.-General Sir Arthur P. Phayre, G.C.M.G., K.C.S.I., and C.B. Pp. xii.-312. 1883. 14s.

A SKETCH OF THE MODERN LANGUAGES OF AFRICA. Accompanied by a Language-Map. By R. N. Cust, Author of "Modern Languages of the East Indies," &c. 2 vols., pp. xvi. and 566, with Thirty-one Autotype Portraits. 1883. 25s.

RELIGION IN CHINA; containing a brief Account of the Three Religions of the Chinese; with Observations on the Prospects of Christian Conversion amongst that People. By Joseph Edkins, D.D., Peking. Third Edition. Pp. xvi. and 260. 1884. 7s. 6d.

OUTLINES OF THE HISTORY OF RELIGION TO THE SPREAD OF THE UNIVERSAL RELIGIONS. By Prof. C. P. TIELE. Translated from the Dutch by J. Estlin Carpenter, M.A., with the Author's assistance. Third Edition. Pp. xx. and 250. 1884. 7s. 6d.

The following works are nearly ready:—

THE LIFE OF THE BUDDHA AND THE EARLY HISTORY OF HIS ORDER. Derived from Tibetan Works. By W. W. Rockhill.

MANAVA-DHARMA-CASTRA; or, Laws of Manu. A New Translation, with Introduction, Notes, &c. By A. C. Burnell, Ph.D., C.I.E., Foreign Member of the Royal Danish Academy, and Hon. Member of several learned societies.

THE APHORISMS OF THE SANKHYA PHILOSOPHY OF KAPILA. With Illustrative Extracts from the Commentaries. By the late J. R. Ballantyne. Second Edition, edited by Fitzedward Hall.

BUDDHIST RECORDS OF THE WESTERN WORLD, being the Si-Yu-Ki by Hwen Thsang. Translated from the original Chinese, with Introduction, Index, &c. By Samuel Beal, Trinity College, Cambridge, Professor of Chinese, University College, London. In 2 vols.

UNGER.—A SHORT CUT TO READING: The Child's First Book of Lessons. Part I. By W. H. Unger. Fourth Edition. Cr. 8vo, pp. 32, cloth. 1873. 5d.

SEQUEL to Part I. and Part II. Fourth Edition. Cr. 8vo, pp. 64, cloth. 1873. 6d. Parts I. and II. Third Edition. Demy 8vo, pp. 76, cloth. 1873. 1s. 6d. In folio sheets. Pp. 44. Sets A to D, 10d. each; set E, 8d. 1873. Complete, 4s.

UNGER.—W. H. UNGER'S CONTINUOUS SUPPLEMENTARY WRITING MODELS, designed to impart not only a good business hand, but correctness in transcribing. Oblong 8vo, pp. 40, stiff covers. 1874. 6d.

UNGER.—THE STUDENT'S BLUE BOOK: Being Selections from Official Correspondence, Reports, &c.; for Exercises in Reading and Copying Manuscripts, Writing, Orthography, Punctuation, Dictation, Précis, Indexing, and Digesting, and Tabulating Accounts and Returns. Compiled by W. H. Unger. Folio, pp. 100, paper. 1875. 2s.

UNGER.—TWO HUNDRED TESTS IN ENGLISH ORTHOGRAPHY, or Word Dictations. Compiled by W. H. Unger. Foolscap, pp. viii. and 200, cloth. 1877. 1s. 6d. plain, 2s. 6d. interleaved.

UNGER.—THE SCRIPT PRIMER: By which one of the remaining difficulties of Children is entirely removed in the first stages, and, as a consequence, a considerable saving of time will be effected. In Two Parts. By W. H. Unger. Part I. 12mo, pp. xvi. and 44, cloth. 5d. Part II., pp. 59, cloth. 5d.

UNGER.—PRELIMINARY WORD DICTATIONS ON THE RULES FOR SPELLING. By W. H. Unger. 18mo, pp. 44, cloth. 4d.

URICOECHEA.—MAPOTECA COLOMBIANA: Catalogo de Todos los Mapas, Planos, Vistas, &c., relativos a la América-Española, Brasil, e Islas adyacentes. Arreglada cronologicamente i precedida de una introduccion sobre la historia cartografica de América. Por el Doctor Ezequiel Uricoechea, de Bogóta, Nueva Granada. 8vo, pp. 232, cloth. 1860. 6s.

URQUHART.—ELECTRO-MOTORS. A Treatise on the Means and Apparatus employed in the Transmission of Electrical Energy and its Conversion into Motive-power. For the Use of Engineers and Others. By J. W. Urquhart, Electrician. Crown 8vo, cloth, pp. xii. and 178, illustrated. 1882. 7s. 6d.

VAITANA SUTRA.—See AUCTORES SANSKRITI, Vol. III.

VALDES.—LIVES OF THE TWIN BROTHERS, JUÁN AND ALFONSO DE VALDÉS. By E. Boehmer, D.D. Translated by J. T. Betts. Crown 8vo, pp. 32, wrappers. 1882. 1s.

VALDES.—SEVENTEEN OPUSCULES. By Juán de Valdés. Translated from the Spanish and Italian, and edited by John T. Betts. Crown 8vo, pp. xii. and 188, cloth. 1882. 6s.

VALDES.—JUÁN DE VALDÉS' COMMENTARY UPON THE GOSPEL OF ST. MATTHEW. With Professor Boehmer's "Lives of Juán and Alfonso de Valdés." Now for the first time translated from the Spanish, and never before published in English. By John T. Betts. Post 8vo, pp. xii. and 512–30, cloth. 1882. 7s. 6d.

VALDES.—SPIRITUAL MILK; or, Christian Instruction for Children. By Juán de Valdés. Translated from the Italian, edited and published by John T. Betts. With Lives of the twin brothers, Juán and Alfonso de Valdés. By E. Boehmer, D.D. Fcap. 8vo, pp. 60, wrappers. 1882. 2s.

VALDES.—SPIRITUAL MILK. Octaglot. The Italian original, with translations into Spanish, Latin, Polish, German, English, French, and Engadin. With a Critical and Historical Introduction by Edward Boehmer, the Editor of "Spanish Reformers." 4to, pp. 88, wrappers. 1884. 6s.

VALDES.—THREE OPUSCULES: an Extract from Valdés' Seventeen Opuscules. By Juán de Valdés. Translated, edited, and published by John T. Betts. Fcap. 8vo, pp. 58, wrappers. 1881. 1s. 6d.

VALDES.—JUÁN DE VALDÉS' COMMENTARY UPON OUR LORD'S SERMON ON THE MOUNT. Translated and edited by J. T. Betts. With Lives of Juán and Alfonso de Valdés. By E. Boehmer, D.D. Crown 8vo, pp. 112, boards. 1882. 2s. 6d.

VALDES.—JUÁN DE VALDÉS' COMMENTARY UPON THE EPISTLE TO THE ROMANS. Edited by J. T. Betts. Crown 8vo, pp. xxxii. and 296, cloth. 1883. 6s.

VALDES.—JUÁN DE VALDÉS' COMMENTARY UPON ST. PAUL'S FIRST EPISTLE TO THE CHURCH AT CORINTH. Translated and edited by J. T. Betts. With Lives of Juán and Alphonso de Valdés. By E. Boehmer. Crown 8vo, pp. 390, cloth. 1883. 6s.

VAN CAMPEN.—THE DUTCH IN THE ARCTIC SEAS. By Samuel Richard Van Campen, author of "Holland's Silver Feast." 8vo. Vol. I. A Dutch Arctic Expedition and Route. Third Edition. Pp. xxxvii. and 263, cloth. 1877. 10s. 6d. Vol. II. *in preparation.*

VAN DE WEYER.—CHOIX D'OPUSCULES PHILOSOPHIQUES, HISTORIQUES, POLITIQUES ET LITTÉRAIRES de Sylvain Van de Weyer, Précédés d'Avant propos de l'Editeur. Roxburghe style. Crown 8vo. PREMIÈRE SÉRIE. Pp. 374. 1863. 10s. 6d.—DEUXIÈME SÉRIE. Pp. 502. 1869. 12s.—TROISIÈME SÉRIE. Pp. 391. 1875. 10s. 6d.—QUATRIÈME SÉRIE. Pp. 366. 1876. 10s. 6d.

VAN EYS.—BASQUE GRAMMAR. See Trübner's Collection.

VAN LAUN.—GRAMMAR OF THE FRENCH LANGUAGE. By H. Van Laun. Parts I. and II. Accidence and Syntax. 13th Edition. Cr. 8vo, pp. 151 and 120, cloth. 1874. 4s. Part III. Exercises. 11th Edition. Cr. 8vo, pp. xii. and 285, cloth. 1873. 3s. 6d.

VAN LAUN.—LEÇONS GRADUÉES DE TRADUCTION ET DE LECTURE; or, Graduated Lessons in Translation and Reading, with Biographical Sketches, Annotations on History, Geography, Synonyms and Style, and a Dictionary of Words and Idioms. By Henri Van Laun. 4th Edition. 12mo, pp. viii. and 400, cloth. 1868. 5s.

VAN PRAAGH.—LESSONS FOR THE INSTRUCTION OF DEAF AND DUMB CHILDREN, in Speaking, Lip-reading, Reading, and Writing. By W. Van Praagh, Director of the School and Training College for Teachers of the Association for the Oral Instruction of the Deaf and Dumb, Officier d'Academie, France. Fcap. 8vo, Part I., pp. 52, cloth. 1884. 2s. 6d. Part II., pp. 62, cloth. 1s. 6d.

VARDHAMANA'S GANARATNAMAHODADHI. See AUCTORES SANSKRITI, Vol. IV.

VAZIR OF LANKURAN: A Persian Play. A Text-Book of Modern Colloquial Persian. Edited, with Grammatical Introduction, Translation, Notes, and Vocabulary, by W. H. Haggard, late of H.M. Legation in Teheran, and G. le Strange. Crown 8vo, pp. 230, cloth. 1882. 10s. 6d.

VELASQUEZ AND SIMONNÉ'S NEW METHOD TO READ, WRITE, AND SPEAK THE SPANISH LANGUAGE. Adapted to Ollendorff's System. Post 8vo, pp. 558, cloth. 1882. 6s.
    KEY. Post 8vo, pp. 174, cloth. 4s.

VELASQUEZ.—A DICTIONARY OF THE SPANISH AND ENGLISH LANGUAGES. For the Use of Young Learners and Travellers. By M. Velasquez de la Cadena. In Two Parts. I. Spanish-English. II. English-Spanish. Crown 8vo, pp. viii. and 846, cloth. 1883. 7s. 6d.

VELASQUEZ.—A PRONOUNCING DICTIONARY OF THE SPANISH AND ENGLISH LANGUAGES. Composed from the Dictionaries of the Spanish Academy, Terreos, and Salvá, and Webster, Worcester, and Walker. Two Parts in one thick volume. By M. Velasquez de la Cadena. Roy. 8vo, pp. 1280, cloth. 1873. £1, 4s.

VELASQUEZ.—NEW SPANISH READER: Passages from the most approved authors, in Prose and Verse. Arranged in progressive order. With Vocabulary. By M. Velasquez de la Cadena. Post 8vo, pp. 352, cloth. 1866. 6s.

VELASQUEZ.—AN EASY INTRODUCTION TO SPANISH CONVERSATION, containing all that is necessary to make a rapid progress in it. Particularly designed for persons who have little time to study, or are their own instructors. By M. Velasquez de la Cadena. 12mo, pp. 150, cloth. 1863. 2s. 6d.

VERSES AND VERSELETS. By a Lover of Nature. Foolscap 8vo, pp. viii. and 88, cloth. 1876. 2s. 6d.

VICTORIA GOVERNMENT.—PUBLICATIONS OF THE GOVERNMENT OF VICTORIA. List in preparation.

VOGEL.—ON BEER. A Statistical Sketch. By M. Vogel. Fcap. 8vo, pp. xii. and 76, cloth limp. 1874. 2s.

WAFFLARD and FULGENCE.—LE VOYAGE À DIEPPE. A Comedy in Prose. By Wafflard and Fulgence. Edited, with Notes, by the Rev. P. H. E. Brette, B.D. Cr. 8vo, pp. 104, cloth. 1867. 2s. 6d.

WAKE.—THE EVOLUTION OF MORALITY. Being a History of the Development of Moral Culture. By C. Staniland Wake. 2 vols. crown 8vo, pp. xvi.-506 and xii.-474, cloth. 1878. 21s.

WALLACE.—ON MIRACLES AND MODERN SPIRITUALISM; Three Essays. By Alfred Russel Wallace, Author of "The Malay Archipelago," "The Geographical Distribution of Animals," &c., &c. Second Edition, crown 8vo, pp. viii. and 236, cloth. 1881. 5s

WANKLYN and CHAPMAN.—WATER ANALYSIS. A Practical Treatise on the Examination of Potable Water. By J. A. Wanklyn, and E. T. Chapman. Sixth Edition. Entirely rewritten. By J. A. Wanklyn, M.R.C.S. Crown 8vo, pp. 192, cloth. 1884. 5s.

WANKLYN.—MILK ANALYSIS; a Practical Treatise on the Examination of Milk and its Derivatives, Cream, Butter, and Cheese. By J. A. Wanklyn, M.R.C.S., &c. Crown 8vo, pp. viii. and 72, cloth. 1874. 5s.

WANKLYN.—TEA, COFFEE, AND COCOA. A Practical Treatise on the Analysis of Tea, Coffee, Cocoa, Chocolate, Maté (Paraguay Tea), &c. By J. A. Wanklyn, M.R.C.S., &c. Crown 8vo, pp. viii. and 60, cloth. 1874. 5s.

WAR OFFICE.—A LIST OF THE VARIOUS MILITARY MANUALS AND OTHER WORKS PUBLISHED UNDER THE SUPERINTENDENCE OF THE WAR OFFICE may be had on application.

WARD.—ICE: A Lecture delivered before the Keswick Literary Society, and published by request. To which is appended a Geological Dream on Skiddaw. By J. Clifton Ward, F.G.S. 8vo, pp. 28, sewed. 1870. 1s.

WARD.—ELEMENTARY NATURAL PHILOSOPHY; being a Course of Nine Lectures, specially adapted for the use of Schools and Junior Students. By J. Clifton Ward, F.G.S. Fcap. 8vo, pp. viii. and 216, with 154 Illustrations, cloth. 1871. 3s. 6d.

WARD.—ELEMENTARY GEOLOGY: A Course of Nine Lectures, for the use of Schools and Junior Students. By J. Clifton Ward, F.G.S. Fcap. 8vo, pp. 292, with 120 Illustrations, cloth. 1872. 4s. 6d.

WATSON.—INDEX TO THE NATIVE AND SCIENTIFIC NAMES OF INDIAN AND OTHER EASTERN ECONOMIC PLANTS AND PRODUCTS, originally prepared under the authority of the Secretary of State for India in Council. By John Forbes Watson, M.D. Imp. 8vo, pp. 650, cloth. 1868. £1, 11s. 6d.

WATSON.—SPANISH AND PORTUGUESE SOUTH AMERICA DURING THE COLONIAL PERIOD. By R. G. Watson. 2 vols. post 8vo, pp. xvi.-308, viii.-320, cloth. 1884. 21s.

WEBER.—THE HISTORY OF INDIAN LITERATURE. By Albrecht Weber. Translated from the Second German Edition, by J. Mann, M.A., and T. Zachariae, Ph.D., with the sanction of the Author. Second Edition, post 8vo, pp. xxiv. and 360, cloth. 1882. 10s. 6d.

WEDGWOOD.—THE PRINCIPLES OF GEOMETRICAL DEMONSTRATION, reduced from the Original Conception of Space and Form. By H. Wedgwood, M.A. 12mo, pp. 48, cloth. 1844. 2s.

WEDGWOOD.—ON THE DEVELOPMENT OF THE UNDERSTANDING. By H. Wedgwood, A.M. 12mo, pp. 133, cloth. 1848. 3s.

WEDGWOOD.—THE GEOMETRY OF THE THREE FIRST BOOKS OF EUCLID. By Direct Proof from Definitions Alone. By H. Wedgwood, M.A. 12mo, pp. 104, cloth. 1856. 3s.

WEDGWOOD.—ON THE ORIGIN OF LANGUAGE. By H. Wedgwood, M.A. 12mo, pp. 165, cloth. 1866. 3s. 6d.

WEDGWOOD.—A DICTIONARY OF ENGLISH ETYMOLOGY. By H. Wedgwood. Third Edition, revised and enlarged. With Introduction on the Origin of Language. 8vo, pp. lxxii. and 746, cloth. 1878. £1, 1s.

WEDGWOOD.—CONTESTED ETYMOLOGIES IN THE DICTIONARY OF THE REV. W. W. SKEAT. By H. Wedgwood. Crown 8vo, pp. viii. and 194, cloth. 1882. 5s.

WEISBACH.—THEORETICAL MECHANICS: A Manual of the Mechanics of Engineering and of the Construction of Machines; with an Introduction to the Calculus. Designed as a Text-book for Technical Schools and Colleges, and for the use of Engineers, Architects, &c. By Julius Weisbach, Ph.D., Oberbergrath, and Professor at the Royal Mining Academy at Freiberg, &c. Translated from the German by Eckley B. Coxe, A.M., Mining Engineer. Demy 8vo, with 902 woodcuts, pp. 1112, cloth. 1877. 31s. 6d.

WELLER.—AN IMPROVED DICTIONARY; English and French, and French and English. By E. Weller. Royal 8vo, pp. 384 and 340, cloth. 1864. 7s. 6d.

WEST and BUHLER.—A DIGEST OF THE HINDU LAW OF INHERITANCE, PARTITION, AND ADOPTION; embodying the Replies of the Sástris in the Courts of the Bombay Presidency, with Introductions and Notes. By Raymond West and J. G. Bühler. Third Edition. Demy 8vo, pp. 1450, sewed. 1884. £1, 16s.

WETHERELL.—THE MANUFACTURE OF VINEGAR, its Theory and Practice; with especial reference to the Quick Process. By C. M. Wetherell, Ph.D., M.D. 8vo, pp. 30, cloth. 7s. 6d.

WHEELDON.—ANGLING RESORTS NEAR LONDON: The Thames and the Lea. By J. P. Wheeldon, Piscatorial Correspondent to "Bell's Life." Crown 8vo, pp. viii. and 218. 1878. Paper, 1s. 6d.

WHEELER.—THE HISTORY OF INDIA FROM THE EARLIEST AGES. By J. Talboys Wheeler. Demy 8vo, cloth. Vol. I. containing the Vedic Period and the Mahá Bhárata. With Map. Pp. lxxv. and 576, cl. 1867, o. p. Vol. II. The Ramayana, and the Brahmanic Period. Pp. lxxxviii. and 680, with 2 Maps, cl. 21s. Vol. III. Hindu, Buddhist, Brahmanical Revival. Pp. xxiv.-500. With 2 Maps, 8vo, cl. 1874. 18s. This volume may be had as a complete work with the following title, "History of India; Hindu, Buddhist, and Brahmanical." Vol. IV. Part I. Mussulman Rule. Pp. xxxii.-320. 1876. 14s. Vol. IV. Part II. completing the History of India down to the time of the Moghul Empire. Pp. xxviii. and 280. 1881. 12s.

WHEELER.—EARLY RECORDS OF BRITISH INDIA: A History of the English Settlements in India, as told in the Government Records, the works of old Travellers, and other Contemporary Documents, from the earliest period down to the rise of British Power in India. By J. Talboys Wheeler, late Assistant Secretary to the Government of India in the Foreign Department. Royal 8vo, pp. xxxii. and 392, cloth. 1878. 15s.

WHEELER.—THE FOREIGNER IN CHINA. By L. N. Wheeler, D.D. With Introduction by Professor W. C. Sawyer, Ph.D. 8vo, pp. 268, cloth. 1881. 6s. 6d.

WHERRY.—A COMPREHENSIVE COMMENTARY TO THE QURAN. To which is prefixed Sale's Preliminary Discourse, with additional Notes and Emendations. Together with a complete Index to the Text, Preliminary Discourse, and Notes. By Rev. E. M. Wherry M.A., Lodiana. 3 vols. post 8vo, cloth. Vol. I. Pp. xii. and 392. 1882. 12s. 6d. Vol. II. Pp. vi. and 408. 1884. 12s. 6d.

WHINFIELD.—QUATRAINS OF OMAR KHAYYAM. See Trübner's Oriental Series.

WHINFIELD.—See GULSHAN I. RAZ.

WHIST.—SHORT RULES FOR MODERN WHIST, Extracted from the "Quarterly Review" of January 1871. Printed on a Card, folded to fit the Pocket. 1878. 6d.

WHITNEY.—LANGUAGE AND THE STUDY OF LANGUAGE: Twelve Lectures on the Principles of Linguistic Science. By W. D. Whitney. Fourth Edition, augmented by an Analysis. Crown 8vo, pp. xii. and 504, cloth. 1884. 10s. 6d.

WHITNEY.—LANGUAGE AND ITS STUDY, with especial reference to the Indo-European Family of Languages. Seven Lectures by W. D. Whitney, Instructor in Modern Languages in Yale College. Edited with Introduction, Notes, Tables, &c., and an Index, by the Rev. R. Morris, M.A., LL.D. Second Edition. Crown 8vo, pp. xxii. and 318, cloth. 1880. 5s.

WHITNEY.—Oriental and Linguistic Studies. By W. D. Whitney. First Series. Crown 8vo, pp. x. and 420, cloth. 1874. 12s. Second Series. Crown 8vo, pp. xii. and 434. With chart, cloth. 1874. 12s.

WHITNEY.—A SANSKRIT GRAMMAR, including both the Classical Language and the older Dialects of Veda and Brahmana. By William Dwight Whitney, Professor of Sanskrit and Comparative Philology in Yale College, Newhaven, &c., &c. 8vo, pp. xxiv. and 486. 1879. Stitched in wrapper, 10s. 6d; cloth, 12s.

WHITWELL.—IRON SMELTER'S POCKET ANALYSIS BOOK. By Thomas Whitwell, Member of the Institution of Mechanical Engineers, &c. Oblong 12mo, pp. 152, roan. 1877. 5s.

WILKINSON.—THE SAINT'S TRAVEL TO THE LAND OF CANAAN. Wherein are discovered Seventeen False Rests short of the Spiritual Coming of Christ in the Saints, with a Brief Discovery of what the Coming of Christ in the Spirit is. By R. Wilkinson. Printed 1648; reprinted 1874. Fcap. 8vo, pp. 208, cloth. 1s. 6d.

WILLIAMS.—A SYLLABIC DICTIONARY OF THE CHINESE LANGUAGE; arranged according to the Wu-Fang Yuen Yin, with the pronunciation of the Characters as heard in Pekin, Canton, Amoy, and Shanghai. By S. Wells Williams, LL.D. 4to, pp. 1336. 1874. £5, 5s.

WILLIAMS.—MODERN INDIA AND THE INDIANS. See Trübner's Oriental Series.

WILSON.—WORKS OF THE LATE HORACE HAYMAN WILSON, M.A., F.R.S., &c.

Vols. I. and II. Essays and Lectures chiefly on the Religion of the Hindus, by the late H. H. Wilson, M.A., F.R.S., &c. Collected and Edited by Dr. Reinhold Rost. 2 vols. demy 8vo, pp. xiii. and 399, vi. and 416, cloth. 21s.

Vols. III., IV., and V. Essays Analytical, Critical, and Philological, on Subjects connected with Sanskrit Literature. Collected and Edited by Dr. Reinhold Rost. 3 vols. demy 8vo, pp. 408, 406, and 390, cloth. 36s.

Vols. VI., VII., VIII., IX., and X. (2 parts). Vishnu Puráná, a System of Hindu Mythology and Tradition. Translated from the original Sanskrit, and Illustrated by Notes derived chiefly from other Puránás. By the late H. H. Wilson. Edited by FitzEdward Hall, M.A., D.C.L., Oxon. Vols. I. to V. (2 parts). Demy 8vo, pp. cxl. and 200, 344, 346, 362, and 268, cloth. £3, 4s. 6d.

Vols. XI. and XII. Select Specimens of the Theatre of the Hindus. Translated from the original Sanskrit. By the late H. H. Wilson, M.A., F.R.S. Third corrected Edition. 2 vols. demy 8vo, pp. lxxi. and 384, iv. and 418, cloth. 21s.

WISE.—COMMENTARY ON THE HINDU SYSTEM OF MEDICINE. By T. A. Wise, M.D. 8vo, pp. xx. and 432, cloth. 1845. 7s. 6d.

WISE.—REVIEW OF THE HISTORY OF MEDICINE. By Thomas A. Wise. 2 vols. demy 8vo, cloth. Vol. I., pp. xcviii. and 397. Vol. II., pp. 574. 10s.

WITHERS.—THE ENGLISH LANGUAGE AS PRONOUNCED. By G. Withers. Royal 8vo, pp. 84, sewed. 1874. 1s.

WOOD.—CHRONOS. Mother Earth's Biography. A Romance of the New School. By Wallace Wood, M.D. Crown 8vo, pp. xvi. and 334, with Illustration, cloth. 1873. 6s.

WOMEN.—THE RIGHTS OF WOMEN. A Comparison of the Relative Legal Status of the Sexes in the Chief Countries of Western Civilisation. Crown 8vo, pp. 104, cloth. 1875. 2s. 6d.

WRIGHT.—FEUDAL MANUALS OF ENGLISH HISTORY, a series of Popular Sketches of our National History compiled at different periods, from the Thirteenth Century to the Fifteenth, for the use of the Feudal Gentry and Nobility. Now first edited from the Original Manuscripts. By Thomas Wright, M.A., F.S.A., &c. Small 4to, pp. xxix. and 184, cloth. 1872. 15s.

WRIGHT.—THE HOMES OF OTHER DAYS. A History of Domestic Manners and Sentiments during the Middle Ages. By Thomas Wright, M.A., F.S.A. With Illustrations from the Illuminations in Contemporary Manuscripts and other Sources. Drawn and Engraved by F. W. Fairholt, F.S.A. Medium 8vo, 350 Woodcuts, pp. xv. and 512, cloth. 1871. 21s.

WRIGHT.—ANGLO-SAXON AND OLD ENGLISH VOCABULARIES. By Thomas Wright, M.A., F.S.A., Hon. M.R.S.L. Second Edition, Edited and Collated by Richard Paul Wulcker. 2 vols. demy 8vo, pp. xx.-408, and iv.-486, cloth. 1884. 28s. Illustrating the Condition and Manners of our Forefathers, as well as the History of the forms of Elementary Education, and of the Languages Spoken in this Island from the Tenth Century to the Fifteenth.

WRIGHT.—THE CELT, THE ROMAN, AND THE SAXON; a History of the Early Inhabitants of Britain down to the Conversion of the Anglo-Saxons to Christianity. Illustrated by the Ancient Remains brought to light by Recent Research. By Thomas Wright, M.A., F.S.A., &c., &c. Third Corrected and Enlarged Edition. Cr. 8vo, pp. xiv. and 562. With nearly 300 Engravings. Cloth. 1875. 14s.

WRIGHT.—THE BOOK OF KALILAH AND DIMNAH. Translated from Arabic into Syriac. Edited by W. Wright, LL.D., Professor of Arabic in the University of Cambridge. Demy 8vo, pp. lxxxii.-408, cloth. 1884. 21s.

WRIGHT.—MENTAL TRAVELS IN IMAGINED LANDS. By H. Wright. Crown 8vo, pp. 184, cloth. 1878. 5s.

WYLD.—CLAIRVOYANCE; or, the Auto-Noetic Action of the Mind. By George Wyld, M.D. Edin. 8vo, pp. 32, wrapper. 1883. 1s.

WYSARD.—THE INTELLECTUAL AND MORAL PROBLEM OF GOETHE'S FAUST. By A. Wysard. Parts I. and II. Fcap. 8vo, pp. 80, limp parchment wrapper. 1883. 2s. 6d.

YOUNG MECHANIC (THE).—See MECHANIC.

ZELLER.—STRAUSS AND RENAN. An Essay by E. Zeller. Translated from the German. Post 8vo, pp. 110, cloth. 1866. 2s. 6d.

PERIODICALS
PUBLISHED AND SOLD BY TRÜBNER & CO.

AMATEUR MECHANICAL SOCIETY'S JOURNAL.—Irregular.

ANTHROPOLOGICAL INSTITUTE OF GREAT BRITAIN AND IRELAND (JOURNAL OF).— Quarterly, 5s.

ARCHITECT (AMERICAN) AND BUILDING NEWS.—Contains General Architectural News, Articles on Interior Decoration, Sanitary Engineering, Construction, Building Materials, &c., &c. Four full-page Illustrations accompany each Number. Weekly. Annual Subscription, £1, 11s. 6d. Post free.

Periodicals. 77

ASIATIC SOCIETY (ROYAL) OF GREAT BRITAIN AND IRELAND (JOURNAL OF).—Irregular.
BIBLICAL ARCHÆOLOGICAL SOCIETY (TRANSACTIONS OF).—Irregular.
BIBLIOTHECA SACRA.—Quarterly, 3s. 6d. Annual Subscription, 14s. Post free.
BRITISH ARCHÆOLOGICAL ASSOCIATION (JOURNAL OF).—Quarterly, 8s.
BRITISH CHESS MAGAZINE.—Monthly, 8d.
BRITISH HOMŒOPATHIC SOCIETY (ANNALS OF).—Half-yearly, 2s. 6d.
BROWNING SOCIETY'S PAPERS.—Irregular.
CALCUTTA REVIEW.—Quarterly, 8s. 6d. Annual Subscription, 34s. Post free.
CAMBRIDGE PHILOLOGICAL SOCIETY (PROCEEDINGS OF).—Irregular.
ENGLISHWOMAN'S REVIEW.—Social and Industrial Questions. Monthly, 6d.
GEOLOGICAL MAGAZINE, or Monthly Journal of Geology, 1s. 6d. Annual Subscription, 18s. Post free.
GLASGOW, GEOLOGICAL SOCIETY OF (TRANSACTIONS OF).—Irregular.
INDEX MEDICUS.—A Monthly Classified Record of the Current Medical Literature of the World. Annual Subscription, 50s. Post free.
INDIAN ANTIQUARY.—A Journal of Oriental Research in Archæology, History, Literature, Languages, Philosophy, Religion, Folklore, &c. Annual Subscription, £2. Post free.
LIBRARY JOURNAL.—Official Organ of the Library Associations of America and of the United Kingdom. Monthly, 2s. Annual Subscription, 20s. Post free.
MANCHESTER QUARTERLY.—1s. 6d.
MATHEMATICS (AMERICAN JOURNAL OF).—Quarterly, 7s. 6d. Annual Subscription, 24s. Post free.
ORTHODOX CATHOLIC REVIEW.—Irregular.
PHILOLOGICAL SOCIETY (TRANSACTIONS AND PROCEEDINGS OF).—Irregular.
PSYCHICAL RESEARCH (SOCIETY OF).—PROCEEDINGS.
PUBLISHERS' WEEKLY.—THE AMERICAN BOOK-TRADE JOURNAL. Annual Subscription, 18s. Post free.
SCIENTIFIC AMERICAN.—WEEKLY. Annual subscription, 18s. Post free.
SUPPLEMENT to ditto.—WEEKLY. Annual subscription, 24s. Post free.
SCIENCE AND ARTS (AMERICAN JOURNAL OF).—Monthly, 2s. 6d. Annual Subscription, 30s.
SPECULATIVE PHILOSOPHY (JOURNAL OF).—Quarterly, 4s. Annual Subscription, 16s. Post free, 17s.
SUNDAY REVIEW.—Organ of the Sunday Society for Opening Museums and Art Galleries on Sunday.—Quarterly, 1s. Annual Subscription, 4s. 6d. Post free.
TRÜBNER'S AMERICAN, EUROPEAN, AND ORIENTAL LITERARY RECORD.—A Register of the most Important Works Published in America, India, China, and the British Colonies. With occasional Notes on German, Dutch, Danish, French, Italian, Spanish, Portuguese, and Russian Literature. Subscription for 12 Numbers, 5s. Post free.
TRÜBNER & CO.'S MONTHLY LIST of New and Forthcoming Works, Official and other Authorised Publications, and New American Books. Post free.
WESTMINSTER REVIEW.—Quarterly, 6s. Annual Subscription, 22s. Post free.
WOMAN'S SUFFRAGE JOURNAL.—Monthly, 1d.

TRÜBNER & CO.'S CATALOGUES.

Any of the following Catalogues sent per Post on receipt of Stamps.

Africa, Works Relating to the Modern Languages of. 1d.

Agricultural Works. 2d.

Arabic, Persian, and Turkish Books, printed in the East. 1s.

Assyria and Assyriology. 1s.

Bibliotheca Hispano-Americana. 1s. 6d.

Brazil, Ancient and Modern Books relating to. 2s. 6d.

British Museum, Publications of Trustees of the. 1d.

Dictionaries and Grammars of Principal Languages and Dialects of the World. 5s.

Educational Works. 1d.

Egypt and Egyptology. 1s.

Guide Books. 1d.

Important Works, published by Trübner & Co. 2d.

Linguistic and Oriental Publications. 2d.

Medical, Surgical, Chemical, and Dental Publications. 2d.

Modern German Books. 2d.

Monthly List of New Publications. 1d.

Pali, Prakrit, and Buddhist Literature. 1s.

Portuguese Language, Ancient and Modern Books in the. 6d.

Sanskrit Books. 2s. 6d.

Scientific Works. 2d.

Semitic, Iranian, and Tatar Races. 1s.

TRÜBNER'S
COLLECTION OF SIMPLIFIED GRAMMARS
OF THE
PRINCIPAL ASIATIC AND EUROPEAN LANGUAGES.
EDITED BY REINHOLD ROST, LL.D., PH.D.

The object of this Series is to provide the learner with a concise but practical Introduction to the various Languages, and at the same time to furnish Students of Comparative Philology with a clear and comprehensive view of their structure. The attempt to adapt the somewhat cumbrous grammatical system of the Greek and Latin to every other tongue has introduced a great deal of unnecessary difficulty into the study of Languages. Instead of analysing existing locutions and endeavouring to discover the principles which regulate them, writers of grammars have for the most part constructed a framework of rules on the old lines, and tried to make the language of which they were treating fit into it. Where this proves impossible, the difficulty is met by lists of exceptions and irregular forms, thus burdening the pupil's mind with a mass of details of which he can make no practical use.

In these Grammars the subject is viewed from a different standpoint; the structure of each language is carefully examined, and the principles which underlie it are carefully explained; while apparent discrepancies and so-called irregularities are shown to be only natural euphonic and other changes. All technical terms are excluded unless their meaning and application is self-evident; no arbitrary rules are admitted; the old classification into declensions, conjugations, &c., and even the usual *paradigms* and tables, are omitted. Thus reduced to the simplest principles, the Accidence and Syntax can be thoroughly comprehended by the student on one perusal, and a few hours' diligent study will enable him to analyse any sentence in the language.

NOW READY.
Crown 8vo, cloth, uniformly bound.

I.—**Hindustani, Persian, and Arabic.** By the late E. H. Palmer, M.A. Pp. 112. 5s.

II.—**Hungarian.** By I. SINGER, of Buda-Pesth. Pp. vi. and 88. 4s. 6d.

For continuation see next page.

Trübner's Simplified Grammars—continued.

III.—**Basque.** By W. VAN EYS. Pp. xii. and 52. 3s. 6d.
IV.—**Malagasy.** By G. W. PARKER. Pp. 66. 5s.
V.—**Modern Greek.** By E. M. GELDART, M.A. Pp. 68. 2s. 6d.
VI.—**Roumanian.** By M. TORCEANU. Pp. viii. and 72. 5s.
VII.—**Tibetan.** By H. A. JÄSCHKE. Pp. viii. and 104. 5s.
VIII.—**Danish.** By E. C. OTTÉ. Pp. viii. and 66. 2s. 6d.
IX.—**Turkish.** By J. W. REDHOUSE, M.R.A.S. Pp. xii. and 204. 10s. 6d.
X.—**Swedish.** By Miss E. C. OTTÉ. Pp. xii. and 70. 2s. 6d.
XI.—**Polish.** By W. R. MORFILL, M.A. Pp. viii. and 64. 3s. 6d.

The following are in preparation :—

SIMPLIFIED GRAMMARS OF

Albanian, by WASSA PASHA, Prince of the Lebanon.
Assyrian, by Prof. SAYCE.
Bengali, by J. F. BLUMHARDT, of the British Museum.
Burmese, by Dr. E. FORCHAMMER.
Cymric and Gaelic, by H. JENNER, of the British Museum.
Egyptian, by Dr. BIRCH.
Finnic, by Prof. OTTO DONNER, of Helsingfors.
Hebrew, by Dr. GINSBURG.
Icelandic, by Dr. WIMMER, Copenhagen.
Lettish, by Dr. M. I. A. VÖLKEL.
Lithuanian, by Dr. M. I. A. VÖLKEL.
Malay, by W. E. MAXWELL, of the Inner Temple, Barrister-at-Law.
Pali, by Dr. EDWARD MÜLLER.
Portuguese, by WALTER DE GRAY BIRCH.
Russian, Bohemian, Bulgarian and Serbian, by W. R. MORFILL, of Oxford.
Sanskrit and Prakrit, by HJALMAR EDGREN, Lund, Sweden.
Sinhalese, by Dr. EDWARD MÜLLER.

Arrangements are being made with competent Scholars for the early preparation of Grammars of **German, Dutch, Italian, Chinese, Japanese,** *and* **Siamese.**

LONDON : TRÜBNER & CO., LUDGATE HILL.

www.ingramcontent.com/pod-product-compliance
Lightning Source LLC
Chambersburg PA
CBHW030254170426
43202CB00009B/741